The Changing Economic Environment in Asia

Also by Bernadette Andreosso-O'Callaghan

INDUSTRIAL ECONOMICS AND ORGANIZATION: The European Experience (*with David Jacobson*)

Also by Jacques Jaussaud

CHINA AND INDIA: Economic Performance and Business Strategies of Firms in the Mid-1990s (*with Sam Dzever*)

PERSPECTIVES ON ECONOMIC INTEGRATION AND BUSINESS STRATEGY IN THE ASIA-PACIFIC REGION (*with Sam Dzever*)

The Changing Economic Environment in Asia

Firms' Strategies in the Region

Edited by

Bernadette Andreosso-O'Callaghan
Jean Monnet Professor of Economics
Euro-Asia Centre
University of Limerick
Ireland

Jean-Pascal Bassino
Associate Professor of Economics
Paul Valéry University
Montpellier, France

and

Jacques Jaussaud
Professor of Management
Université François Rabelais de Tours
France

palgrave

First published 2001 by
PALGRAVE
Houndmills, Basingstoke, Hampshire RG21 6XS and
175 Fifth Avenue, New York, N. Y. 10010
Companies and representatives throughout the world

PALGRAVE is the new global academic imprint of St. Martin's Press LLC Scholarly and Reference Division and Palgrave Publishers Ltd (formerly Macmillan Press Ltd).

ISBN 0–333–96437–3

This book is printed on paper suitable for recycling and made from fully managed and sustained forest sources.

A catalogue record for this book is available from the British Library.

Library of Congress Cataloging-in-Publication Data
The changing economic environment in Asia : firms' strategies in the region / edited by Bernadette Andreosso-O'Callaghan, Jean-Pascal Bassino, Jacques Jaussaud.
p. cm.
Includes bibliographical references and index.
ISBN 0–333–96437–3
1. Strategic planning—Asia. 2. Industrial management—Asia. 3. Corporations—Asia. 4. Investments, Foreign—Asia. 5. Financial crises—Asia. 6. Asia—Economic conditions—1945– I. Andreosso-O'Callaghan, Bernadette, 1959– II. Bassino, Jean-Pascal, 1959– III. Jaussaud, Jacques, 1957–

HD30.28 C462 2001
658.4'012'095—dc21

2001032122

10 9 8 7 6 5 4 3 2 1
10 09 08 07 06 05 04 03 02 01

Printed in Great Britain by Antony Rowe Ltd, Chippenham, Wiltshire

Contents

List of Figures and Tables

Figures

Tables

Notes on the Contributors

Bernadette Andreosso-O'Callaghan is Jean Monnet Professor of European Economic Integration and Director of the Euro-Asia Centre, University of Limerick. Her major research interests lie in the area of economic integration, with a specific focus on EU–Asian relations, and on structural change in European and Asian countries. Her recent publications include 'An Analysis of Structural Change in China using Biproportional Methods', in *Economic Systems Research*, 12: 1 (2000, with Guoqiang Yue) and 'The Distribution of Foreign Direct Investment in Vietnam: An Analysis of its Determinants' in R. Strange, J. Slater and C. Molteni (eds), *The European Union and Asean* (Palgrave, 2000, with J. Joyce).

Jean-Pascal Bassino is Associate Professor of Economics at Paul Valéry University (Montpellier, France). He is at present on research leave as a Visiting CNRS Research Fellow at the Center for International Economics and Finance, UMR CNRS 6126, Aix-en-Provence, France. His research interests and publications are in the areas of international economic cooperation in Asia, the Euro-Mediterranean region, and the quantitative and institutional economic history of Asia, with a special reference to Japan and Vietnam.

Charles Chittle is currently Professor Emeritus of Economics at Bowling Green State University, Bowling Green, Ohio, USA. He has served as Visiting Professor of Economics and Fulbright Professor of Economics in Lebanon, Russia, and Jordan and as Research Associate at the Institute of World Economics (Kiel, Germany). He has also been a consultant for the World Bank. He has authored and contributed to books and has had many articles published in a variety of economics journals. His research has been in the areas of international trade, regional economic integration, industrialization and trade policies, and the socialist market economy.

Nathalie H. Fabry is an Associate Professor of Economics and International Business at the University of Marne-la-Vallée (France). She holds a PhD from the University of Paris 1-Panthéon-Sorbonne. Her current research interests are in the field of multinational enterprises, transition economies, and knowledge transfer. She was a Fulbright research fellow at the Wharton School of the University of Pennsylvania (Fall 1999).

Guy Faure is a senior research fellow at the French National Center for Scientific Research (CNRS), and a member of the Institute of East Asian Studies of Lyon, France. He is also Director of the Asian program (DUMEOC) at the Institute of Political Studies, Lyon, France, and he teaches on the Asian Business post-graduate course delivered in the School of Economics and Management of the University of Lyon.

Pierre Grou is Professor of Economics at the University of Versailles-Saint-Quentin-en-Yvelines (Paris 15). He has published widely on the theme of multinational enterprises. Among his publications is *The Financial Structure of Multinational Capitalism* (Berg Publishers, 1985). His current research relates to socio-economic aspects of structural and technological change.

Françoise Guelle is Associate Professor at the University Jean Moulin of Lyon, France. She is also a Researcher at the Institute of East Asian Studies, Lyon, France. Her major research expertise is in the area of the Japanese economy. Between 1990 and 1994, she served as a Japanese Industry Economist at the French Ministry of Trade and Industry, Observatory of Industrial Strategies, Paris. She has been a Visiting Researcher at Keio University, Hosei University and Waseda University in Tokyo, Japan.

Yong He is a research fellow at the National Center for Scientific Research (CNRS). His major research interest is in the area of development economics, with a specific focus on the Chinese economy, its industrialization process, and its open-door policy. He is currently working on some more general theoretical topics such as industrial price discrimination and the division of labor.

Hyun Jae-Hoon is a doctoral candidate at the University of Sheffield.

Jacques Jaussaud is Professor of Management, IAE, University François Rabelais de Tours, France. His research interests are in the areas of business strategy and human resource management (with a particular focus on Japan, China, and other Asian countries). He has published widely in these areas, and is the editor of the French Management Journal '*Japon in Extenso*'.

Doryane Kermel-Torrès received a PhD in Geography from the University of Bordeaux, France. While as a Research Fellow at the IRD (Institut de Recherche pour le Développement, Paris, France), she has conducted comparative studies on several Asian countries, particularly India and Thailand, on the themes of rural transformation and public policies. She is now working on the transitional process from agriculture to industry in South-East Asia. She is also coordinating the *Atlas of Thailand* (Bangkok: White Lotus) to be published in English and in French.

Kyoo H. Kim is Professor of Economics at Bowling Green State University, Ohio, USA. His research interests revolve mostly around the areas of economic integration (in particular, trade and FDI in the emerging markets of Asia), monetary economics and finance, and fiscal issues.

Bertrand Maximin is an Associate Professor at the University René Descartes, Paris, France. He teaches in the areas of international economics, political economy, and development economics. His research deals mostly with the issues of the labor contribution to industrial development, and the competitiveness of the newly industrialized countries of Asia.

Christian Milelli is a Research Fellow at the National Center for Scientific Research (CNRS) and he is a member of FORUM. His current areas of research are the impact of globalisation at industry and corporate levels. He is the author of *Les firmes multinationales: des entreprises au coeur d'industries globalisée* (Vuibert, 1995, with M. Delapierre). He has also written numerous articles on structural change in those areas, particularly relating to the Japanese economy.

Xiaolin Pei is a research fellow at the University of Lund, Sweden and is currently a visiting research scholar on the East Asia Program of Cornell University, USA. His research interests are development economics and institutional economics in general, and China's transition to market economy in particular. Author of many articles published in international refereed journals, he has recently published *The Institutional Root of China's Rural Industry and Gradual Reform* (Lund University Press, 1998).

Philippe Schar completed his PhD in Geography at the University of Bordeaux, France. He is a Research Fellow at the National Center for Scientific Research (CNRS) where he specializes on industrialisation, agrarian change, and development in India and Thailand. He has also a broader interest in the comparative social and spatial patterns of the transition process from agricultural to industrial economies in the case of South and Southeast Asian economies.

Jean-Christophe Simon is Senior Economist at the Research Institute for Development (IRD), Paris, France and a Research fellow at the Centre Asie (IREPD) of the University of Grenoble, France. From 1985 to 1994, he was a visiting Research Fellow at CUSRI (Chulalongkorn University), Bangkok, and served as an adviser to the Government of Thailand. He has contributed to or coordinated several research projects focusing on the newly industrialized economies of Asia, on issues ranging from the current dynamics of industrial sectors (entrepreneurship, expansion of manufacturing activities, particularly export oriented) to the analysis of development patterns and regional integration in emerging economies (State intervention, institutional aspects, such as investment or export promotion). His publications in English include: *Entrepreneurship and Socio-economic transformation in Thailand and Southeast Asia* (Chulalongkorn University Press, 1994), and 'The New Pattern of Expansion of the Manufacturing Sector in Thailand', in M. Parnwell (ed), *Uneven Development in Thailand* (Avebury, 1996).

Robert Taylor is Reader in Modern Chinese Studies and Co-Director of the Centre for Chinese Studies at the University of Sheffield. He has published widely, and his work includes *Greater China and Japan* (Routledge, 1996).

Cho Yong-Doo was formerly a lecturer in the School of East Asian Studies at the University of Sheffield and is currently a member of staff at the Posco Research Institute of Pohang Steel in Seoul. His publications include *Financial Factors and Corporate Investment* (Avebury, 1996).

Hua Wang has been a PhD student in the area of Applied Economics at the Pierre Mendès France University, Grenoble, France, since 1998. His research interests are in the areas of industrial organization, transaction economics, Governmental policy in developing countries, the economics of the division of labor, and the Chinese automobile industry. He has published *The Structure of Chinese Inter-Provincial Trade* (CERDI, Université d'Auvergne, 1998, with Yong He), 'L'industrie automobile en Chine, panorama et réflexions' (Working Paper, IREPD, UPMF, 1998), and 'FDI in the Chinese Automobile Industry: Country of Origin Effects' (3rd EACES Workshop, Paris 2000, with Xavier Richet).

Zhong-Yu Zhang holds a PhD in International Business from the University of Poitiers, France. She developed an expertise in the area of the organization and control of Sino-French joint ventures in China. She greatly contributed to the development of international relations studies at the University of Poitiers, particularly towards China. Very sadly, Zhong-Yu passed away in November 2000, after a battle with cancer.

List of Abbreviations and Acronyms

AICO	ASEAN Industrial Cooperation Committee
ANOVA	Analysis of Variance
APEC	Asia-Pacific Economies
ASEAN	Association of South-East Asian Nations
BOI	Board of Investment (Thailand)
BOT	Build-Operate-Transfer
CEEC	Central and Eastern European Country
Chaebol	Korean conglomerate
CIS	Commonwealth of Independant States
CP	Charoen Pokphand (Group) (Thailand)
CPI	Consumer Price Index
DFI	Direct Foreign Investment
EU	Europen Market
FDI	Foreign Direct Investment
FIE	Foreign Invested Enterprise
FIPA	Foreign Investment Promotion Act (Korea) (1998)
FIZ	Free Investment Zone (Korea)
FPI	Foreign portfolio Investment
FTA	Free Trade Area
GDP	Gross Domestic Product
GNP	Gross National Product
HRM	Human Resources Management
IDE	Investissement Direct à l' Étranger
IFI	Institute for International Finance (US)
IIT	Inter-Industry Trade
IMF	International Monetary Fund
IO	input–output
IPZ	Investment Promotion Zone (Thailand)
ISI	Import Substitution Industrialization
JETO	Japan's External Trade Organization
JIT	Just In Time
KOTRA	Korean Trade Organization
Kudôkâ	Hollowing Out
LDC	Less Developed Country
M&A	Mergers and Acquisition
MERCOSUR	Latin American Common Market

MITI	Ministry of International Trade and Industry (Japan)
MNC	Multinational Corporation
MNE	Multinational Entrerprise
MOF	Ministry of Finance (Japan)
NAFTA	North American Free Trade Area
NEKK	Nihon Enerugi- Keizai Kenkyûjo
NFDI	Net Foreign Direct Investment
NFI	Net Foreign Investment
NFPI	Net Foreign Portfolio Investment
NIC	Newly Industrializing Country
NIE	Newly Industrialized Economy
NSI	Net Stock Investment
NTB	Nontariff Barier
OECD	Organization for Economic Cooperation and Development
OEM	Original Equipment Manufacture
OLI	Ownership-Location-Internalization
OLS	Ordinary Least Squares
PCA	Principal Components Analysis
PEE	Poste d'Expansion Economique
PPC	Production Possibility Curve
PPF	Production Possibility Frontier
PRC	Poeple's Republic of China
QC	Quality Circle
R&D	Research and Development
SEM	Single European Market
SEZ	Special Economic Zone (China, Vietnam)
SIC	Standard Industrial Classification
SME	Small and Medium-Sized Enterprise
SOE	State-Owned Enterprise
TFP	Total Factor Productivity
TVE	Township and Village Enterprise
UN	United Nations
US	United States
VAT	Value Added Tax
VCP	Vietnamese Communist Party
WTO	World Trade Organization

Introduction

Bernadette Andreosso-O'Callaghan, Jean-Pascal Bassino and Jacques Jaussaud

In the eyes of many observers and analysts, the 1997 'Asian Crisis' has abruptly put an end to a mode and cycle of uninterrupted economic growth in a number of Asian countries,[1] by highlighting the many inherent contradictions characterizing the chosen unsustainable development paths. Others see in the crisis the manifestation of hidden weaknesses that compel these economies to put in motion regulatory mechanisms that will, after a given time for adjustment, secure high growth rates in the future, without fundamentally challenging the chosen mode of development. Although there is today quasi-consensus, among economists and business analysts on the type and nature of these contradictions and weaknesses, the different weights accorded to them explain the two broad diverging views referred to above. We can group these contradictions and weaknesses into two major categories. The first category refers to the so-called 'structural weaknesses' of the Asian economies, and encompasses the lack of corporate governance; the laxity of public policy makers; the proliferation of incestuous relationships between corrupted governments, large domestic financial institutions, and large domestic manufacturing conglomerates,[2] opaque accountancy and legal systems; and nonsustainable business practices accounting for low levels of total factor productivity (TFP). The other category refers to external variables such as an excessive liberalization of capital markets; persistent levels of overinvestment since the mid-1980s; the slowdown in the growth of Asian exports in the mid-1990s; and the chosen exchange rate policy which, through a system of currencies pegged to the US dollar, has contributed to massive inflows of capital and to the large current account deficits recorded before the crisis in the respective countries.

In spite of their unprecedented surge during the 1990s, foreign direct investment (FDI) flows represented less than a third of all private capital flows in Asia between 1984 and 1995. Although the crisis can only be marginally explained by FDI flows, through their contribution to the high levels of overinvestment before the outbreak of the crisis, FDI flows have in any case been severely affected by the extent of the crisis. In other words, FDI is the vehicle through which the Asian crisis might have been transmitted to the Western economies. How have foreign investors responded to the crisis? What type of 'new' strategies have been put in place? In the immediate post-crisis era, can we notice a substitution effect between Europe and Asia on the part of Japanese firms? Does the crisis reveal a need for a change in the Japanese human resource management (HRM) system, for a radical restructuring, perhaps disappearance, of the conglomerates? Thanks to a number of learning effects, are Asian and European investors in China, a late opener to trade and investment flows, adopting a more cautious approach? The collection of selected essays included in the present volume provides a critical reappraisal of the impact of the Asian crisis on the strategies of firms operating in the Asian and ASEAN regions. These papers are an updated and revised version of a selected number of contributions that were presented at the Fifth International Euro-Asia Research Conference held in Poitiers, France, in November 1998. Although the impact of the crisis on the behavior of European firms in the region is a recurrent theme in this work, the book leaves also some room for the analysis of Japanese and Asian firms' behavior as well. In endeavoring to represent a substantial contribution to the understanding of the changes generated by the Asian crisis, in the area of trade and investment relations, industrial structures and employment relations, this volume provides some answers to the above questions.

The six chapters in Part I of the book all relate to direct investment links, and suggest that the crisis should be viewed in the context of global business relations.

Centered around the theme of the determinants of economic growth in the case of South Korea, Malaysia, and Thailand, Nathalie Fabry and Bertrand Maximin's Chapter 1 underlines the stages approach to comparative advantage and to FDI, with a shift to the skill-intensive investment goods sector, as economic development proceeds (Ozawa, 1992). The authors stress the role and importance of FDI in the growth process of countries. The findings of an econometric study suggest that South Korea stands out as the country that has benefitted most from FDI. The authors argue that although inward FDI has an impact on host countries' growth rates in general, this impact is greater the more qualified the host countries' labor force. Thanks to its national system of innovation, Korea has demonstrated a real ability to absorb foreign technologies and to diffuse them into the domestic production structure. Chapter 1 highlights the increasing role accorded to qualitative factors such as the level of training and the absorptive capacity of recipient economies, and warns against overreliance on cheap and unqualified workers as an element to attract foreign investors. The insufficient level of expertise and training are seen as the greatest of all structural handicaps present in Thailand and Malaysia.

By proposing a comparative analysis of Japanese FDI flows to the European Union and Asia, Bernadette Andréosso-O'Callaghan and Jean Pascal Bassino's Chapter 2 aims to analyze the degree of interdependence between the two large geo-economic areas. Europe and Asia appear to be increasingly complementary locations for Japanese foreign investors, and the Asian crisis has only very marginally challenged this global pattern of investment. The prospects of Japanese investment relocation in Europe because of the instability in the Asian region are only very limited. The specific cases of motor-vehicles, electrical, telecommunication and optical equipment corroborate the absence of substitution effects between the two regions. Intra-firm trade between the two regions is far from being insignificant and is not only confined to the largest Japanese firms.

The link between direct investment (and beyond that, relocation) and de-industrialization applied to the case of Japan (*kûdôka*) is the central theme of Françoise Guelle's Chapter 3. Illustrating Schumpeter's 'creative destructions' concept, the strategy of Japanese firms has, for a number of years, been to relocate low-value added activities in Asia, while key or high-value added activities were kept in the home country. The phenomenon of de-industrialization is mirrored by a decreasing share of the manufacturing sector in domestic gross domestic product (GDP), and by corresponding decreases in manufacturing employment. Through export substitution effects and re-imports, the phenomenon has been responsible for a deterioration of the Japanese trade balance since 1996. The specific case of the electronics and electrical equipment industry clearly shows the negative impact of relocation on domestic employment since 1991. Although the seven biggest firms are able to maintain employment levels in Japan in spite of large investment outflows, many small and medium-sized enterprises (SMEs) are forced to contract, relocate in the peripheral areas of Japan, or close down.

Jean-Christophe Simon's Chapter 4 analyzes the unprecedented changes brought about by the crisis in Thailand, an economy that had experienced steady growth rates for 40 years. Having an impact beyond the financial sphere, the crisis further damaged the sluggish demand trends in the property sector. It triggered a sharp fall in retail trade, and was responsible for a doubling of the company bankruptcy rate in 1998, leading to important layoffs. This chapter goes on to assess the response of Thai firms to the new challenge, and the development and implementation of new 'adaptive' strategies, such as a greater emphasis on the nonprice elements of competitiveness (durability of products, design . . .). However, the author warns that the access to finance and an efficient management structure are critical elements that are indispensable to the implementation of pro-active strategies.

Breaking with the tradition of studying FDI in China originating from 'high-profile manufacturers' from Western economies, Robert Taylor, Cho Yong-Doo, and Hyun Jae Hoon focus in Chapter 5 on the specific issue of human resource strategies of light-industry South Korean firms in Beijing and Qingdao province, most of them being wholly owned Korean companies. Devolution of power from Korean headquarters to China, high involvement of Chinese managers in the decision making process, a relatively high level of trust, changing recruitment procedures, evolving employment and evaluation patterns, and dedication to training, are all elements that characterize these firms. The Korean firms surveyed show a long-term commitment to China, a strategy which contrasts with that of many foreign firms investing there, who are motivated primarily by low-cost labor and raw materials.

The theme of foreign direct investment (FDI) in China as well as the results obtained from a survey of foreign invested firms, are also the central feature and topic of Zhong-Yu Zhang's Chapter 6. After a brief review of the different organizational collaborative modes that are on offer to foreign firms investing in China, the chapter analyzes the performances of Sino-French firms in China by relating them, for instance, to the quality of the relationship between partners. The author confirms the hypothesis that performance, defined as the managers' subjective appreciation of the results of the firm, is positively influenced by a good relationship between partners. A positive correlation is found between performance and longevity of the firm. The – relatively high – degree of autonomy enjoyed by the equity joint venture in the area of HRM is another contributory factor to better performance. However, the statistical link between the relative share of the respective partners in the capital is not confirmed by this study.

Part II of the book is devoted to seven chapters exploring the impact of the crisis on the financial as well as on the productive spheres of the Asian economies. Pierre Grou and Christian Milelli's challenging title to Chapter 7 announces a study aimed at examining the impact of the 1997 financial crisis on Asian conglomerates. Assuming that the causes of the

Asian crisis are partly structural, it appears indeed that the industrial groups, epitomized by large conglomerates, have reached a feasibility limit. The indebtedness of many South Korean *chaebols* was common before the crisis. Other weaknesses of these *chaebols* included their lack of positioning and mastery of key technologies, a relatively poorly qualified workforce, and their insulation from domestic competitive forces owing to their privileged relationship with the state. In the view of the authors, these large productive structures will need to restructure into specialized groups or firms. Although centered on the case of South Korean *chaebols*, the chapter also briefly explores the counter-tendency visible in the People's Republic of China (PRC) where the restructuring of state-owned enterprises (SOEs) allows for the emergence of conglomerates with the objective of their mutation into future world-class competitors.

Guy Faure in Chapter 8 sees the Asian crisis as having produced an 'electroshock' on policy makers in the Asian economies. The crisis accelerated a number of structural reforms. Although new de-regulation and liberalization programs emerged during the post-crisis era in the real spheres of countries such as Thailand, Malaysia, and South Korea, the author emphasizes the fact that many Asian countries had been trying to ease their regulatory framework for many years prior to the crisis. Chapter 8 addresses the importance of this new environment in four selected economies, and its likely impact on FDI. The author argues that the reform process was indispensable to rebuild investors' confidence in countries that need FDI to fuel their economic recovery.

An econometric investigation of the variables influencing net portfolio and net direct investment in South Korea before the crisis is undertaken in Kyoo Kim and Charles R. Chittle's Chapter 9. The results, in line with economic theory and with the results of other studies, suggest that a 1 percentage point increase of the domestic real interest rate leads to a substantial decrease in both domestic and net foreign investment in Korea (–\$271 million and –\$326 million, respectively). Given the positive impact of FDI on the Korean economy's growth, the authors calculate the amount of FDI needed in the Korean economy in order to increase GDP by a given percentage. The authors highlight the large surge of portfolio investment in the six or seven years preceding the crisis, during the same period of time, net FDI has been negative. These figures give an idea of the extent of the financial bubble and of the level of overprotection of the Korean Banking sector before the crisis. Consequently, the authors test the moral hazard model as an explanation of the financial crisis in the case of Korea. The results, confirming that domestic firms crowd out more FDI if they can borrow more capital from the international financial market, lend support to the moral hazard behavior of domestic firms, banks, and government, as an explanation for the financial crisis in Korea. Finally, the chapter outlines the changes in government economic policy in response to the crisis (e.g. liberalization of capital inflows and increased flexibility of the labor market)

In Chapter 10, Jacques Jaussaud highlights the fact that the Japanese model of HRM was under enormous pressure in the 1990s. Confronted with a negative performance in a depressed environment, companies were forced to put into place drastic cost measures, including the dismissal of permanent employees. Long-term growth and an ageing population will put more and more strains on HRM systems in Japan. Although one may have at least two different interpretations of the so-called 'Japanese model' of HRM, Jacques Jaussaud questions whether this model will remain a major point of reference in the field.

Doryane Kermel-Torrès and Philippe Schar's Chapter 11 deals with the case of industrialization in Thailand and critically analyzes the nature of the crisis there. The authors' emphasis is on the structural features of the Thai economy, i.e. the productive system favoring an export-led growth model, and the problem of the labor force. The methodology used is a survey of 100 firms situated in the North-East and Southern regions of Thailand, i.e. those regions given status of Investment Promotion Zones (IPZs) in the early 1990s and that have benefitted from generous decentralization incentives from the Thai Board of Investment (BOI). After a description of the major salient features characterizing these firms during the year preceding the crisis (1996), such as an important reliance on institutional credit channels and the dependence of these firms on foreign markets, the authors place a great emphasis on the poor educational level of the workforce and the problem of skill shortages. Acute skill shortages are mostly felt in the industrial parks and slow down the mechanization process of the economy. However, the inadequacy of the general training level of the workforce in relation to the needs of a rapidly developing economy inhibits the progression of the country on the value added and labor productivity ladder.

Yong He and Xiolin Pei's Chapter 12 explores the important question whether China's unprecedented growth is sustained only by an overall increase in inputs (rather than by input substitution mirroring structural change). If so, then this model of development is not sustainable in the long term. The ways rationalization of the industrial structure – or structural change – can take place is through specialization and economies of scale and scope. These lead to higher concentration ratios in some selected industries.

The calculations made by the authors show that concentration has generally decreased over the 1990–96 period for the 33 industries under review. This should be seen in parallel with the restructuring process affecting the Chinese SOEs. Ferrous metals, nonferrous metals, mining, smelting and food are particular industries showing large declines in the concentration ratio over the period. On the other hand, petroleum refinery, furniture, timber, and printing are industries with increasing concentration ratios over the period. An econometric investigation of the variables influencing the degree of concentration is also undertaken in Chapter 12. The authors claim that the decrease in concentration ratios in the area of raw materials and of some equipment good industries may reflect the fact that the development of the Chinese industry is based essentially upon an extensive mode of production, i.e. an increase in inputs rather than on a qualitative improvement. Profit rate, as defined as profit before tax divided by total real capital employed, contributes favorably to concentration, whereas other variables such as demand conditions, home market size and export conditions have only a limited impact on the level of concentration. The decrease in the average profit rate of Chinese enterprises is partly responsible for declining concentration ratios over the period, and the demise of the SOEs contributes largely to this phenomenon. Other explanations for the decrease in concentration ratios are low entry barriers, incentives of all kinds given by the government, and therefore the high rate of firms' entry into the many individual markets.

The theme of the open door policy and its impact on the Chinese economy is also the leading thread of Hua Wang's Chapter 13. The objective is to determine the exact contribution of foreign trade to GDP growth, restricting the analysis to the case of the Shanghai area, and using a modified version of Denison's growth model (Denison and Poullier, 1967). Although the case of Shanghai represents a pilot study, it is nevertheless an interesting example of how a designated city has responded to the new challenges brought about by the open door policy. The annual average growth rate of foreign trade in Shanghai exceeded 18 percent during the first half of the 1990s. Using data covering the period 1978–95, but focussing on the sub-period 1991–95, the calculations show that the capital input is the engine of economic growth over the period. It contributed more than 83 per cent to the average annual growth rate of GDP, whereas the labor input contributed only marginally to GDP increases. TFP changes are fairly low over this period; this reflects the decline of the 'advance of knowledge.' The annual average contribution of foreign trade to GDP has been slightly more than 9 per cent of GDP growth over the same period.

Notes

1 In particular in Thailand, Malaysia, Indonesia, Philippines, and South Korea.
2 This view has been the 'official view' espoused by the International Monetary Organizations.

References

Ozawa, T. (1992) 'Foreign Direct Investment and Economic Development,' *Transnational Corporations,* 1: 1, 27–54.

Denison E. F. and Poullier, J. P. (1967) *Why Growth Rules Differ* (Washington, DC: The Brooking Institution).

Part I

Regional Integration and Firms' Strategies: Drastic Changes

1
FDI, Industrial Labor Transformation and Growth: The Cases of South Korea, Malaysia, and Thailand

Nathalie Fabry and Bertrand Maximin

Introduction

Developing countries used to be rather hostile to inward Foreign direct investment (FDI); they feared that FDI might lead to uneven global development. This attitude changed radically in the mid-1980s, particularly in Asia (Calvo, Laderman and Reinhart 1996; Markusen and Venables, 1997; Lall, 1998). Since then, host countries' governments have welcomed increasing flows of inward FDI, essentially in the manufacturing sector. They now consider that FDI may be an 'industrialization instrument' less dangerous than international indebtedness (Rodriguèz-Clare, 1996). The most visible characteristic of this change was the surge of FDI from developed countries in Asia until the Asian crisis broke out in the summer of 1997 (Hill and Athukorala, 1998).

Developing host countries used to receive foreign firms whose activities were intensive in cheap and abundant labor. Thus, FDI determinants were mainly supply oriented, and typically, FDI took place in order to reduce production costs and to maintain foreign firms' price competitiveness on export markets. However, since the 1990s, competition has no longer been exclusively based on cost advantages, but rather on quality. Foreign firms look for a combination of low labor costs, technological capabilities, labor qualifications, dynamic local demand, efficient market organization, stable political, institutional and legal environment, and safe and reliable infrastructures (Van Den Bulcke and Zhang, 1998). The progressive erosion of a labor cost-based attractiveness suggests that host countries must perform a quality shift to enhance sustained growth. This shift relies mainly on labor qualifications and workers' learning aptitudes in order to facilitate knowledge transfer (Cullen and Johnson, 1995). This challenge is of a great importance, particularly if countries do not want to see the 'Asian miracle' turning into a 'myth' as described by Krugman (1994), Lall (1994), or Amsden (1994).

In the literature, FDI from developed to developing countries is thought of as a package of capital stock, know-how, managerial skills, and technology (Jansen, 1995; Balasubramanian, Salisu and Sapsford, 1996; Borensztein, de Gregorio and Lee, 1998). Its impact on growth is expected to be multifold: industrial employment, upgrading of labor qualifications, job training, and technology transfer (Blomström Kokko and Zejan, 1994). The ultimate impact of FDI on the growth of output in the recipient economy depends on the spillover effects to the domestic firms (Blomström and Kokko, 1998). FDI leads to increasing returns in domestic production, and to increases in the value added content of FDI-related production (Haddad and Harrison, 1993; Lucas, 1993a). But the relation between FDI and growth is not straightforward. Unskilled human capital, unsafe and unreliable infrastructures, weak absorption capacities of the transferred technology, and weak financial institutions can indeed block the transmission phenomenon and reduce the impact of FDI on growth.

While determinants of inward FDI have been discussed extensively (Lucas, 1993b; Fabry and Maximin, 1998; Fabry and Zeghni, 1998), little research has been undertaken on the nature and direction of the relationship between inward FDI and growth, especially when applied to Asian countries (De Melo, 1999). Our study will endeavor to fill a gap by arguing that in order to remain attractive, Asian countries must upgrade their resources, and particularly the qualification of their labor force. If they fail to do so, they may have to cope with fierce competition from transition economies and they may encounter difficulties to generate an endogenous growth process. As Perkins (1994) noted, there is no unique Asian model but rather different ways leading to rapid growth in a relatively cohesive social context. Thus, we will focus on three Asian countries: a Newly industrialized economy (NIE) of the first generation (Korea) and two NIEs of the second generation that are also ASEAN members (Malaysia and Thailand).

Inward FDI and the upgrading of local competencies

As mentioned in the Introduction, inward FDI is a major vehicle for technology transfer. It is indeed its ability to transfer knowledge that differentiated FDI from other capital transfers such as portfolio investment or international aid. Knowledge transfer may improve the host country's industrial framework, but to benefit from positive effects of inward FDI, host countries may have to upgrade their local competencies and skills.

Inward FDI and technology transfer

Technology transferred through FDI generates externalities at an inter- and intra-industrial level. This transfer may generate a pattern of comparative advantage based on a regional hierarchy. At the inter-industrial level, FDI and the transferred technology may improve the local supply of intermediate products. It may help the host country subcontractors to decrease their production cost and to enhance the quality of their products. More generally, the development of a local subcontractor network is a way through which the host country may improve its industrial structure. How? Foreign subsidiaries need to buy inputs on the local market. Thus, FDI generates subcontracting activities. But the quality and the price of the local inputs are a main concern for foreign firms. Thus, foreign investors have an important role to play in helping local suppliers in upgrading their production processes and their outputs. Foreign firms' support and help can be composed of technical assistance, technological support, and information about management or distribution (Blomström, 1989). Thanks to foreign production and to an upgrading of the local production, host country consumers may benefit from a wider range of products and may enjoy better quality products. Moreover, the products are available in the host country at a lower price. This phenomenon is particularly true for micro-electronic devices. The counterpart is a relative dependence towards foreign firms, foreign knowledge, and technology.

At the intra-industrial level, the direct impact of inward FDI may be analyzed through the eclectic paradigm proposed by Dunning, based on the three concepts of asset specificity, internalization, and location advantages (Dunning, 1988, 1995; Markusen, 1995).

To overcome local entry barriers, foreign investors may offer to transfer part of their intangible assets (mainly knowledge) to the host country. In the case where the foreign subsidiaries re-export their local production, this transfer may facilitate the host country's international insertion. Foreign investors may also contribute to improving the skills and abilities of local workers. Thanks to the education and training received from foreign investors, some of these workers may become local entrepreneurs (subcontractors). They may also move towards other firms. Moreover, the upgrading of local workers' skills may give the foreign investors the opportunity to transfer most of its management methods. For example, Japanese firms who invested in the electronics sector in Korea and

Malaysia were able to introduce 'just in time' (JIT) production processes and quality circles (QCs) within their plants. Moreover, local producers belonging to the same industry introduced the Japanese management framework (Rassiah, 1994). The success of foreign subsidiaries is closely related to the complementarity between their specific assets and the general productivity of factors within the host country. The success relies also on the complementarity created between their subsidiaries and the local firms (Haddad and Harrison, 1993; Kokko and Blomström, 1995).

Finally, in a meso-economic perspective of international technology transfer, as presented by Vernon (1966), the Asian model suited the 'flying-geese' framework, starting from Japan and diffusing to other Asian countries (Akamatsu, 1962). This analytical pattern stresses the fact that the firms having lost their comparative advantage in their home country during the 1980s (e.g. Korea) have been using FDI in ASEAN countries to benefit from cheap and abundant labor. The firms' strategy created a regional and hierarchical shift of comparative advantages (Maximin, 1992, 1994). Moreover, technology transfer and inward FDI make more relevant the qualitative upsurge of host countries.

Technology transfer as an irreversible bias for host countries

Inward FDI implies that the price of exported goods must increase more rapidly than that of imported inputs in the host countries. One can also show that the trade generated by inward FDI may transform the host countries' patterns of production and consumption. They may also create inequalities and lead to redundancies and exit of nonqualified workers from the labor market. This can be illustrated by the following figure, inspired by the work of Richardson (1995).

In Figure 1.1, the production of equipment goods is located on the vertical axis. To produce such goods, firms need research and development (R&D), as well as qualified and skilled workers. The consumer goods are located on the horizontal axis. These goods require more unskilled work. The production possibility frontier (PPF) is convex and reveals the existence of decreasing economies of scale.

In *autarky*, the initial production possibility frontier is represented by the curve FPP_0 for a capital/consumption ratio determined at the point c_0. An increase in the capital stock will normally increase the production level, which may shift, for example, to $FPPC_1$.

In a situation of *international trade*, comparative advantages will shift to the investment goods sector, which uses skilled workers intensively. Firms from dynamic Asian countries (NIEs) may take advantage of the host country's attractiveness and venture into FDI. But in order to face the competition

Figure 1.1 Inward-FDI and host country's labor

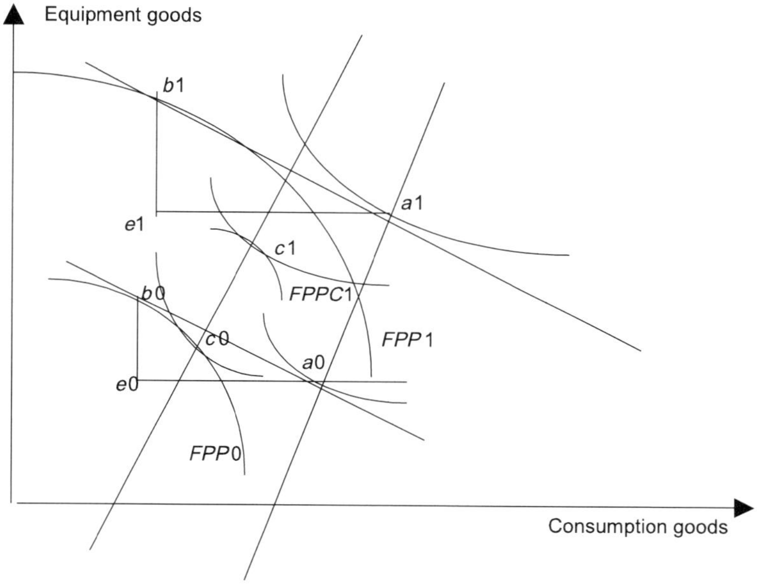

Source: Derived from Richardson (1995)

from low-labor cost countries and also from more advanced ones, they may choose the technologies and the production methods that involve more skilled workers. Thus, skilled workers within the host country appear to be complementary with inward FDI (Bartel and Lichtenberg, 1987; Krueger, 1993; Bhagwati, 1994). International trade will move the PPF of the host country. On the graph, it will move to the point b_0 along the FPP_0 curve. The consumption curve will shift to a_0. The host country becomes able to promote more capitalistic and skilled labor-intensive production (e_0b_0). The increase of more value added exports gives the host country the opportunity to import more consumer goods (e_0a_0). The slope of the line (b_0a_0) is the relative world price of the two categories of goods.

Finally, thanks to an internal dynamism of local producers and to an exogenous growth of the capital stock provided by inward FDI, the host country will see its PPF move to FPP_1. Production is at point b_1, and consumption at a_1. The simultaneous variations of consumption and production create a new expansion path. The slope of this new expansion path (a_0a_1) represents the level of welfare obtained from international trade and inward FDI. This welfare improvement is the result of a decrease in domestic consumption goods prices relative to equipment goods prices. The share of capital-intensive goods changes more rapidly than that of consumption goods (b_0b_1). The shift in relative prices leads necessarily to a more intensive use of qualified workers by local firms and thus, increases the demand for such skilled workers (Ozawa, 1992). This situation may create inequalities between qualified and less qualified workers. The workers whose qualifications no longer correspond to the firms' needs may face redundancies. Further training is a solution for such workers, but most of them have to shift towards service activities.

Inward FDI allows the host country to rapidly improve and upgrade its attractiveness and more generally to improve the global efficiency of its factors of production. We will see next that these qualitative improvements rely primarily on educational systems.

Inward FDI and the need to improve the host country's human capital

Asian countries rapidly came to acknowledge that, in a context of fierce international competition mainly based on knowledge, they had to improve their human capital in order to remain competitive (Lucas, 1993a; Young, 1994). Knowledge may be acquired through many ways: technical and professional learning, R&D promotion, new products development. All of these ways may create positive externalities, once acquired and mastered. Consequently, in order to benefit from these externalities and to generalize the learning capabilities of workers, governments and large firms have actively taken part in the upgrading of their educational systems. As a result, the share of public spending for education and/or R&D in GNP has been soaring. In the same way, enrolment ratios in secondary schools and at post-secondary levels have been increasing.

Between 1965 and 1995, the share of public spending in GNP doubled in the Asian NIEs. In Korea, for example, the enrolment ratio in higher education is similar to that of most industrialized countries. The same increase is also observable in Malaysia and Thailand. In those countries, the evolution is more recent and more selective. In all cases, specific fields such as mathematics, technologies and management are emphasized (Maximin, 1992). During the 1990s, more than 20 percent of the working population in both Thailand and Malaysia had third-level education (Young, 1994).

The modernization of the educational system was made possible owing to the participation of the private sector and the support of families in promoting social upgrading through knowledge acquisition. Professional training within firms is a particular concern for host 'countries' governments. In Korea, to promote such training, the state gives specific tax reductions to firms who finance professional training programs.

Professional training and technological development are deeply interlinked. Consequently, as training and technological competencies increased locally, firms were able to invest in R&D to improve the quality, the scale, and the scope of their product lines. At the beginning of the 1990s there were more than 700 R&D units in Korea, thanks to the government and the firms' involvement in training and knowledge-based assets development (Kim and Dahlman, 1992). In 1995, Korea spent 2.7 percent of its GNP on R&D. This compares with a figure of 2.4 percent for France and for the United States. However, the GNP share spent on R&D does not suffice to derive any satisfactory conclusions on the efficiency of a national system of innovation. In spite of a relatively high expenditure level, Korea's innovation system is characterized by many inefficiencies linked to the *chaebols* system (Mowery and Oxley, 1995; Ernst, 1998).

The R&D share in GDP is 0.2 percent in Thailand and 0.4 percent in Malaysia, two figures that are far below that of Korea (Table 1.1). However, Malaysia seems to be willing to overcome rapidly its disadvantage. In 1989, a training center was created in Penang (Penang Skill Development), located on a major inward FDI site. But this specific action can not fill the gap existing between the need for technicians and engineers in the local economies and the numbers of such skilled workers available. To improve the qualitative aspect of its attractiveness, Malaysia also upgraded its legal system, with more protection for the firms' intangible assets and more attention to intellectual property rights.

Within a context where quality improvement is a major concern, FDI may create positive externalities in host countries. The creation of local absorptive capabilities is the only way to make local firms and workers able to benefit from technologies and knowledge transferred via FDI. The upgrading of local competencies and skills may also enable foreign firms to transfer even more complex technologies and knowledge to host countries. Only such a progressive and continuous process of technology transfer and increasing absorptive capabilities can lead to an endogenous growth process in the host country.

Inward FDI and the endogenous growth process

The economic literature on growth has for a long time been composed of two main strands. On one side, the Keynesian literature focuses on savings

Table 1.1 Public spending, R&D, and enrollment ratio, Korea, Malaysia, and Thailand 1970 and 1994

Country	Public spending (% of GDP)		Public spending on R&D (% of GDP)	Enrollment ratio (%)				
				Primary	Secondary		Third-level	
	1970	1994	1994	1994	1970	1994	1970	1994
Korea	3.6	4.5	2.8	101	46	93	16	48
Malaysia	4.4	5.3	0.4	93	34	59	4	7
Thailand	3.5	3.8	0.2	98	17		13	19

Source: *World Bank*: *Annual Report on World Development, 1993–1995.*

and domestic investment (Harrod–Domar models 1939 and 1946) and on the other, neo-classical studies focus on technical progress, following Solow's seminal work (Solow, 1956). The literature on endogenous growth opens the door to a new direction. In that body of literature, human capital, R&D, and infrastructure are considered as key determinants of growth. Furthermore, the externalities and structural transformations thus created are themselves important determinants of growth. This leads to study the impact of inward FDI on the host country's growth. We study the relationship between FDI and growth in Korea, Malaysia and Thailand during the period 1981–95 (so before the 1997 Asian crisis).

Inward FDI and host-country growth

As mentioned above, FDI may transfer new technologies, new managerial practices, and know-how, and may upgrade the workers' skills. Consequently, inward FDI is expected to generate externalities in the host country and, thus, to enhance a sustainable growth process. Exports are supposed to be the partial result of the foreign firm's production and are supposed to be technology-intensive. They are also a signal that the host country is open to international trade, and this may give foreign firms the opportunity to allocate resources according to the comparative advantage principle. Writing the production function as follows:

$$y = g(L, K, F, X, T) \tag{1.1}$$

Where Y is real GNP; L the labor force available in the host country proxied by the population; K the stock of domestic capital; F the stock of foreign capital; X the exports; and T technological progress. By taking the logarithm of the two sides of the equation and by differentiating them, we obtain the following growth function, which may help us to understand the main growth determinants:

$$y = \alpha + \beta l + \chi k + \psi f + \phi x \tag{1.2}$$

β, χ,ψ and ϕ represent the elasticity of production relatively to labor, capital, inward FDI, and exports. The stock of capital (domestic and foreign) is difficult to evaluate, particularly in the case of developing economies. Therefore, as a proxy for this stock, we chose the share of domestic investment in GNP (called *IY*). The same method has been applied to inward FDI and the resulting variable has been called *FDIY* (Balasubramanyan, Salisu and Sapsford, 1996). The elasticity of production relatively to domestic capital, to FDI, and to exports is particularly relevant to understand the nature of the host country's growth. From this model, we can derive a model in line with the work of authors such as

Table 1.2 Explanatory variables for the empirical test

Variable	Definition	Expected signs
POPU	Population of country *i*, as proxy of available labor force *Sources*: IMF.	(+)
FDIY	Share of inward FDI in GNP of the host country *i*, as proxy of stock of foreign capital in country *i* *Sources*: IMF.	(+)
IY	Share of domestic investment in GNP of the host country *i*, as a proxy of the stock of domestic investment in country *i* *Sources* : IMF.	(+)
X	Total exports of country *i* *Sources*: IMF	(+)

Balasubramanyan, Salisu and Sapsford (1996) or Borenzstein, de Gregorio and Lee (1998). This model is written as follows (see Table 1.2 for a definition of the variables):

$$\log GNP_i = \beta_1 + \beta_2 \log POPU_i + \beta_3 FDIY_i + \beta_4 IY_i + \beta_5 \log X_i + \varepsilon \qquad (1.3)$$

It should be noted that the relation between FDI and growth is not straightforward. Among other things, unskilled human capital and a weak capacity of absorption of the transferred technology can indeed block the transmission phenomenon and reduce the impact of inward FDI on growth. Moreover, FDI may also be attracted by a domestic dynamic demand (catch-up demand). Consequently the relationship between FDI and GNP raises a causality problem. In order to resolve this problem, we performed a causality test (Granger) to obtain more information about each factor's contribution to growth. Although this test could not determine any strong causality between FDI and GNP, it did not determine any reverse causality between GNP and FDI either. Thus, the Granger test can not help us to understand the growth determinants of the selected countries. The best this test can do is to reveal a possible link between FDI and GNP. Following this avenue, we will focus below on the contribution of FDI to the host country's growth.

Table 1.3 GDP determinants, Korea, Malaysia, and Thailand, 1981–95

Variables	Korea	Malaysia	Thailand
Intercept	–2.017835 (–0.720521)	7.911078**** (131.7029)	7.911078**** (–1.838549)
log*POPU*	3.563247*** (3.761537)	0.208899** (2.181342)	3.646195*** (3.172835)
FDIY	21.18351**** (4.896672)	1.204982*** (3.636284)	0.062608*** (3.338340)
IY	–0.568765*** (–2.735380)	0.081085* (1.455135)	–0.112510 (–0.601565)
log*X*	0.073316 (0.920062)	0.270935**** (10.27969)	0.003066 (0.036029)
R_2 adjusted	0.981845	0.998182	0.996509
D–W	2.186283	2.893764	2.337313
Method	MCO	MCO	MCO
Period	1981–95 etc	1981–95 etc	1986–95 etc
Observations	15	15	10

Inward FDI as an initiator of growth

The following log-linear statistical model will be tested with the ordinary least squares (OLS) method:

$$\log GDP_{it} = \beta_1 + \beta_2 \log POPU_{it} + \beta_3 FDIGDP_{it} + \beta_4 IGDP_{it} + \beta_5 \log X_{it} + \varepsilon_{it}$$

This log-linear model allows us to consider the coefficients as elasticities. The results of the test are presented in Table 1.3. The adjusted R^2 ratio and the Durbin–Watson statistic are significant.

In *Korea,* FDI's contribution to GDP growth is positive and significant; this is also the case for the *POPU* variable. The latter may represent both the size of the local market and its dynamism. On the other hand, the proxy of the domestic capital stock and exports do not have an impact on the growth rate. Thus, the contribution of FDI to growth seems to be mainly qualitative. We can observe that Korea's growth may be explained by a demand variable (*POPU*) but also by structural variables such as a national system of innovation, which may contribute to enhance the FDI efficiency (Hobday, 1995). Moreover, Korea is a country poor in raw materials and natural resources. Thus FDI is in value added activities such as manufacturing or services activities. These activities benefit from a relatively highly educated labor force. In that sense, Korea differs from other countries such as Malaysia or Thailand.

In the case of Malaysia, all the retained variables may explain the growth during the period 1981–95. This is true for the population variable, which is a proxy for domestic demand, seen as a structural and quantitative variable. Inward FDI and exports have the most significant contributions. Both may be associated to a technology transfer process to Malaysia. Finally, domestic investment has a positive and significant link with growth. Thus, Malaysian growth seems to be more dependent on foreign than on domestic demand. In such a context, the host country needs to pay particular attention to its attractiveness, especially with regard to qualifications and infrastructure. The positive sign of the exports variable shows that Malaysia has incorporated foreign technology; however, the coefficient is still low. This may reveal a low absorptive capacity of the country and a small ability to diffuse the imported technology to the local firms (subcontractors).

In Thailand, only two variables are significant and have the expected sign. These are the population (*POPU*) and the proxy for foreign capital invested in the country (*FDIY*). The relationship between GDP and *FDIY* is not reinforced by a similar one between GDP and exports. One explanation may be that Thailand's growth is driven by a demand for goods intensive in non-qualified workers and does not include imported technology and knowledge. Such a situation may impede the future growth of the country.

Finally, inward FDI has an impact on host countries' growth. The more qualified the host countries' labor force, the greater the impact. This is particularly true for Korea where a real ability to absorb foreign technology and to diffuse it into the local production framework exists. This is less true for Malaysia and Thailand. However, the relationships between GDP and exports do not match our expectations. That is to say that exports do not, as would be expected, drive growth. This is a kind of vulnerability for these countries in a quality-based competition. The only issue for host countries is to be less dependent on an international demand in constant flux. To perform this challenge, countries need to introduce more flexibility into their production systems and to have a more diversified supply.

Conclusion

Our study has shown that inward FDI may boost the host countries' growth in Asia. FDI played a major role in generating externalities and helping these countries to insert themselves into international trade. To gain even more inward FDI, host countries must manage a global shift toward a more qualitative-based attractiveness. The availability of cheap and unqualified workers is no longer a way to attract foreign investors. Host countries need to adjust their attractiveness to the quality requirements of foreign firms. If not, they may no longer stimulate inward FDI. We have shown in this chapter that the best way to perform this upgrading is to introduce more diversification and flexibility into the production process and to boost qualification and knowledge. This seems to be the only way to improve the credibility of Asian host countries, which has been partly undermined by the Asian crisis of summer 1997.

References

Amsden, A. (1994) 'Why Isn't the Whole World Experimenting with the East Asian Model to Develop?,' *World Development*, 22: 4, 627–33.

Akamatsu, K. (1962) 'A Historical Pattern of Economic Growth in Developing Countries,' *Developing Economies*, 1, 2–25.

Bhagwati, J. (1994) 'Free Trade: Old and New Challenges,' *The Economic Journal*, 104, 231–46.

Bartel, A. and Lichtenberg, F. (1987) 'The Comparative Advantage of Educated Workers in Implementing New Technology,' *The Review of Economics and Statistics*, 1, 1–11.

Balasubramanyam, V., Salisu, M., and Sapsford D. (1996) 'Foreign Direct Investment and Growth in EP and IS Countries,' *The Economic Journal*, 106, 92–105.

Blomström, M., and Kokko, A. (1998) 'Multinational Corporations and Spillovers,' *Journal of Economic Survey*, 12: 3, 247–77.

Blomström, M., Kokko, A., and Zejan, M. (1994) 'Host Country Competition, Labour Skills, and Technology Transfer by Multinationals,' *Weltwirtschaftliches Archiv*, Band 130, Heft 3, 521–33.

Blomström, M. (1989) *Foreign Investment and Spillovers* (London: Routledge).

Borensztein, E., de Gregorio, J., and Lee, J-W. (1998) 'How Does Foreign Direct Investment Affect Economic Growth?,' NBER, 5057.

Calvo, G., Leiderman, L., and Reinhart, C. (1996) 'Inflows of Capital to Developing Countries in the 1990s,' *Journal of Economic Perspectives*, 10: 2, 123–39.

Cullen, J. and Johnson, J. (1995) 'Japanese and Local Partner Commitment to IJVs: Psychological Consequences of Outcomes and Investments in the IJVs' Relationship,' *International Journal of Business Studies*, 1, 91–116.

De Melo, J. (1999) 'Foreign Direct Investment-led growth: Evidence from Time Series and Panel Data,' *Oxford Economic Papers*, 51, 133–51.

Domar, E. (1946) 'Capital Expansion, Rate of Growth and Employment,' *Econometrica*, 14, 137–47

Dunning, J. (1988) *Explaining International Production* (London: Unwin Hyman).

Dunning, J. (1995) 'Reappraising the Eclectic Paradigm in a Age of Alliance Capitalism,' *Journal of international Business Studies*, 26: 3, 461–93.

Ernst, D. (1998) 'Catching-up, Crisis and Industrial Upgrading: Evolutionary Aspects of Technological Learning in Korea's Electronic Industry,' *Asia Pacific Journal of Management*, 15: 2, 247–83.
Fabry, N. and Maximin, B. (1998) 'Les déterminants macro-économiques des investissements directs étrangers en Asie du Sud-est: le cas du Japon et des USA,' in Guerraoui D. and Richet X. (eds), *Les investissements directs étrangers, facteurs d'attractivité et de localisation* (Casablanca: Toubkal and Paris: l'Harmattan), 201–27.
Fabry, N. and Zeghni, S. (1998) 'Les investissements directs japonais en Chine: attractivité comparée de Dalian et Shanghai,' *Revue d'économie du développement*, 2, 91–114.
Haddad, M. and Harrison, A. (1993) 'Are There Positive Spillovers From Foreign Investment?,' *Journal of Development Economics*, 42: 1, 51–74.
Harrod, R. (1939) 'An Essay in Dynamic Theory,' *The Economic Journal*, 49: 193, 14–33.
Hill, H. and Athukorala, P-C. (1998) 'Foreign Investment in East Asia: A Survey,' *Asian Pacific Literature*, 12: 2, 23–50.
Hobday, M. (1995) *Innovation in East Asia* (Aldershot: Edward Elgar).
Jansen, K. (1995) 'The Macroeconomic Effects of DFI: The Case of Thailand,' *World Development*, 23: 2, 193–210.
Kim, L. and Dahlman, C J. (1992) 'Technology Policy for Industrialisation: an Integration Framework and Korea Experience,' *Research Policy*, 21: 12, 437–52.
Kokko, A. and Blomström, M. (1995) 'Policies to Encourage Inflows of Technology Through Foreign Multinationals,' *World Development*, 23: 4, 602–11.
Krueger, A.O. (1993) 'Virtuous and Vicious Circles in Economic Development,' *The American Economic Review*, 83: 2, 351–5.
Krugman, P. (1994) 'The Myth of Asia's Miracle,' *Foreign Affairs*, November–December, 62–78.
Lall, S. (1994) 'The East Asian Miracle: Does the Bell Toll for Industrial Strategy?,' *World Development*, 22: 4, 645–54.
Lall, S. (1998) 'Changing Perceptions of FDI in Development,' in P. K. Tharakan and D. Van Den Bulcke (eds.), *International Trade, FDI and the Economic Environment* (London: Macmillan).
Lucas, R. (1993a) 'Making A Miracle,' *Econometrica*, 2, 251–72.
Lucas, R. (1993b) 'On the Determinants of FDI: Evidence from East and Southeast Asia,' *World Development*, 21: 3, 391–406.
Markusen, J. and Venables, A. (1997) 'Foreign Direct Investment as a Catalyst for Industrial Development,' *NBER Working Paper*, 6241.
Markusen, J. (1995) 'The boundaries of Multinational Enterprises and the theories of International Trade', *Journal of Economic Perspectives*, 9: 2, 169–89.
Maximin, B. (1992) 'Marché du travail et dynamique de l'avantage comparatif dans les nouveaux pays industrialisés d'Asie,' *Revue d'Economie Politique*, 102: 3, 423–48.
Maximin, B. (1994) 'L'enjeu de l'investissement direct international en Thaïlande: l'émergence d'un NPI de la deuxième génération,' *Mondes en développement*, 22: 86, 9–22.
Mowery, D. C. and Oxley, J. E. (1995) 'Inward Technology Transfer and Competitiveness: The Role of National Innovation Systems,' *Cambridge Journal of Economics*, 19, 67–93.

Ozawa, T. (1992) 'Foreign Direct Investment and Economic Development,' *Transnational Corporation*, 1:1, 27–54.
Perkins, D. (1994) 'There Are At Least Three Models of East Asian Development,' *World Development*, 22: 4, 655–61.
Rassiah, R. (1994) 'Flexible Production Systems and Local Machine Subcontracting: Electronics Components Transnationals in Malaysia,' *Cambridge Journal of Economics*, 18: 3, 279–98.
Richardson, J. D. (1995) 'Income Inequality and Trade: How to Think, What to Conclude,' *Journal of Economic Perspectives*, 9: 3, 33–55.
Rodriguèz-Clare, A. (1996) 'Multinationals, Linkages, and Economic Development'' *American Economic Review*, 86: 4, 852–73.
Solow, R. (1956) 'A Contribution to the Theory of Economic Growth,' *Quarterly Journal of Economics*, 70: 1, 65–94
Van Den Bulcke, D. and Zhang, H. (1998) 'Foreign Equity Joint Ventures in China: Interactions between Government Policies and Multinational Investment Strategies,' in P. K. Tharakan and D. Van Den Bulcke (eds), *International Trade, FDI and the Economic Environment* (London: Macmillan, 1998).
Vernon, R. (1996) 'International Investment and International trade in the Product Cycle,' *Quarterly Journal of Economics*, 88, 190–207.
Young, A. (1994) 'The Tyranny of Numbers: Confronting the Statistical Realities of East Asian Growth Experiences,' *The Quarterly Journal of Economics*, 10: 3, 641–80.

2

Japanese Direct Investment in Asia and the European Union: Is There an Interdependence?

Bernadette Andreosso-O'Callaghan[*] and Jean-Pascal Bassino[**]

Introduction

The 1997–8 Asian financial crisis indicates the growing interdependence existing between EU and Asian economies. Excessive reliance upon international capital flows is currently seen as one of the main explanatory factors of this turmoil, combined with an inappropriate allocation of domestic resources and the many distortions induced by market-unfriendly policies. The rapid depreciation of most Asian currencies against both the US dollar and major European currencies may enhance the comparative advantage of these countries. However, the collapse of domestic demand in the ASEAN countries has induced a cautious attitude on the part of foreign investors, who had to postpone or cancel several projects. In addition, they had to reconsider or even to change drastically their strategy aimed at implementing – within their business group – an international division of labor, and therefore international trade flows between their subsidiaries.

The purpose of this chapter is to investigate the connection between the various subsidiaries of global firms, and the interdependence of the EU and Asian markets through the global operations of Japanese multinational firms. The choice of Japanese firms is justified both by the availability of data and by the size of Japanese firms and foreign direct investment (FDI) flows. Undoubtedly, a comparison with US firms could be informative. But, since Europe seems less attractive for Japanese investors, when compared with US investors, our main concern lies in evaluating the interdependence between investment choices of Japanese firms in the European Union and Asia, and the possible repercussions of the Asian crisis on the Union via the Japanese plants. By 'interdependence', we mean the extent to which a firm separates out its components parts and, for our purpose, locates them in the Union and Asia. The ultimate result of this strategy is the building-up of a *filière* at the quasi-global (that is at the Union, Asia or ASEAN level), with either two-way trade flows or alternatively one-way trade flows in different types of finished goods between these two areas.

The study will highlight the case of a number of selected technology-based industries: motor-vehicles and electrical, telecommunications, and optical equipment. By concentrating on the Union and ASEAN, this chapter will analyze the spatial form of the firm's internal division of labor. In addition, this research implies a comparison between investment choices between alternative developed or developing countries: towards the ASEAN rather than China on the one hand, towards the Union and other European countries rather than the United States or NAFTA and perhaps MERCOSUR countries, on the other. This will involve the use of statistical sources provided by the Ministry of Finance in Tokyo and of micro-data collected and published by Toyo Keizai, a private Japanese data bank and publishing company.

The current debate on Japanese FDI and new research avenues

Research on Japanese investment and location has normally focused on the motives for investing abroad.[1] Sekiguchi (1979), Nagamoto (1990), and Beamish, Delios and Lecraw (1997) appraise Japanese investment on a global scale. Other studies either compare Japanese and US FDI (Horaguchi, 1992), or concentrate on particular regions of the world. For example Tokunaga (1992) studies the case of Asia; Yamawaki (1991), Strange (1993), Thomsen (1993), Thiran and Yamawaki (1995), Darby (1996), Mayer and Mucchielli (1998) and Nemoto (1999) have documented the case of Japanese FDI in the Union. However, research on the specific case of Japanese investment in the Union as a competing or alternatively complementary destination to Asia, and more specifically to ASEAN, is in its infancy.

A synthesis of the major findings derived from the many different empirical and less empirical studies on Japanese location decisions enables us to posit that location decisions by Japanese firms are to be viewed in the context of a step approach. A first step involves the investment decision *per se*. The decision to invest abroad is primarily the result of a conjunction of many 'push factors' that compel the firm to contemplate foreign as opposed to domestic production.

These 'push factors' encompass: firm-specific advantages[2] in line, in some cases, with the product-cycle hypothesis; rising domestic production costs, due partly to an appreciation of the yen; saturation of the production and consumption capacity represented by the domestic economy; and stringent domestic environmental laws.[3] These factors push the firm to seek market access on a global scale.

This first step implies choosing a broad geographical area (Western Europe, as opposed to either Asia or North America). As a result of a first feasibility study, a 'long list' of candidate locations – within the chosen geographical region, and equally attractive – will ensue (Nemoto, 1999). Although it is still possible to segment the Union market into two broad subareas, i.e. the more free market oriented, industrially and technologically developed north on one hand, and the relatively less advanced south with lower technological levels, lower skills and with a more traditional manufacturing sector on the other, harmonisation and factor price equalisation render the Union a relatively homogeneous geographical area, compared with Asia.

This implies that, and with the exception of those industries where the comparative advantages are irrevocably connected with a long established know-how (textile and clothing industry in Italy, toiletries and perfume production in France), there are, for each Japanese investment project in the Union, many competing locations. A second step in the process of FDI refers to the location decision *per se*. Whereas the 'push factors' were paramount in the decision to manufacture abroad, the 'pull factors' will be crucial for the determination of the ultimate location choice.

The 'short list' of location decisions in the Union, and subsequently the final location choice, are greatly determined by the government's attitude towards inward investment, and by the promotional role exercized by the regional development agencies.

Although the motives for investing in different regions of the world have been largely documented, far less attention has been devoted to the issue of interdependence or connection between the different affiliates located in the same region, and furthermore, *between the different affiliates situated in the different regions of the world*. In the last 10–15 years, economic integration in the Union – with the advent of the Single European Market (SEM) – combined with the rapid emergence of the East and South-East Asian economies (and, more recently the trend towards increasing ASEAN economic integration), have greatly stimulated the establishment of these regional headquarters.

Most studies touching on the issue of interdependence hypothesize that the Union, Asia (and North America) are distinct in terms of location.

If there is some connection between different locations of the same Japanese multinational, this connection is intra-regional (intra-Union, intra-ASEAN). Indeed, recent developments in economic theory suggest that the combination of multilateral agreements and regionalism may constitute a strong incentive for foreign investors to locate in an economically integrated area (Japan and the United States in the case of the Union and its associated countries), eventually at the expense of other possible – less integrated – locations (Ethier, 1998). Using an empirical approach, Morris's survey of Japanese plants in the Union highlights some degree of connection between EU sites, a concept defined loosely by the existence of two or more sister plants of the same company in two or more Union countries (Morris, 1987).

According to JETRO (1995), the electric appliance *filière* is increasingly visible in Asia. In this industry, each production base specializes in certain products to meet the demand requirements for the entire Asian region. Kobayashi (1997) notes that coherent networks of affiliates transcend the boundaries of the company. Whereas in Japan, Nissan' s subsuppliers sell parts to Nissan only, in South-East Asia the same subsuppliers would sell parts to other Japanese manufacturers such as Mitsubishi. These studies highlight the geographical sphere of influence of the traditional Japanese (or indeed American) multinational enterprises (MNEs) by referring to the constitution of regional headquarters offices that coordinate the activities of the MNEs' affiliates in the region with that of the corporate headquarters (Dicken, 1998).

Further challenging studies relate to the extent of interdependence between these increasingly integrated regions with respect to the dynamic pattern of investment and also dis-investment. Surprisingly, very little research has been performed on Japanese dis-investment, either in Asia, Europe or other regions. Horaguchi (1992) presents a documented study and an empirical analysis on Japanese dis-investment from various countries during the 1980s. The results indicate that while most of the cases concerned Asia, this phenomenon concentrated on mining and other raw material-based industries (such as food manufacturing, metals, paper, or textile) and on several services (real estate and transportation). In line with the product-cycle model, and considering also exit barriers, a low rate of dis-investment in other manufacturing industries, especially in electrical machinery and transportation equipment, was observed. These remarks, and also the fact that manufacturing industries are perhaps more likely than services to induce complementarities at a global level, justify our emphasis on technology and knowledge oriented manufacturing, a sector which is obviously more prone to product-cycle effects and to technology diffusion.

With respect to investment itself, our study takes as a point of departure the new insights developed by the contemporary international trade theorists. These 'new' international trade theories focus on the growing incidence of intra-industry trade and argue that countries with similar production structures trade more between themselves in manufacturing products, and exchange similar products.[4] Going beyond this reasoning, our study takes another angle by arguing that there is evidence of growing intra-industry trade between substantially different economic regions of the world, namely the Union and Asia, and that this is increasingly possible because of the increasingly global strategies of MNEs, and in particular of Japanese manufacturing groups. Wakasugi (1997) had already noted a share of Japanese intra-industry trade (IIT) with some Asian countries (namely South Korea and Taiwan) being as high as – if not higher than – the shares observed for the United States and for European countries over the 1986–92 time period.[5] Wakasugi comments on this 'puzzling' finding by stressing that FDI, and in particular the increasing incidence of intra-firm trade within Japanese groups, is responsible for increased IIT between more structurally dissimilar countries. Being partly an extension of Wakasugi's work, our study will shed some light on the impact of the building up of vertically integrated systems of production at the global level (or *filières*) on intra-industry and intra-regional trade flows. First, we will briefly review the patterns of Japanese direct investment in Europe and Asia in general.

Patterns of Japanese manufacturing investment in Europe and Asia, 1975–97: cycles and trends

A description of general and sectoral patterns of Japanese FDI in the manufacturing sector, based on data by country of destination and sectors and published by the Ministry of Finance[6] is suggested here. It should be noted that only a selected number of European and Asian countries were considered for data publication before 1980. Accordingly, the figures for the 1975–97 period concern Europe as a geographic entity rather than as an integrated economic region of 15 member countries. Similarly, data on Japanese FDI in ASEAN do not include the new ASEAN member countries for the 1975–85 subperiod. Finally, as a consequence of the change in the currency used by the Ministry of Finance (MoF) for these data – the US dollar before 1992, and the yen thereafter – we had to choose between these two currencies. It is assumed that a large part of foreign investment actually consists of capital goods imported from Japan, or of other yen-denominated assets (such as patents or technologies). For this reason, US dollar values have been converted at yearly exchange rates.

General features of Japanese manufacturing FDI: is there a possible substitution effect between Europe and Asia, or within these two regions?

Although there is a steady increasing trend for the different FDI flows to these regions, and considering that current yen values are not a good indicator for the late 1970s owing to the inflation rate of these years, the increase in FDI is characterized by waves combined with a partial catching-up process. The initial attractiveness of Asia and North America persists, but Europe emerged during the late 1980s as an important target before a decline started to set in during most of the 1990s. However, the initial level of FDI in Europe, abnormally high, should be kept in mind, in order to avoid misleading conclusions based on short-term observations.

Indeed, the fear of an emerging 'Fortress Europe' represented a strong investment incentive in Europe during the late 1980s. However, it appears that Japanese firms' expectations in relation to the growth of the European market, and the negative consequence of economic integration for outsiders, were ill-conceived. The post-bubble Japanese direct investment patterns of the mid-1990s were characterized by a relative decline of the share represented by Europe, but from an exceptionally high level.

Regarding the comparison between Japanese FDI in manufacturing in Europe and in ASEAN, relatively similar patterns have been followed with comparable aggregate yearly levels since the early 1980s. A different pattern is noticeable for Asia as a whole, owing to unprecedented FDI flows towards China. When compared with North America, FDI towards Europe is still lagging behind; the gap remains at a 3:1 ratio during the entire period, except during the peak years.

This overview suggests that, *a priori*, since FDI flows to Europe and to ASEAN are broadly equivalent over time, North America and China, rather than South-East Asian countries may be the most prominent competitors of Europe for attracting Japanese investment. In a multilateral international trade system, Japanese firms may prefer to export to Europe, not only from ASEAN, but also from either the United States or China, according to the possibility of labor–capital substitution.

A further appreciation of the yen after 1994 induced a new wave of capital outflows, especially towards China and the United States, with a peak in 1995 and 1996, respectively. The decline was spectacular in China in 1997. According to estimates for the final years of the 1990s, the figure may have fallen to the lowest level achieved during that decade, not only for the ASEAN countries but also for China. Even if some kind of a geographical substitution exists, the decline of Japanese FDI to Asia does not necessarily imply an increase in the flows directed towards Europe since the United States is, in the case of some industries, an alternative destination.

The absence of catching-up by Europe as an attractive destination for Japanese investment may partially be explained by the intra-EU breakdown of these flows. Furthermore, a comparison with ASEAN may shed some light on these matters. The intense geographical concentration of Japanese FDI in a very few selected European countries has been widely documented (Thiran and Yamawaki, 1995; Mayer and Mucchielli, 1998; Andréosso-O'Callaghan, 1999). As highlighted by these various authors, there are two major attractive countries for Japanese investors in Europe, after correction for their size: the United Kingdom and the Netherlands. The rest accounts for only a third of cumulated Japanese FDI in Europe over the period 1951–96. Even Spain did not manage to capture more than a short-lived attention. Japanese FDI towards each of the four largest European countries (Germany, France, Italy, and Spain) merely reached the level of Japanese investment in the Philippines, by far the least attractive country of the ASEAN group among Japanese business circles (see Figures 2.1–2.3).

By contrast, the main five ASEAN countries and, more recently, Vietnam, received relatively comparable flows regardless of the size of their population or economy. This may be interpreted as a diversification strategy aimed at both avoiding political country risks and at capturing a significant share of the domestic market. Obviously, this kind of concern does not exist in the case of politically stable and economically integrated European countries.

Patterns of Japanese FDI in Europe and in Asia in two selected sectors

The two sectors under investigation are motor-vehicles and electrical, telecommunication, and optical equipment. Motor-vehicles is a mature industry, characterized by homogeneous products, although quality standards and requirements differ in developing and developed countries. The other sector is extremely heterogeneous, but strong spillover effects are common among the different technologies used for audio–video, telecommunication and electronic products; electrical equipment is also used either as a capital good or as a domestic appliance. Furthermore, this sector is characterized by similar quality standards worldwide and by short product cycles.[7]

In the case of both electrical and transportation equipment industries, high levels of Japanese investment flows, first in North America and then in Europe, can again be observed during the late 1980s and early 1990s. Although some kind of cyclical pattern is also noticeable, flows towards ASEAN countries are much more stable. In addition, the second peak of

Figure 2.1 Japanese manufacturing FDI in Europe, Asia, ASEAN, China, and North America, 1975–98 (million yen)

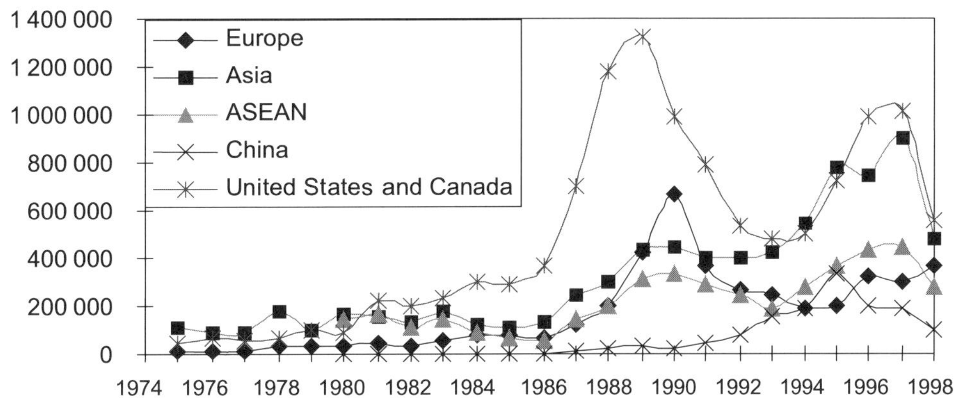

Note: Asia including ASEAN.

Figure 2.2 Japanese manufacturing FDI in selected European countries 1980–98 (million yen)

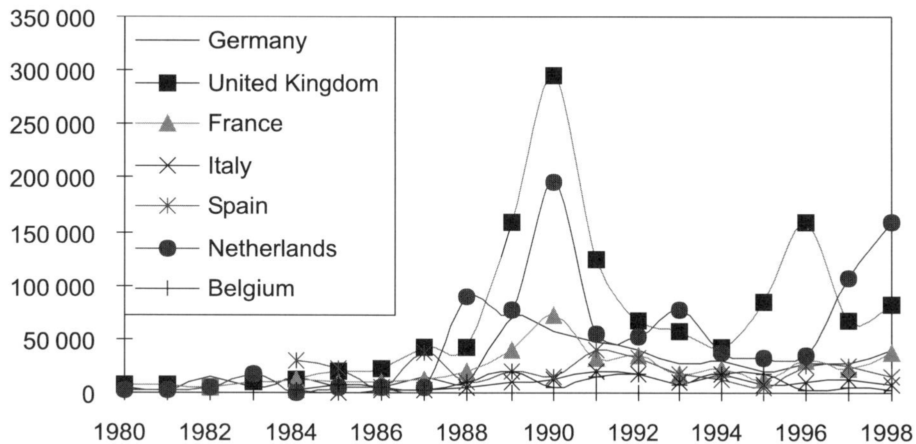

Figure 2.3 Japanese manufacturing FDI, five ASEAN countries 1980–98 (million yen)

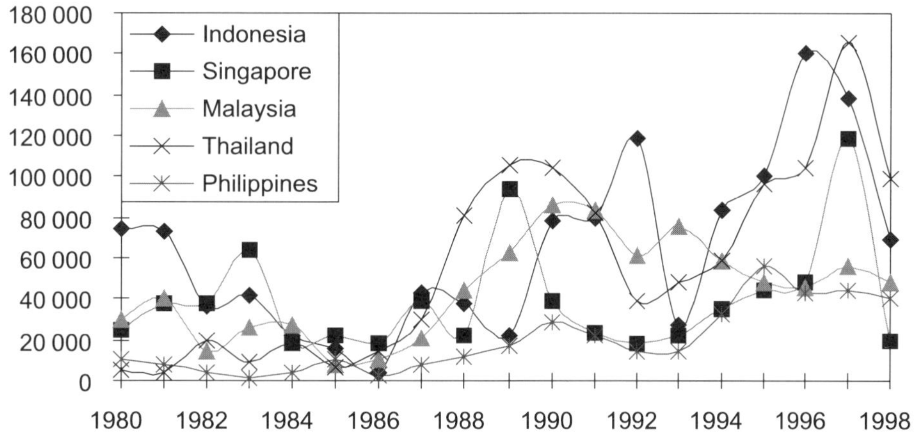

1996–7, experienced by North America is not observed with the same magnitude in the case of Europe (figures 2.4, 2.5).

Case studies on Japanese FDI in manufacturing industry

Purpose and sample

Case studies provide complementary information based upon analyses and comparisons of Japanese companies' international business strategies. The purpose is to describe the visible features of recent investment strategies of a sample of selected Japanese manufacturing groups, using data collected and published by Toyo Keizai Co. (Toyo Keizai, 1998a, 1998b). For a sample of 12 companies, we check the number and characteristics of subsidiaries created by the companies during each year of 1990s and in each country, or group of countries. This gives an indication of new trends, although it is obviously a rough proxy for actual Japanese investment patterns. It is assumed that the year of creation of a new foreign subsidiary is an acceptable and significant indicator of a potential shift in location strategy. Our main interest lies in the comparison of global strategies of firms belonging to different industries, and in their possible shift to alternative target countries.

Quantitative indicators such as business activity, the size of the workforce (when available in the data), and the motivation of the Japanese group for the investment (when indicated) were taken into account.[8] A gradual increase in the size of the capital invested is actually a commonly used method for avoiding risks in the creation and development of a new venture. In addition to the increase in the social capital resulting from Japanese or local investment, a large share of capital formation results from re-invested profits. This last source of financing used to account for a total amount estimated to be the equivalent of Japanese direct investment officially recorded by the Ministry of Finance (MoF) of Japan in the case of subsidiaries in China or ASEAN countries before the outbreak of the Asian financial turmoil (MITI, 1997).

The transportation and electrical equipment industries have been investigated so far at a meso-economic level. They are now considered from a micro-economic viewpoint. The identification of similar business strategies in the geographical breakdown of direct investment for these two industries may allow us to formulate interpretations of the recent trends, especially regarding the perspective of an eventual shift in Japanese direct investment from Asia to Europe. Accordingly, the sample consists of large companies that are expected to develop an adequate

Figure 2.4 Japanese FDI, electrical equipment 1980–98 (Asia, ASEAN, China, Europe and North America) (million yen)

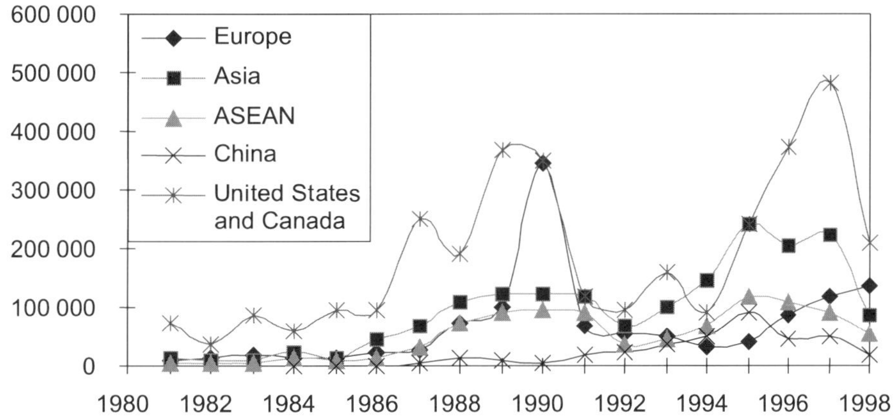

Figure 2.5 Japanese FDI, transportation equipment 1980–98 (Asia, ASEAN, China, Europe and North America) (million yen)

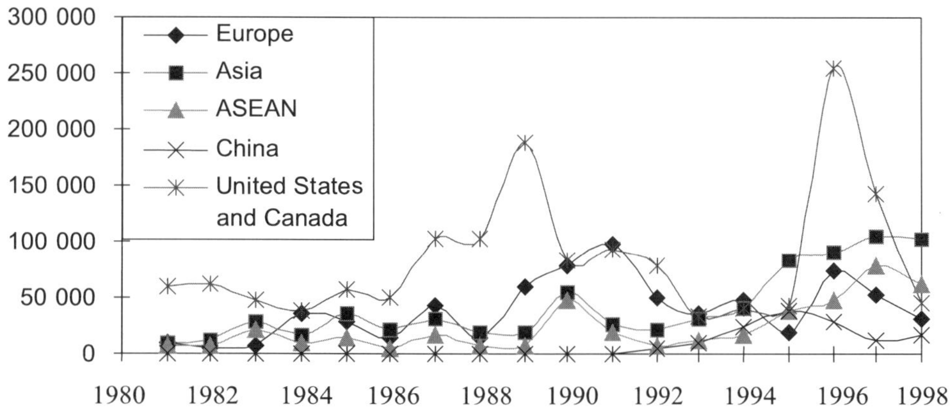

response to the East Asian economic crisis. This sample can be taken as a proxy for the Japanese manufacturing sector as a whole. The following companies are included in the sample:

- For the motor-car industry (including trucks and motorcycles): Toyota, Nissan, Honda, Mitsubishi, Suzuki, and Isuzu.
- For the electrical, telecommunication, and optical equipment industry: Matsushita, Sony, NEC, Canon, Nikon, and Ricoh.

Fuji-Xerox and Mazda were not considered as possible representative firms to be included in the sample owing to the influence of American top-rank managers and American shareholders in the international strategic choices of these companies.

Lessons from case studies on Japanese investment in the 1990s: Europe versus Asia

An observation of the selected case studies in these two industries allow us to identify the following features (Tables 2A.1 and 2A.2 in the Appendix, p. 000):

- Investment in China and ASEAN may involve relatively capital-intensive and technology-intensive products in many cases. Therefore, these countries/regions appear increasingly as alternative locations to Europe and to the United States (or Japan), when exports to these countries are not restricted, (which is normally the rule).
- The pattern of diversification within Asia and, more specifically within ASEAN, has been confirmed and amplified during recent years in the case of the companies in the sample. This means that further economic liberalization with the opening-up of Vietnam and Myanmar (and eventually India and Central Asia), could invite Japanese investors to pay attention to these new potential locations. This may apply to the different parts of China, given the new orientation of the Chinese regional policy contained in the 1990-Five-Year Plan (1996–2000).
- The United States is increasingly important in terms of investment in the areas of high-tech manufacturing, services, and R&D. The United States is by far the most attractive developed country for the companies in the sample. At the other end of the spectrum, investment in the Union tends to focus on logistics or on the presence of new headquarters for business operation in Europe. Except for the continuation of previous investment patterns in both the United Kingdom and the Netherlands, few recent ventures in manufacturing

are observed. The creation of research centres in Europe does not necessarily induce the setting-up of local manufacturing bases.

- Central Europe appears as a possible new attractive destination, but this concerns only a short list of winners, such as Hungary, Poland, and the Czech Republic. These countries have signed Europe Agreements with the Union and display labor costs comparable with those of the more advanced ASEAN countries for the skilled worker category. A possible scenario would be that the first wave of investment would focus on distribution and that manufacturing would eventually follow. Finland, Sweden, and Austria are likely to benefit from the growing interest for a wider Europe, albeit marginally. Russia and other Eastern Europe countries may benefit from investments in the area of financial services and distribution.
- Unless substantial subsidies for Japanese investors compensate for production cost differentials, and unless strong attractive packages are developed by the countries and regions themselves, there are almost no incentives left for choosing France or Germany rather than say, Hungary or Poland. One of the few country-specific advantages left to these more developed countries is the existence of specific skills – as in the case of R&D centers – and the higher level of economic integration achieved by these countries,[9] which would induce Japanese firms to choose Germany rather than the United Kingdom for the localisation of their headquarters in Europe (Sony versus Matsushita).

Further information gathered on a microeconomic basis shows that some degree of interdependence,[10] between the Asian (excluding Japan) and European markets exists among the biggest groups (such as Toyota, Suzuki Motor Corp., Canon Inc., Nikon Corp.). However, far from being confined to the biggest groups, this interdependence is noticeable also in the case of smaller companies such as Hoya Corp., Terumo, and Omron Electronics. Intra-group sales from one region to the other are more common in the case of finished products than in the case of intermediate products. This interdependence concerns up to 40 percent of products manufactured in one region, and implies in most of the cases trade flows from Asia to Europe.

The responses of Japanese firms to the Asian crisis: implications for future Japanese investment in Europe

The local and global responses of Japanese management to the Asian crisis

As a whole, Japanese investment in China and in the ASEAN countries is much too recent to allow Japanese firms to consider immediately an eventual plan of massive disinvestment. Whatever the difficulties faced by the business groups in particular countries, especially in Thailand and Indonesia, top management still remembers the huge profit rates and rapid returns on investment experienced during the 1980s and early 1990s. However, in the case of either ASEAN or China, production is mainly domestic or regionally demand oriented. Depending on the type of product and on the industry, significant differences in quality standards still exist between Japanese products made in ASEAN countries and China, and those geared to the markets of developed countries. Therefore, a dramatic export shift, which is obviously the easiest way to keep up production levels in the Asian subsidiaries, is limited in scale. Using various reports published by Toyo Keizai Co. (1998b), different local and global responses could be observed during the course of the diffusion and the aggravation of the Asian crisis.

The first kind of immediate response proffered by Japanese management to the expected decline in domestic demand in either Thailand or Indonesia was the temporary adjustment of production levels to the new level of effective domestic demand. In the motor-car industry, production lines of pick-up trucks in Nissan's Thailand factory were stopped as early as August 1997. In addition, a reduction of the working time to 4 days per week was implemented on the production lines of other types of cars. Similar decisions were adopted in September 1997 at Honda's Thailand automobile factory where Thai production was halved, with a shift from two teams to one only. The same kind of adjustment was implemented in the following months in many other Japanese subsidiaries in Thailand, Indonesia, and Malaysia. At Matsushita Electric in Malaysia, a 10 percent decrease in the planned level of refrigerators and air-conditioner production was implemented in December 1997; the two local subsidiaries produced more than 50 percent of the Matsushita group total production. The production lines were almost stopped at Toyota's Astra Motor factory (Jakarta) in January 1998, and also in February at Toyota Motor Philippines (Manila).

The second kind of immediate response was to acknowledge the increasing cost of components imported from Japan and at the same time the decline in living standards resulting from the acceleration of inflation. In order to avoid a further decline in the level of effective demand, only modest price increases were implemented. In January 1998, a 10 percent price increase in rupiah was allowed for Toyota models produced in Indonesia (following a 4.3 percent increase in August 1998). In fact, significant differences were observed in the magnitude of price increases, depending on the ratio of local components. In February 1998, Sharp Co.

decided a price increase in the ASEAN countries reaching 100 percent in Indonesia and 20 percent in Malaysia and Thailand (following a previous 20 percent increase between October and December). In addition, significant wage increases were implemented for local staff in order to keep their skills available within the firm. Among others, in February 1998, Oki Electric announced an increase of local employees' wages following a previous increase in November 1997. These measures were obviously inadequate to change the trend and to improve the profitability of local subsidiaries.

The global response of Japanese management consisted, at a micro-level, of significant shifts from the previous model of international specialisation among subsidiaries of the same group. Although labor costs in ASEAN countries declined in dollar or in yen terms, the crisis induced a diffusion of new technologies, and the relatively high-tech production operations shifted from Japan to local subsidiaries or subcontractors in these countries. In December 1997, Honda announced publicly its decision to export from Japan auto-parts of a new model of recreational vehicle to be assembled in Thailand and in the Philippines. It should be noted that this acceleration of the product-cycle process took place in the context of declining Japanese manufacturing production (–10 percent in 1998) to the lowest level since the early 1980s. In January 1998, Isuzu decided to improve quality standards as a requirement for exporting Thai produced pick-up trucks to Australia, and engine components to Japan. In February 1998, the local component rate was increased from around 20 percent to 50 percent at Matsushita Indonesia factories. In January 1998, Canon decided to double the production of ASP compact cameras in Malaysia (15 000 to 30 000 units per month) and to use the yen as the reference currency for exports.

The Japanese government accepted the application by industrial groups for permits allowing temporary foreign staff to work in Japan within the same group. This labor factor mobility occurred in a context of growing unemployment and job destruction in the manufacturing sector. One of the most important cases was that of Nissan allowing Thai workers to come from the Nissan subsidiaries in Thailand in order to avoid layoffs of relatively skilled blue-collar employees. Labor mobility was accepted by these Thai workers owing to the attractive wage differentials and to the positive impact expected on their carreer as a consequence of their being on a training scheme in Nissan's factories in Japan. One of the surprising consequences of the Asian crisis was therefore to induce Japan to renounce one of its basic rules governing its national immigration policy, according to which the supply of foreign labor should not interfere in the

Japanese labor market, except in the case where there were short-term labor shortages.

But equally important for the future role of manufacturing production in Asian subsidiaries was the collective involvement of Japanese producers (Toyota, Matsushita, Sony, etc.), in February 1998, asking the ASEAN Industrial Cooperation committee (AICO) to reduce intra-ASEAN tariffs on manufactured goods from 30–40 percent to 0–5 percent. This quest for an increase in South-East Asian regional economic integration demonstrates that, for the Japanese business community, one of the most important engines in terms of economic recovery lies in the increase of local components in ASEAN-based manufacturing plants, either for the domestic or for the international market.

Implications for Japanese FDI in Europe

The current strategy of Japanese groups in the ASEAN countries could be interpreted as an indication that regionalism is an additional and strong incentive to locate in the countries of the regions where comparative advantages are relatively higher, even if more attractive countries could be found in other parts of the world.

This undoubtedly represents a favorable outcome for several Central and Eastern European countries (CEECs). As a whole, the potential for attracting new Japanese investment in Europe seems extremely low. However, this remark does not apply to Central Europe. Hungary, Poland, and the Czech Republic have become the main targets of a re-deployed strategy in Europe. In the medium term, other countries that have been found to satisfy all the conditions of membership i.e. Cyprus, Slovenia, and Estonia can be added to this list (EC, 1997). In the case of relatively technology-intensive products for export to the Union, Japanese groups will face multiple opportunities and will eventually enjoy the same kind of competition between public authorities for attracting foreign investment that they already experienced inside the Union. However, the reduction of the effective investment cost in the Union during the 1990s was not a strong enough incentive for the Japanese groups.

On the other side and as a consequence of the rejection of Turkey's application for full EU membership, this country could be considered as an outsider with negative implications from the viewpoint of Japanese investors. The Free Trade agreement signed by the Union and 11 Mediterranean developing countries (the 1995 Barcelona Declaration) will increase the number of possible target countries as far as labor-intensive production for re-export to the Union is concerned. In a world trade system combining multilateral agreements and regionalism, economic theory suggests that foreign investment may focus on one or a few number of countries rather than being distributed equally among the new members of the regional agreement (Ethier, 1998).

Conclusions

Japanese direct investment has traditionally followed different patterns in Asia when compared with Europe. In the Union, investment flows are polarised in a few selected countries; in Asia, and more specifically in ASEAN, they are spread more evenly on a geographical basis. Japanese investment flows have been stable in Asia; in the case of Europe, these flows have followed cyclical patterns.

Through the growing incidence of FDI, Europe and Asia appear increasingly as complementary locations not only in the view of the largest Japanese manufacturing groups, but also for smaller ones. Intra-group trade between the two regions is far from being insignificant. In a typical case, Asian countries are used as a manufacturing base for finished products exported to Europe. Will the Asian crisis jeopardize this international division of production and distribution patterns?

From a European viewpoint, it could be expected that the Asian crisis could have a significant impact on the Asian economies' comparative advantages, and that instability in the region may stimulate Japanese FDI in Europe. However, in addition to the past experience of high profit rates in Asian subsidiaries, strong public incentives, in both Japan and the Asian countries, are likely to exert pressure in order to avoid disinvestment in Asia. In particular, China continues to be considered as one of the most attractive locations in Asia. On the other hand, the enlargement of the Union to include a few selected CEE countries with labor costs comparable to those of the ASEAN countries is a further and strong incentive for future new Japanese investment increasing in China and in ASEAN countries, rendering the prospects for increased intra-group trade between Europe and Asia even more feasible.

Appendix

Table 2A.1 Foreign investment trends, Japanese motor-vehicles companies (including trucks and motorcycles)

	ASEAN and China	Europe	United States, Canada, Mexico and MERCOSOR
Toyota	Investment in Vietnam (1996) and also in China (1998), in Tianjin. In the 1990s, increase in production in other Asian subsidiaries: Thailand (1962, 1978, 1987, 1988, 1993, 7500 employees), Taiwan (1984, 2400), Philippines (1988 and 1990, 2600), Indonesia (1971, 5400).	Investment in France (1997) following previous production plants in United Kingdom (1988, 1989). Investment limited to distribution in Poland (1990), the Czech Republic (1993), Hungary (1991), and Turkey (1990). Same in Italy (1990) and Spain (1992)	Following massive investment in the 1980s, no recent subsidiaries in the United States and Canada, except in California for the control of five former factories. Production subsidiary in Argentina (1994).
Nissan	Production subsidiaries in Thailand (1996), Indonesia (1996), and for distribution in Myanmar (1997). Also producing in Taiwan (1978, 1985, 1987) and in the Philippines (1983).	Investment in Finance in the United Kingdom (1997), following production (1986, 1987, 1991, 1992). Production subsidiaries in Spain (1995, 1995), following investment in 1980 and 1990; also in the Netherlands (1982, 1985, 1987, 1988, 1990, 1990, 1995). Only sale and design in Germany, France and Italy.	Subsidiaries in the United States (1990, 1991, 1991) in services business (finance, insurance logistics) following massive investment in production subsidiaries between the 1960s and the 1980s. Same in Canada (1990). Production increasing in Nissan Mexicana.
Honda	Investment in China (Guangdong, 1995, 1995, 1997), India (1995), and Vietnam (1996). Increasing production during the mid-1990s, in Malaysia, Thailand, Indonesia, and the Philippines (many subsidiaries established from the 1960s).	Participation in the United Kingdom (1996) in a joint venture with a subcontractor for auto-parts production following previous investment (1986, 1989). Investment in Italy (1996) in motorcycles production.	Investment in the United States (1995, 1996, 1997) in auto-parts production following massive investment in the 1980s. Production subsidiary in Brazil for auto-parts.
Mitsubishi	Investment in Vietnam (1995), following those in Indonesia (1975), Thailand (1987), and Philippines (1987) (3000 and 2000 employees, respectively) No subsidiary in China. Important participation in the Proton Project in Malaysia in the 1980s.	R&D subsidiary in Germany (1993). Sale subsidiaries: Sweden (1995), Hungary (1991), Czech Republic (1993). Investment in 1999 in Portugal for the production and sale of light trucks (400 employees).	R&D subsidiary (1996), in Illinois (USA), following previous investment in production subsidiaries in the same state (1985, 1988, 1991).

Table 2A.1 Foreign investment trends, Japanese motor-vehicles companies (including trucks and motorcycles) (*continued*)

	ASEAN and China	**Europe**	**United States, Canada, Mexico and MERCOSOR**
Suzuki	Suzuki's four first subsidiaries in China between 1993 and 1996 z(in Shandong, Sichuan). Fifth subsidiary in India in 1993; investment in Vietnam (1996).	Subsidiary created in Hungary for production in 1992, for marketing in Poland in 1992, and in Austria in 1993.	
Isuzu	Massive investment in China in 1995, Beijing and Sichuan. New production subsidiaries in Vietnam (1997), in Taiwan (1995), and in the Philippines (1995); also in Thailand (1996) for auto-parts following previous investment.	Subsidiaries for production in Poland (1997), and in the United Kingdom (1996) following previous investment in the United Kingdom (1987) (2000 employees). A subsidiary for distribution in continental Europe: Germany (1996).	Subsidiary in Indiana (1995), for services, following previous investments in Indiana (1989), California (1981) and Michigan (1975).

Source: Toyo Keizai Co. (1998b).

Table 2A.2 Foreign investment trends, Japanese electrical and optical equipment companies

	ASEAN and China	Europe	United States, Canada, Mexico and MERCOSOR
Matsushita Electric Industrial	In China, eight companies established in 1994, five in 1995, seven in 1996 and two in 1997. In 1996, three new companies in Indonesia; same in India. Also in Vietnam (1996), in Thailand (1997), in Malaysia (1996), in the Philippines (1995) and in Singapore (1996), Sony's first R&D center in Asia.	Four new companies established in the United Kingdom (1992, 1993, 1995, 1997) for logistics and nonfinance services. Also in Germany, four new companies (1995, 1996, 1997) for production, services and Matsushita Headquarters in Europe. Finance company in Austria (1994) and Finland (1996) for trade with Central Europe and Russia or other CIS countries. Production companies in Poland (1995) and the Czech Republic (1995, 1996); distribution in Hungary (1994), Romania (1996) and Slovakia (1997).	13 new companies established in the United States between 1995 and 1998 (doubling the total number of Matsushita subsidiaries in the United States) for production, services and R&D. In 1997, production subsidiary in Mexico.
Sony	Sony's five first subsidiaries in China established between 1993 and 1996. Also in Thailand, Indonesia and India (1995) and the Philippines (1997).	Only three investments in the Union since the late 1980s: In the Netherlands, for logistics (1990, 1993) and Germany for managing business operations in the Union (1995). Investment in Hungary (1994) and Slovakia (1996) for production purposes.	Four company established in the United States in 1995 and 1996 (manufacturing and TV programs). Distribution company established in Argentina (1995).

Table 2A.2 Foreign investment trends, Japanese electrical and optical equipment companies (*continued*)

	ASEAN and China	Europe	United States, Canada, Mexico and MERCOSOR
NEC	Nine new subsidiaries established in China since 1994 (Guangdong, Fujian, Shanghai, Liaoning, Beijing). Investment (1997) in Vietnam, the Philippines, and Indonesia.	Only two recent investments in Europe: NEC Europe in London as central office for Union and a subsidiary in St Petersburg (Russia) for manufacturing.	Three new subsidiaries established in 1996 and 1997 for R&D purposes.
Toshiba	12 new subsidiaries established in China since 1994 (Guangdong, Wuhan, Shanghai, Tianjin, Beijing). Investment (1995, 1996) in Thailand, the Philippines, and Indonesia.	Only one investment in Europe: Toshiba Research Centre (United Kingdom) for semi-conductors technology.	Four new subsidiaries established in the United States since 1995 (production of semi-conductors and R&D), following an investment in 1993 in finance (Toshiba America Capital Co.). Also in Mexico in 1995 for distribution purposes.
Nikon	Subsidiaries in South Korea for services (1993). for marketing in Thailand (1994). No investment in China since 1991.	No investment in the Union since 1990 (Canon Research Centre, France) and 1991 (copiers recycling factory in the United Kingdom). Three new marketing subsidiaries in Poland, the Czech Republic and Hungary (1994).	No investment in the United States since the last two in 1990 (Canon Research Center, Canon Finance) and 1992 (Canon Trading, export to Japan, Canon Computer, manufacturing).
Ricoh	In China, Ricoh's five first subsidiaries established in 1991 (one), 1993 (one), 1995 (three). Also three subsidiaries in Hong Kong (1995, 1996), one in Singapore (1996), and in India (1993).	Subsidiary established in Spain for manufacturing (1996). Marketing subsidiaries established in 1995 and 1996 in Hungary, Poland, and Austria.	Three new subsidiaries established in the United States for marketing in 1994 and 1995 and also in 1997 for R&D.

Source: Toyo Keizai Co. (1998b).

Notes

* Funding from the CNRS/ Forbairt program is greatly acknowledged.
** Funding from the CNRS, Forbairt program and Japan Foundation are greatly acknowledged.

1 Note that even before potential investors in foreign countries opt for offshore manufacturing, they are faced with a trade-off between three alternative choices: FDI, exports, and licensing (Horagushi, 1992). Japanese firms are notorious for their exceptional reluctance to adopt licensing as an international business strategy except when investment barriers are associated with a fast-growing domestic market: this was the case in Korea during the 1970s and 1980s, and it explains to a large extent the low level of Japanese investment there. This remark does not apply, however, to the rest of Asia.
2 'Ownership' in the traditional literature on FDI (Dunning, 1981). On the applicability of the OLI paradigm to the case of Japanese investors, see Hasegawa (1996) and Andréosso-O'Callaghan (1999).
3 The latter explain overseas manufacturing activities of Japanese chemical firms during the 1970s (Darby, 1996a).
4 For example, Helpman (1987) hypotheses that the share of IIT is explained by the similarity of factors between countries, and by the size of their national income. See also Helpman and Krugman (1985).
5 In this study, the share values have been calculated on the basis of bilateral trade flows relating to 11 fairly aggregated industry sectors (raw materials and mineral fuels, nonmetal mineral products, foodstuffs, textile, light industrial products, chemicals, metals, general machinery, electrical machinery, transportation equipment, and precision instruments).
6 The data for 1997 were not published by the MOF at the time of the submission of this chapter; we rely upon figure kindly provided by the administration during a visit to the MOF in July 1998.
7 Other technology- and knowledge-intensive industries, such as machine-tools, are not investigated here because of the relatively small number of affiliates, owing to the relatively small size of parent companies. The chemical and pharmaceutical industry was also neglected owing to its extreme heterogeneity; to the magnitude of reliance on foreign technology and patents; to the negative impact of the shortage of skilled labour (blue-and especially white-collar workers) in Asia, with perhaps the exception of Korea, Taiwan, and Singapore.
8 Information on the social capital of the local subsidiary, which is not necessarily a relevant indicator for the size of the capital actually invested, was neglected.
9 An advantage suddenly brought to the fore by the creation of the euro-area
10 We have defined 'interdependence' as the percentage of sales of finished and intermediate products manufactured in one region, say Asia (except Japan) and sold in another (Europe).

References

Andreosso-O'Callaghan, B. (1999) 'Japanese Manufacturing Investment in France in a EU Comparative Framework – Theory and Practice,' in F. P. Cerase, F. Mazzei, and C. Molteni (eds.) *Japan and the Mediterranean World* (Napoli: Fridericiana Varia), 145–77.

Beamish, P. W., Delios, A., and Lecraw, D. (1997) *Japanese Multinationals in the Global Economy* (Aldershot: Edward Elgar).

Darby, J. (1996a) 'Less Successful Strategies: Japanese Manufacturing in Southern Europe,' *South European Society & Politics*, 1: 1, 24–46.

Darby, J. (1996b) *Japan and the European Periphery* (London: Macmillan).

Dicken, P. (1998) *Global Shift – Transforming the World Economy* (London: Paul Chapman).

Dunning, J. H. (1981) *International Production and the Multinational Enterprise* (London: Allen & Unwin)

Ethier, W. J. 'Regionalism in a Multilateral World,' *Journal of Political Economy*, 106: 6, 1214–45.

European Commission (EC) (1997), 'Agenda 2000 – For a Stronger and Wider Union,' *Bulletin of the European Union*, Supplement 5/97, Brussels.

Hasegawa, S. (1996) 'Determinants of Japanese Firms' Entry Modes in Europe,' Globalisation et Regionalisation, Conference Internationale en Sorbonne, Paris (May 29–30).

Helpman, E. (1987) 'Imperfect Competition and International Trade: Evidence from Fourteen Industrial Countries'. *Journal of the Japanese and International Economies*, 1, 62–81.

Helpman, E. and Krugman, P. (1985) *Market Structure and Foreign Trade: Increasing Return, Imperfect Competition and the International Economy* (Cambridge, Mass., MIT Press).

Horaguchi, H. (1992) *Nihon kigyo no kaigai chokusetsu toshi, Asia he no shinshutsu to tettai* (Foreign Direct Investment in Japanese Firms, Investment and Disinvestment in Asia) (Tokyo: University of Tokyo Press).

JETRO (various issues) (Japan's External Trade Organization), *White Paper on FDI* (Tokyo: Jetro).

Kobayashi, H. (1997) 'Globalization Strategy of the Japanese Automobile Industry,' Conference Proceedings, Economic Relations between Europe and East Asia, Université Paul Valéry, Nîmes (June).

Mayer, T. and Mucchielli J. L. (1998) 'Strategic Location Behaviour: The Case of Japanese Investments in Europe,' *Journal of Transnational Management Development,* 3: 3/4, 131–67.

MITI (1997) *Kaigai jigyo katsudo chosa gaiyo* (1997 A Survey of Japanese Firms' Overseas Subsidiaries' Activities) (Tokyo: MITI).

Morris, J. (1987) 'Japanese Manufacturing Investments in the European Economic Community: The Effects of Integration' (Brussels: Report to DG1, Commission of the EC).

Nagamoto, Y. (1990) 'Japanese Investments Abroad: Past, Present and Future Japanese Presence in Europe,' *IRES Discussion Paper* (Université Catholique de Louvain).

Nemoto, E. (1999) 'Japanese Investments in Spain,' in F. P. Cerase, F. Mazzei and C. Molteni (eds) *Japan and the Mediterranean World* (Napoli: Fridericiana Varia) 197– 212.

Sekiguchi, S. (1979) *Japan Direct Foreign Investment* (London: Macmillan).

Strange, R. (1993) *Japanese Manufacturing Investment in Europe – Its impact on the UK Economy* (London: Routledge).

Thiran, J. M. and Yamawaki, H. (1995) 'Regional and Country Determinants of Locational Decisions: Japanese Multinational Firms in European Manufacturing,' *IRES Discussion Paper,* 95/7 (Université Catholique de Louvain).

Thomsen, S. (1993) 'Japanese Direct Investment in the European Community: The Product Cycle Revisited,' *World Economy,* 16: 3, 301–15.

Tokunaga S. (ed) (1992), *Japan's Foreign Investment and Asian Economic Inderdependence: Production, Trade and Financial System* (Tokyo: University of Tokyo Press).

Toyo Keizai Co. (1998a) *Kaigai shinshutsu kigyo soran, kunibetsu hen* (Yearbook of Japanese Foreign Subsidiaries, Classification by Countries) (Tokyo: Toyo Keizai Shinposha).

Toyo Keizai Co. (1998b), *Kaigai shinshutsu kigyo soran, kaishabetsu hen* (Yearbook of Japanese Foreign Subsidiaries, Classification by Companies) (Tokyo: Toyo Keizai Shinposha).

Wakasugi, R. (1997) 'Missing Factors of Intra-industry Trade: Some Empirical Evidence Based on Japan,' *Japan and the World Economy,* 9, 353–62.

Yamawaki, I. (1991) 'Locational Decisions of Japanese Multinational Firms in European Manufacturing Industry,' Department of Economics (Université Catholique de Louvain, mimeo).

3

The Links between Japanese Investment in Asia and De-Industrialization in Japan

Françoise Guelle

Faced with industrial maturity since the mid-1980s, Japan has entered a phase in which manufacturing industry no longer attracts talented young people, where small and medium-size (SMEs) companies are losing their technological basis, and where the Japanese regions, experiencing a depopulation effect, are forced to compete with other Asian countries in order to maintain a certain level of manufacturing investment.

The rise in the unemployment rate highlights the decline of manufacturing industry in Japan. It is tempting to draw a parallel with the rise of the country's direct investment flows abroad. The extent of production transfer to Asia since the 1990s is often cited as one of the principal reasons for this evolution. Underlying this assertion is the acknowledgment that these transfers lead to fewer direct exports for a greater number of imports, and that they have a tendency to weaken the industrial structure and to reduce employment (Katoh, 1994; Saitoh, 1996; Seki, 1997). Thus de-industrialization, or *kûdôka*, appears to go hand in hand with industrial maturity.

Western industrial countries experienced de-industrialization well before Japan. In the United States, two terms define this phenomenon: 'de-industrialization' refers to industries in decline, while the 'hollow corporation' is a reference to the managerial aspects of the firms in question. The expression 'de-industrialization' was originally used to describe the breaking up of basic industries in the United States: 'a widespread, systematic disinvestment in the nation's basic productive capacity' (Bluestone and Harrison, 1982, p. 6). It referred to the closing of firms, the departure of employees, and the appearance of deserted towns surrounded by industrial wasteland.

Others have a less pessimistic view of the situation. Some authors such as Bell and Naisbitt (1982) maintain that de-industrialization affecting manufacturing firms emptied of their productive substance is only an inevitable stage which every manufacturing company in decline must go through in its transition to find a place in post-industrial society or in the information society. Whatever the difficulties, they are temporary and they will be overcome, promoting the adjustments of the international industrial structure.

In Japan, the question is of great interest within the framework of domestic industrial policies; the ideal adjustment would consist in transferring resources of industries having lost their competitive advantage in international markets to industries that are becoming competitive. This is what Japan has done since the beginning of its internationalization strategy: transfer the low-value added industries to Asia and keep the high-value added industries in Japan. But with the emergence of disturbances in the internal regulation of employment, is this mythical slogan showing signs of wear?

The less widespread term in Japanese economics literature, *datsukôgyôka*, corresponds to de-industrialization that is specific to an industrial sector, while *sangyôkûdôka* concerns its consequences for the surrounding social and industrial structure. This is also what Japanese specialists mean by 'hollowing out'. The Japanese notion of *kûdôka* would be situated between the restrictive definition of the IMF (1997), which refers to a long-term decrease in manufacturing employment, and a wider definition, according to which the gradual loss of international competitiveness leads to an increase in imports and direct investment which, in turn, have a negative effect on employment levels and industrial production of developed countries.

The impact of relocation on the Japanese industrial system

Let us consider the indicators which will help us to set up a diagnosis of de-industrialization of the Japanese economy. In terms of manufacturing jobs, since the peak of 1992, the manufacturing industry lost 1.24 million employees (nearly 8 percent) in four years without provoking a major social crisis. The number of employees dropped from 24.4 percent to 22.3 percent of the total working population; the share of value added from the manufacturing industry in the nation's gross domestic product dropped from 27.1 percent to 24.6 percent (Table 3.1). As for the imports of manufactured goods, these reached nearly 60 percent of total imports, though in the early 1990s, Japan was still considered as being only a big importing country of raw materials.

Table 3.1 Changes in selected Japanese manufacturing de-industrialization indicators, 1991–6

Indicators/years	1991	1992	1993	1994	1995	1996
Wages (million)	15.50	15.69	15.30	14.96	14.56	14.45
% of working population in industry	24.3	24.4	23.7	23.2	22.5	22.3
% of GDP	27.1	27.0	26.3	25.6	24.9	24.6
% of manufactured goods in imports	50.8	50.2	52.0	55.2	59.1	59.4

Source: *Keizai kikakuchô, Sômuchô tôkeikyoku* (Economic Planning Agency, Bureau of Statistics, Management and Coordination Agency).

The evolution of these indicators suggests that important changes are taking place in Japanese industrial structure. The presumption of a risk of de-industrialization is leading the Japanese authorities to devote careful attention to studying the impact of Japanese direct investment abroad.

Experts identify several effects on the industrial system. These effects are variable and often contradictory, and they can be typologically divided into four large categories:

- *Substitution effect for exports*: the production exported from Japan until now has been relocated in a third country to supply foreign markets and markets of host countries directly: this creates direct substitution, and a decrease in Japanese exports.
- *Stimulation effect on exports*: Japan's supply of capital goods for relocated firms, as well as exports of intermediary goods to ensure the functioning of these firms, are phenomena that stimulate exports.
- *Re-import effect*: goods produced outside Japan are re-imported to supply the Japanese market. In relation to these goods, Japanese based firms have lost their comparative advantage. This causes a growth in imports.
- *Non import effect*: production transfers reduce the volume of raw material imports to Japan: this causes a decrease in imports. This effect is currently considered negligible.

Effects on the trade balance

The Ministry of International Trade and Industry (MITI) has estimated the cumulated result of these effects (Figure 3.1). Until 1993, the result in terms of trade balance was positive. In 1996, the negative effect reached

Figure 3.1 Estimation of FDI effects on the Japanese trade balance, 1991–6

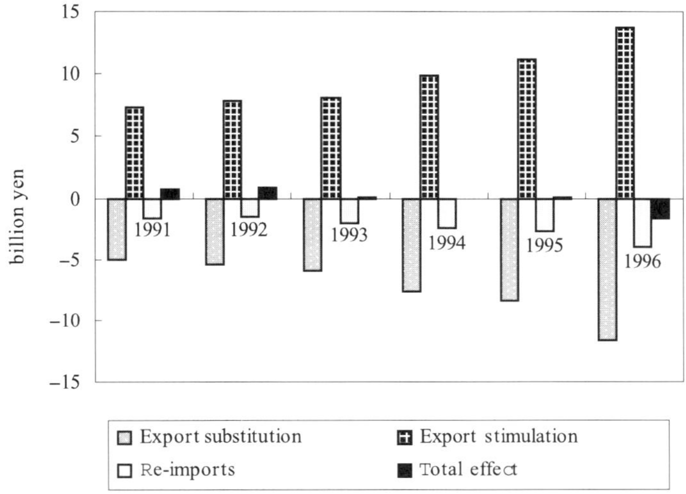

Source: *Tsûsanshô* (MITI) (1998–5), 71–2.

1.617 billion yen, an increase of 2.514 billion yen when compared to the best recorded figures in 1992 (equivalent to 35 percent of the favorable trade balance). Each effect tends to expand with the cumulative growth of the stock of direct foreign investment (DFI). In 1996, the positive effect on exports from Japan (+13.75 billion yen) improved by 24 percent, but this was thwarted by the acceleration of the negative effect stemming from re-imports (–3.91 billion yen, +47 percent) and from export substitution (–11.59 billion yen, +39 percent). Since the mid-1990s, Japan entered a new phase where relocations are beginning to lose their advantageous nature as complements to exports and are becoming true substitutes.

Effects on domestic production

The effects of the activity of Japanese firms abroad on the volume of domestic production are estimated in various ways. The discrepancies according to the estimation methods used are significant, but the tendencies are identical: all converge towards a negative effect.

In 1994, these were estimated at –10.4 billion yen (corresponding to a 1.6 percent reduction of domestic production) (NEKK, 1996). In 1995, for the first time, the value of the production of relocated firms exceeded the

Table 3.2 Estimation of FDI effects on the production of two industries, 1996 (billion yen)

Effects	Motor-vehicles	Precision machinery
Export stimulation	+4.7	+6.8
Export substition	–10.8	–5.7
Re-imports	–0.2	–1.8

Source: Based on *Tsûsanshô* (1998–5), 74.

value of Japanese exports. This effect is attributed to the growth of transfers to Asia.

Estimates by MITI focused on a global negative impact of -6 billion yen in domestic production loss in 1996. The motor-vehicles industry, with a 25 percent rate of production relocation, was hit hard by the highest negative effects, -6.3 billion yen. The effects on the precision machinery industry, for example, were virtually balanced, in spite of high levels of re-imports, which were offset by export support (Table 3.2).

Effects on employment

Relocation has had negative implications since 1993. In that year only, 6000 jobs were lost. According to MITI estimations, the loss reached 225 000 jobs in 1996 (Figure 3.2).

Figure 3.2 Estimation of FDI effects on employment, 1991–6 (thousands of jobs)

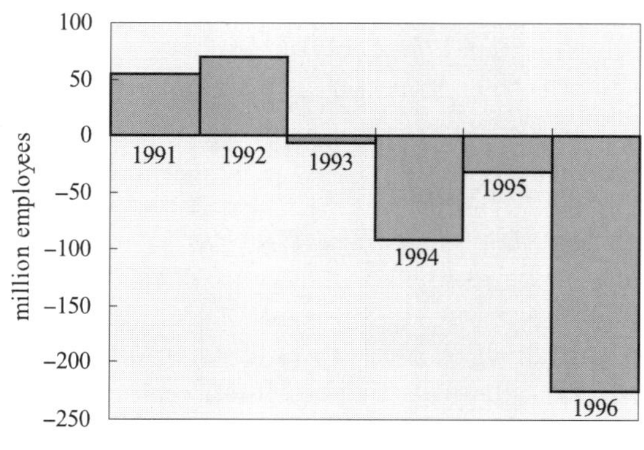

Source: based on *Tsûsanshô*, 1998–5, p. 74.

Figure 3.3 Evolution of employment, Japanese electronics industry, 1976–95, (millions of employees)

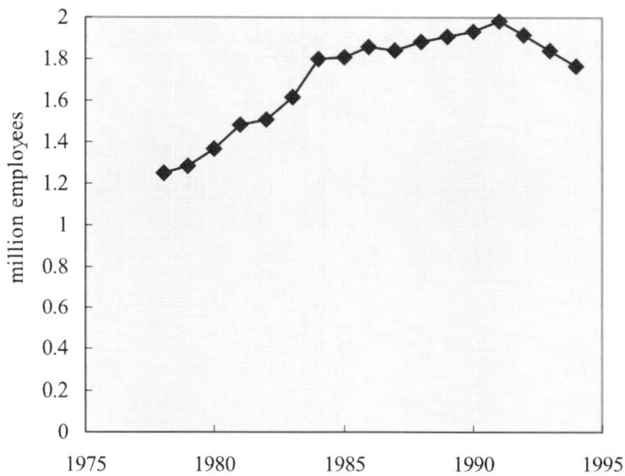

Source: *Kôgyô tôkeihyô* (Industrial Census).

The electronics industry and urban depopulation

Employment in the electrical and electronic appliances manufacturing industry has experienced a significant increase since the late 1970s. Numbers rose from 1.25 million employees in 1978 to nearly 2 million in 1991 (Figure 3.3). After reaching this peak, employment in this area steadily decreased. In 1993, figures dropped to the 1987 level, 1.84 million employees.

This industry, totaling more than 31 000 firms, is dominated by seven large firms actively involved in a worldwide relocation process. As far as these large firms are concerned, employment in Japan globally did not slow down during this period, in spite of some visible divergence for each individual firm. Few new firms were created, and the number of establishments increased from 101 to 104. In total, employment generated by large firms increased slightly from 226 096 to 240 949 employees (Table 3.3).

At the same time, these firms reinforced their foreign presence abroad: the number of foreign invested projects abroad increased by 181 establishments. Employment created outside Japan (+118 895) was almost equal to half the direct employment existing on Japanese territory. The large electronics firms of Japan found themselves in an employment

Table 3.3 The electronics industry in Japan: evolution of the number of establishments and of jobs, 1987 and 1993

Establishments / Jobs	**1987 Establishments**	**1993 Establishments**	**1987 Jobs**	**1993 Jobs**
Total for largest seven	101	104 +3	226 096	240 949 +14 853
Total for sector	31 066	31 803	1 844 011	1 844 725

Source: Adapted from Horaguchi, 1998, I.

situation whereby they managed to hold two workforce pools of equivalent numbers both inside and outside Japan (Table 3.4).

In spite of their expansion abroad, these large firms continued to keep employment in Japan, investing in high-value added and high-technology sectors, while labor-intensive small and medium-sized (SMEs) company suffered. Local statistics underlined these trends.

Urban concentration of large groups/de-concentration of small and medium-sized companies

The 'lean' concentration of large firms in two large Japanese urban poles and in their periphery was accompanied by the disappearance of small businesses. The seven largest Japanese firms concentrated 40 percent of their total employment in localities that recorded the highest net job losses during this period. Parallel with job creations carried out by the large groups, the emptying of large urban centers was confirmed: small businesses in Tokyo's center lost half of their workforce (–19 098) and 621 companies closed. In Tokyo and Osaka. 1194 establishments and 67 851 jobs disappeared (Horaguchi, 1998,I).

Given a context of stable employment during this period, which regions benefitted from the transfers? Urban centers and their near periphery found themselves de-populated to the benefit of more distant suburbs or other locations outside the cities. For example, the prefecture of Kanagawa lost 138 establishments and 16 010 jobs in Yokohama–Kawasaki–Yokosuka, the most urbanized and industrialized zone along its coastal border, but it gained 308 companies and 18 225 jobs in its western inland area. In the Kansai area, Kyoto, Shiga, and Kobe were the cities which benefited from the draining of Osaka. As for the other regions, the remote southern island of Kyûshû attracted new businesses.

This type of flow between urban centers/suburbs, province/center and province/province, tends to invalidate the hypothesis of a total de-industrialization by non urban areas. It seems to be a much more diffuse

Table 3.4 Large Japanese electronics firms abroad: number of establishments and jobs created per geographical zone, 1987 and 1993

	Asia		North America		Europe		World	
	1987	**1993**	**1987**	**1993**	**1987**	**1993**	**1987**	**1993**
Establishments	117	195	69	114	73	132	328	509
1993/87		+78		+45		+59		+181
Jobs	57 951	119 933	21 633	67 330	9 799	26 319	108 193	227 088
1993/87		+61 982		+45 697		+16 720		+118 895

Source: Adapted from *Kaigai shinshutsu kigyô sôran* (Directory of Overseas Affiliates of Japanese Companies) (Tokyo: Toyo Keizai Shinpo Sha).

phenomenon over the whole territory, where the pyramid-style structure of manufacturing which has given Japanese industry its wealth will continue to crumble in the face of changes initiated by large firms in the context of the international division of labor and of regional development.

Qualitative changes in the industrial structure

The productive structure and the regional strategy of large groups, which depended on an internal division of region/labor within the firm, are being modified. During the period of Japan's high economic growth, the large companies situated in the urban centers started by applying the spatial division of labor throughout Japan. Because of the intensity of cost competitiveness strategies, they were compelled to massively transfer their production outside the cities. This was done in an effort to secure an excellent workforce at a lower cost, and to benefit from the financial advantages created as a solution to the regional imbalances on a national scale. This regional relocation strategy was accompanied by the development of SMEs around the establishments of large groups, and by the diffusion of a certain technological know-how outside the cities. Another characteristic of this relocation phenomenon was the fact that the concentration of key managerial functions was held in the headquarters. In particular, R&D remained in the great metropolitan areas.

Large firms began subsequently to transfer their production facilities abroad, a phase called 'second regionalization abroad' (Katoh, 1994). These relocations remained nevertheless closely linked to production cost reductions, so as to keep prices of mass-produced finished products competitive. Simple, repetitive, and labor-intensive tasks were those which were prioritized for relocation in Asia. When relocations are not simply equivalent to partial production transfers, but when they are actual disinvestments involving the closure of existing establishments outside cities, an invasive fear develops that the technological level of the surrounding industrial structure will disappear and that these regions will experience technological draining (Seki, 1997). The regions affected by de-industrialization must find new ways to stimulate development (Ogasawara, 1997), when they do not have the possibilities to expand into the services sector that the great urban centers have.

Japanese industry, whose development has until now depended on its hardware sector, is entering a period in which value added and profit will no longer be focussed on hardware, but rather on software, such as the development of networks, and professional services (KBTK, 1994). Japanese firms drew their power from mechatronics, a term combining mechanics and electronics technologies. In the 1980s and 1990s, mechatronics conferred indisputable strengths on Japanese industry. But competition is changing, and producers are being forced to look abroad for new sources of competitiveness. If Japanese firms do not relocate their assembly activities, they will be confronted with a loss of income, all the more so as computer architectural software continues to be dominated by American firms. Japanese firms will have to cooperate in order to enter future sectors of growth, while Japanese industry involved in a phenomenon of segmented de-industrialization must re-invent an effective production network in an environment where it has delegated part of its production to its Asian partners.

References

Bell, D. and Naisbitt, J. (1982) *Megatrends – Ten New Directions Transforming Our Lives* (New York: Warner Books).

Bluestone, B. and Harrison B. (1982) *The Deindustrialization of America – Plant Closings, Community Abandonment and The Dismantling of Basic Industry* (New York: Basic Books).

Horaguchi, H. (1998) 'Nihon no sangyô kudôka – 1987 nen kara 93 nen no shûyô denki meka- ni tsuite' (The De-industrialization of Japan, Concerning the Major Electrical Constructors from 1987 to 1993), Part II, *Hôsei Daigaku keiei gakkai*, 34: 4 131–69.

IMF (1997) 'Deindustrialization: Causes and Implications', *IMF Working Paper*, 1997–4, Washington, DC.

Katoh, H. (1994) *Henkakuki no Nihon sangyô – kaigaiseisan to sangyô kûdokâ –* (Japanese Industry in a Period of Change: Production Abroad and Deindustrialization) (Tokyo: Shinhyoron).

KBTK (1994) *Kypujyûnendai no sangyô kôzô henka to Nihon kigyô no kaigai chokusetsu tôshi senryaku no kenkyii – denki denshi jidôsha seni sangyo wo chûshin ni* (Study of the Changes in the Industrial Structure of the 1990s and of Foreign Direct Investments of Japanese Firms, Principally in the Electric, Electronics, Automobile, and Textile Industries) (Tokyo: Kokusai bôeki tôshi kenkyûjo, March 1994).

MITI (1998) 'Dai 27-kai kaigai jigyô katsudô dôkô chôsa gaiyô' (Presentation of the 27th Survey of the Evolution of Activities of Firms Abroad) (Tokyo: Tsûsanshô daijin kanbô chôsa tôkeibu kigyô tôkeika).

Nihon Enerugi- Keizai Kenkyûjo (NEKK) (1996) 'Wagakuni kigyô no kaigai jigyô katsudô to enerugi- juyô sangyô kûdôka to sono eikyô' (The Activity of Japanese Companies Abroad and the Demand for Energy: De-industrialization and its Influence), Conference Proceedings (Teireikenkyûhôkokukai shiryô 322).

Ogasawara, K. (ed.). (1997) *Chiiki kûdôka jidai ni okeru gyôsei to boranteia* (Policies and Voluntary Participation in an Era of Regional De-industrialization) (Tokyo: Tôkyô Chûô hôken shuppan).

Saitoh, T. (1996) *Nihon sangyô daitenkan* (Major Changes in Japanese Industry) (Tokyo: Tôyô keizai shimpôsha).

Seki, M. (1997) *Kûdôka wo koete – gijutsu to chiiki no saikôchiku* (Overcoming Industrialization: Regional Technological Reconstruction) (Tôkyô: Nition keizai shimbunsha).

4

The Outcome of the Crisis for Emerging Countries in Asia and the Renewal of Industrial Strategies of Foreign Firms: The Case of Thailand

Jean-Christophe Simon

The Asian crisis remains very much a topical issue, in spite of its occurrence more than three years ago. It should still be viewed as a thought-provoking theme – even more so now as it is recognized as much more than a currency crisis, with far-reaching effects well beyond Asia itself. It is indeed a global crisis for societies, national identities and industrial activities, as well as for institutions and for the credibility of governments. Three years after the outbreak of the financial crisis, with economic recovery in sight, some old questions remain unresolved and new issues are emerging.

This chapter will contribute in some way to the thinking about the characteristics of the economic crisis, by considering the strategies of firms in Asia confronted by it, and compelled to adjust to it, and by placing an emphasis on the manufacturing sector. It assumes that Thailand is a good case study that enables us to understand the South-East Asian version of the crisis, for several reasons.

It is well known that Thailand's currency collapse of 2 July 1997 triggered the subsequent monetary instability, that spread in the following months to Malaysia, Indonesia, and even to more mature economies such as Singapore, Hong Kong, Taiwan, and, later, Korea. The approach of the national dimensions of the crisis is particularly revealing of a country that was used to steady growth, even at a time of oil shocks. The 'currency bang' has shaken confidence, and fundamental elements, such as income distribution, employment, consumption, and investment patterns, were strongly altered.

Thailand, to some extent like Malaysia, epitomizes the 'High-performing economies of South-East Asia' – with strong financial and industrial links with Japan, and an aspiration to play a key economic role in the region (hub for Indochina, emerging financial center, with a few aspiring multinational companies). The country was known throughout the 1980s for its careful macroeconomic policy and skillful public-led development strategy. However, neither abroad nor at home did anybody foresee such a drastic crisis in relation to financing and to institutional mismanagement, although some revealing signs were evidence of an underoptimal functioning of the economy. The issue of financial losses, public restructuring of private debts, and banking system changes seems set to last.

The situation of Thailand's industrial crisis sectors (e.g. industry, finance, and trade) is also revealing for other Asian economies, from the point of view of governance and management of institutional requirements, as well as concerning the position of foreign firms, which has drastically improved. For that reason, the strategies of foreign companies are worth considering; they show, at first glance, an interesting range of attitudes.

This analysis presents first a picture of the crisis years, in order to illustrate the extent and characteristics of the downturn. It shows how bad the damages was to the economies, and it suggests that the social costs were substantial but hidden and unevenly borne by Asian countries. This can particularly be observed in Thailand – the epitome of 'South-East Asian tigers'. Focus will then be placed on the crisis in Thailand and on issues of public management to address the need for reform and for institutional renewal (new government policies and regulations). The study is based on two field surveys carried out in Asia in 1998 and 1999.[1] It analyses the crisis of the major sectors, considering elements such as financing, consumption reduction and company restructuring. Finally, we will investigate some prospects for industrial strategies in the region, with special consideration given to foreign companies. Many industries are still facing difficult times although a short-term recovery was confirmed by the end of 1999; one issue is the renewal of financing supply and credit procedures from a moribund banking sector; another is the re-appraisal of export competitiveness and internal demand for manufacturing goods.

Asian economies: flying geese through the Asian crisis

Since early 1997, the focus of many analyses was mostly on the currency and financial crises. Over the following months, the debate shifted to subsequent policy adjustments and to international financial packages.

The currency instability in South-East Asia, was followed by a strong depression, economic restructuring and political tensions in several ASEAN member countries. These phenomena spread to some parts of East Asia: for instance, the Korean economy faced a severe crisis of its financial and industrial organization; part of the Japanese financial sector was on the verge of collapse. With its economy in recession and weak currency deflating imports, Japan contributed to the downward spiral of Asian economies. By the middle of 1998, there were several major elements of crisis stacked up, or rather intertwined, from social tensions to company restructuring and a potential new monetary trigger in China. The focus on China increased, with particular concern about its economic slowdown. Then came the silver lining on the cloud as the Chinese government decided to maintain its currency in order to gain a strategic advantage in the region and to gain some bargaining power with the United States in the globalization and World Trade Organization (WTO) negotiations. When conspicuous signs of recovery appeared in 1999, issues were blurred: fewer analysts were writing and fewer people were thinking about the crisis as a remaining challenge and as a persistent dangerous factor in the economic picture. Indeed, economies appear to be recovering, growth rates gaining momentum, the global world trade situation is brightening and subsequently national economies appear stabilized – will this last?

Recession and turmoil in Asia: from boom to bust, and back?

South-East Asia has shown a considerable transformation: from overall economic prosperity, robust growth, optimistic business climate, increasing political and social confidence, diminishing tensions, and diplomatic assertiveness, to a climate of gloom, uncertainty in most circles, and even frustration and anger for some groups or national leaders. The situation is a complex one, as are the dynamics that lead to such a powerful crisis. The tables in the statistical appendix (p. 000) demonstrate some elements that illustrate this climate of crisis, showing the general slowing down of activity in the emerging Asian countries, and also the relative discrepancies between countries.

Two consequences can be noted at this stage. First, the frequent revision of assumptions, such as growth forecasts – the currency instability and bad macroeconomic indicators have seriously damaged the hitherto well established climate of (over) confidence that prevailed in the business circles of Asia from the late 1980s. This confidence may be difficult to restore for both producers and consumers. Second, at the regional level, it is likely that institutional arrangements aimed at bringing in more trade liberalization will be slower to implement. Some elements of haggling appeared at APEC meetings. It is foreseeable that the ASEAN Free Trade Area (FTA) will face a new challenge because of its members' divergences (discrepancy of economic fundamentals and regarding policy measures implemented to tackle the crisis).

The local scene in Thailand: first in ... first out?

An economic recession was quite an unprecedented experience for Thailand until 1997, since the country had been accustomed to steady growth over the previous 40 years. Some adjustment crises did take place after the two oil shocks, but the main concern of the government and of technocrats after 1980 was to maintain a macroeconomic discipline and to avoid the overheating of the economy. Since the early 1990s, as a consequence of the double-digit growth years (1988–90 for the GNP boom), a bubble economy developed in the property and service sectors. On top of that, some emerging issues – loss of export competitiveness, slow acquisition of industrial skills, etc. – showed already that the scene was less favorable for the aspiring Newly Industrializing Countries (NICs) in 1995–96, and Thailand was first to fall in the currency crisis. The recent recovery trend manifested by improved fundamentals, monetary stabilization, and increased foreign reserves in 1999 did not wipe out the deep cracks created by the crisis in the economic and social dynamism.

Macroeconomic management of the crisis

The issue of macroeconomic management, that partly triggered the crisis, comes at the top of the debate. The years of prosperity certainly made the government complacent about macroeconomic stability, and the foreign exchange rate was taken for granted by both technocrats and industrialists. An aggravating factor is that the brain drain of top civil servants and the intertwining between public technocrats and business circles blurred the norms of macro-management. Vested interests and poor control over legally dubious business deals aggravated the tensions on the Stock Exchange as well as the failure of the Bangkok Bank of Commerce in 1996–7, and resulted in a loss of credibility of the economic authorities.

The currency devaluation was a case of 'too strong because too late'; the rumors of devaluation had spread over several month and the following rates swing was as much a matter of internally induced reactions (industries seeking forex coverage at all cost) as of foreign speculations. The drastic adjustment negotiated with the IMF in mid-1997 was a strong medicine. Both technocrats at the Bank of Thailand and other major economic departments (such as the Ministry of Finance, MOF)[2], and most politicians seemed to agree that there was little room for alternatives. But reluctance was high among some social groups, fueling a strong anti-IMF feeling.

Crisis and deflation of the bubble

The crisis in the financial sector received large coverage.[3] It should be stressed that, beyond the exchange rate issue that triggered the crisis, policies on the part of private banks, namely credit abundance with low risk and collateral control, combined with poor management capability, aggravated the slump.

Beyond the financial sector, another area of turmoil was the property sector; the slump in demand for property that emerged in 1994 was thus aggravated. There was a very visible construction bust in the capital and also provincial cities, for both commercial and residential properties. Considering the huge property accumulation, it is estimated that a span of five years is a minimum to return to a cleared market. Prices did not fall sharply, though, as most owners were trying to maintain the value of their asset. There were few publicized closures of large companies, because the commercial legal system was quite inadequate to deal with foreclosure and nonperforming loans. The bubble burst of 1997 caused the 1998 recession. During the first semester, sales of department stores fell sharply and by May 1998 the retailers' association declared a drop of 20 percent. The rate of company failure doubled compared to 1997; about 4000 firms ceased operation, two-thirds of which were based in Bangkok. Damages to business activity could also be seen by the intense bargain offers. Domestic consumption of all goods, from beer to cars, was severely depressed between 1997 and 1998; it fell by about 70 percent over seven months.[4]

Employment: the inconspicuous crisis

Strikingly, the crisis has not resulted in swelling unemployment; by the first months of 1998, the official figure was only about 0.8 million unemployed. The unemployment rate never climbed to more than 5 percent of the labor force. Why was there such a slow emergence of the employment issue in Thailand?[5] This is due largely to several structural factors, particular to some emerging NICs of South-East Asia such as Thailand and Malaysia. First, since 1997, immigrants in low-paid activities were the first employees to be laid off. This was particularly conspicuous in the construction, fisheries, and agricultural processing sectors, but it also took place in some light manufacturing activities. Second, companies' emergency policies have frequently been to cut higher salaries, bonuses and overtime rather than to lay off massively; this is easily explained by the desire to limit conflict. Actually, some publicized cases of massive lay offs, sometimes after plant strikes in 1995–96 and 1997, may have been a deterrent factor. Third, acceptance of underemployment at the level of the household made the first trench of redundancies bearable; family or group solidarity made it possible for household units to survive on diminishing incomes. Basic items for living remained cheap, and people cut first their expenses on durable consumer goods (for example, installments on motorcycles).

Industries in crisis: recent and current issues

Industries in crisis: some general issues

This section focuses on issues faced by industries and their adjustment strategies, including early warnings of the crisis which were already perceptible by 1995–96.[6]

Some hidden roots of the crisis?

One emerging problem was the loss of export competitiveness. This could be identified in several industrial activities suffering from increasing labor costs, from deficient services (container exports, packing, insurance), from a relative depletion and pollution of natural resources (marine products, agricultural products such as vegetables and seeds), and from a slow progress in upgrading the quality of some manufacturing exports (garments, light electrical parts, etc.). As a result, the growth of major exports slowed down in 1996.

Another major issue for export oriented industries, but also for most labor-intensive economic activities such as construction and commerce, was the shortage of labor and increasing labor unrest. Both skilled and unskilled labor became scarce in the mid-1990s. This made it difficult for industrialists to keep dedicated workers or to improve training at low cost, because of job-hopping and low motivation or commitment.[7]

Three topical issues for industrial activities

First among the complaints of industrialists was the financial problems faced in 1997–8; the high cost of borrowing was caused by the liquidity crunch – the government keeping a tight policy until July 1998, and banks being very conservative and overcareful in their lending policy. The implementation of special financing for SMEs companies was under intense discussion, and was slowly implemented.

Then, the currency instability in the first stage of the crisis made any assumptions on foreign exchange cost very difficult. Industrialists had to pay higher costs for imports but also higher prices for banking forex coverage. In that context, some firms tried to limit trading (quotations and sales) in US dollars when possible (for example, for sales within ASEAN, or exports to Japan) or increase procurements on local markets.

Changes in regulations also contributed to uncertainty. The management of company failures and a bankruptcy law were to be implemented on a large scale in a country with a notoriously weak judicial system. The Labor Protection act and the Foreign Ownership and Alien Business Law are other areas of major relevance to firms' activity that were reformed. Restrictions were first waived on a case-by-case basis,[8] but new regulations passed by Parliament in 1999 considerably improved the picture for most foreign investors.

Finally, the competitiveness issue was not diluted in the crisis, particularly in view of a potential competitive devaluation in China. In 1998–9, reports on efficiency and local competitiveness showed an unfavorable situation for many industries in Thailand, compared to the average developing/emerging economies, because of a lack of investment, and a wait-and-see attitude instead of strategic management.

The challenge of adjustment and restructuring in key activities

Before undertaking our fieldwork, it was assumed that the crisis would be more conspicuous at company level. That is, a visible long cohort of firm failures or serious disruptions in some sectors on the one hand, and proactive or innovative strategies on the other, were expected. Actually, beyond the collapse in banking and financial services, the general impression that prevailed during 1998 was that most companies had managed to weather the storm.

Firms operating for the local market

This was obviously the most critical issue at a time of recession. A first and very visible example was the construction sector, the activity of which collapsed, as most on-going projects (for both private property and public infrastructure) stopped. The burst of the speculative bubble for business properties, offices, hotels, and condominiums halted sales.

Demand for equipment also collapsed. Industrial investment was frozen in most companies, with a few exceptions such as computer systems for productivity improvement, and energy-saving equipment. The consumption of inputs for agriculture also decreased because of increased costs of imported fertilizers and other specific chemicals.

Government spending was also slashed, maintaining only priority social expenditure, and private consumption was seriously trimmed. It completely collapsed for cars or durable consumer goods. This undermined the situation of some foreign subsidiaries, particularly Japanese.

In that context, the general trend for companies was to reduce, or even 'mothball', activity by keeping minimal cost (shelving, or postponing projects) or minimal staff (cut of staff, of bonus and managerial salaries). There was a 'wait for better days' attitude on the local scene. In fact, many companies tried to adapt on a temporary basis. On the local market, as there was little hope of quick recovery, companies tested survival strategies to get a bigger slice of a shrinking cake: new marketing strategies for consumer goods products were implemented (e.g. selection of new sales channels, emphasis on value for price, durability). Some firms increased local procurement, with a change in product packaging or even design.

Export oriented activities

Interviews with exporters, in particular in the textile and jewelry industries, show that they enjoyed a boom because of the devaluation. For jewelry exporters, the import content of their products is low (local or smuggled stones, local manpower), the access to cash for raw material (gold) is easy, and design and quality can be emphasized. Garment producers temporarily benefitted from new lease of competitiveness but the currency instability was a major worry, as was competition with China, demanding adaptive strategies.

Foreign exporters and those firms based on international networks for sourcing and assembly operations (such as electronics and optical equipment) were in a good position to weather the crisis. In that context, some firms benefitted from public measures to encourage more exports, or external financing on favorable conditions.

Owing to improvements in world markets, and perhaps with the exception of Japan (a major customer for Thailand), leading exports such as garments, computers, and consumer electronics surged, pulling the exporters further out of their dire straits.

In the course of the crisis, some exporters opted for market diversification, because of financial constraints and anti-dumping problems on the American market. This is testimony of the flexibility of some components of the local manufacturing sector.

Beyond the crisis: current pro-active strategies for firms

The survey revealed that only those companies that have access to financing, or that have an efficient management structure capable of preparing for a new period of growth, were taking a pro-active stance throughout the crisis in 1998–9. Local companies could still arrange foreign borrowing or keep access to good financing, but foreign firms clearly held a new competitive edge on the Thai market.

Emergence of new strategies

Several types of pro-active strategies emerged and were implemented on a long-term basis.

To escape from the stagnation constraint, some companies suddenly sought salvation through exports. These emerging exporters could be found among heavy industries such as construction material, glass, and paper, and even in the transport equipment sector. Most of them were companies with a coherent management structure that could allocate efforts to master this new strategy.[9]

Another positive ingredient of the new strategies was the tendency to refocus firms' activities on core businesses. Many Thai companies had clearly overstretched their ambitions in terms of product range, and investment diversification. The Charoen Phokphand (CP) Group, originally based on animal feed and agri-business, developed into a multi-sector, multi-countries' conglomerate, without substantially altering its 'overseas Chinese-type' opaque control and management structure. It is now reducing its activities in China.[10] It is also selling off its majority share in retail chain in Thailand. In addition, to secure fresh foreign financing, it is restructuring the agri-business operations that were the source of its wealth, but that were only partly listed because of a persistent Chinese family control.

Siam Cement, another blue chip of Thai manufacturing is also to restructure its operation. It was characterized by overdiversification. It also suffered in its core activities of cement and construction material from the strong merger and acquisition (M&A) strategies of multinational corporations (MNCs) in Asia. There were only three deals in 1996, and about 15 in 1998, increasing the MNC shares at an estimated 60 percent of the Asian market, up from less than 20 percent in 1996.

A special situation for foreign firms?

However serious the economic situation was, there was no atmosphere of panic among the foreign business community. There have been few publicized cases of firm closures. This was observed mostly among East Asian labor-intensive manufacturers, and among a few Western companies re-engineering their global activity.

Foreign firms are starting to show a new assertiveness in their strategies in Thailand. Several elements make the foreign companies' situation a privileged one: they have both the financial resources (magnified by the devaluation), and better management structures, and they can now enjoy more institutional flexibility. Indeed, with current changes in regulations regarding majority ownership, foreign companies face a good challenge: they can choose to increase their investment with weak partners. This is particularly relevant for industries with export prospects; producers for the stagnant local market have to try to weather the storm, making the most of their waiting time by reorganizing their operations, promoting training, etc.). Changes in import content regulations could also seriously transform the picture of industrial organization in South-East Asia.

Firms have to play their part skillfully. Regarding M&A strategies, it is not a 'free for all' situation: competition is increasing among foreigners, and Thai authorities and public opinion are particularly sensitive to this matter. In 1998, the Board of Investment claimed that approximately 20 billion baht (500 million US$) were invested by foreigners to gain control of majority shares in 145 companies, given that the rules had been eased in the case of seven sectors.[11]

New commitment and increased stakes from European investors were monitored in several sectors. In banking, the Dutch giant ABN Amro took control of Bank of Asia, with the ambition of promoting it from 11th to 5th rank. In the steel industry, Ugine Acier took control of Thainox from local and Japanese partners. In the pulp and paper industry, a Norwegian firm bought stakes in mill plus plantation.

Some investors from emerging East Asia have closed down, and some larger companies have reduced their activity. This is particularly true for Korean firms because of their own domestic problems. On the other hand, several firms from Taiwan increased their investment; a very visible case is Tuntex in the petrochemicals industry.

Japan presents a special case as companies have for a long time shown a strong commitment to Thailand. Because of past very profitable operations, many could afford to lose money. This is particularly true in the motor-vehicles sector where patience was the prevailing philosophy, and where firms remained officially optimistic regarding mid-term prospects. For example, Toyota increased its share from 60 to 70 percent. Its registered capital increased ten fold, certainly comforted by the recovery. Other Japanese firms are also increasing their stake.

Conclusion: elements for future scrutiny

The following remarks are inspired by an analysis of the situation in Thailand. Many of them are also useful for the analysis of neighboring large industrial powers in the ASEAN region. In the latest months of 1999, the outcome of the crisis was assumed to be progressive adjustment. Internal reforms and stabilization were due to take place within two to four years. This is in line with the so called 'Mexico 1995' scenario of soft recovery for Asia, suggested by Paul Krugman.

By the year 2000, a noticeable divergence had taken place among the ASEAN-4 countries. The pace of reform has lagged behind, and political upheavals have peaked. It seems that Thailand – and Malaysia too – show stronger resilience as well as better adjustment capabilities, although these two countries face strong challenges in the years to come.. In that context, many firms should have no difficulty in recovering from the crisis and in facing both market transformations and institutional changes:

- *The building of a new competitive advantage.* Just before the crisis, some industrial countries were losing their edge with new competitors (particularly because of Chinese emergence). A country like Thailand was losing in terms of labor costs without making enough progress in terms of product upgrading (quality and productivity). How will this be addressed when companies have fewer financial resources, a greater temptation to tap the scores of unskilled unemployed workers, and when governments have to face social unrest and budget constraints, thus limiting their promotion capacity?
- *The deepening of sector restructuring.* The continuous changes in structures and organizational patterns may gain momentum. A new organization could emerge in spite of pressures to resist increased foreign ownership or reduce protection for national industries. Will the new industrial structures of South-East Asia be more open, with fewer oligopolies and alliances between states and local tycoons?
- *Changes in regional economic conditions.* Considering the frail recovery and the degradation of the position of 'developmentalist states,' should one assume that there will be more global constraints (from the WTO, in terms of international standards and norms), with a risk of slowing down regional integration, particularly the ASEAN FTA project?

Statistical Appendix

Table 4A.1 Monetary context, selected Asian emerging countries, December 1996–September1999 (currency rates to US$)

	Dec. 1996	Jun. 1997	Jan. 98	Jun. 1998	Jul. 1999	Sep. 1999
Thailand	25.5	24.7	52.8	42	37	40.8
Malaysia	2.52	2.52	4.11	3.92	3.79	3.79
Philippines	26,3	26.4	41.0	38.9	38.28	40.69
Indonesia	2377	2428	9888	11 650	6585	8435
Korea	844	891	1660	1393	1183	1210

Source: *The Economist*, Dow Jones.

Table 4A.2 Emerging Asian economies through the crisis, late 1997 and 1st quarter 1998 (percentage change, year on year)

	GDP	Exports change in US$ (%)	Imports change in US$ (%)	Industrial production
Thailand	–0.4	–0.2	–34.3	–17.5
Malaysia	–1.8	–14.3	–16.5	–6.0
Philippines	1.7	21.9	–0.9	–11.8
Indonesia	–6.2	0.7	–43.9	10.7
Korea	–3.8	10.5	–36.6	–13.3

Source: *The Economist* and *Far Eastern Economic Review*.

Table 4A.3 GDP growth trends, selected emerging Asian economies and, 1996–2000

	1996	1997	1998	1999 *	2000 *
Thailand	5.5	–1.3	–9.4	1.5	2.5
Malaysia	8.6	7.5	–7.5	3.0	5.0
Philippines	5.7	5.2	–0.5	2.4	3.0
Indonesia	8.0	4.9	–13.4	–1.7	2.5
Korea	7.1	5.0	–5.8	7.0	5.0

Note:
* Latest estimates or forecast.
Source: Goldman Sachs

Table 4A.4 Foreign trade and industrial activity, selected Asian economies, 1999

	Exports change in US$ (%)*	Imports change in US$ (%)*	Industrial production
Thailand	9.2	17.9	15.4
Malaysia	9.5	19.4	19.3
Philippines	21.9	8.8	14.3
Indonesia	–7.9	–13.4	10.2
Taiwan	7.9	12.9	Nil
Korea	10.5	36.1	18.1

Note:
* Year on year.
Source: *Far Eastern Economic Review* (November 1999).

Notes

* Several colleagues and friends kindly contributed to my investigation and thinking – to cite but a few – Professors Shimokawa (Hosei University), Fujimoto (Tokyo University), Suthipand Chiratiwat (Chulalongkorn University), Françoise Guelle and Yveline Lecler (Université de Lyon). The support of ISEA in Singapore is also gratefully acknowledged.

1 The analysis compiles general data from documents, interviews, and case studies collected during a two-month mission to Japan and Thailand in 1998, and to South-East Asia in early 1999. The surveys were based on interviews with managers/directors in manufacturing firms (20 in 1998, 35 in 1999) complemented by collection of business cases from private sources. The sample of surveyed companies was selected to reflect broadly traditional and advanced activities, both domestic and export oriented.

2 Its job is to be restructured, with many Departments streamlined as part of a government re-engineering package advised by the IMF.

3 About one-third of listed companies suffered a fall of more than 75 percent in their share prices in 1997 (ING Barings FEER, 5 February 1998).

4 The promotion of local products is actively made, to the extent that some unidentified organizations promoted a xenophobic campaign against foreign products.

5 Particularly compared to South Korea where social activism seems currently to be accelerating.

6 These problems were clearly perceived as early as 1995; for example, the Bank of Thailand Quarterly Survey showed concerns, by Fall 1995, about the economic slowdown and pessimism among business circles. But procrastination prevailed among policy makers as well as easygoing attitudes of business leaders.

7 During our interviews conducted in 1998, some industrialists declared that they had changed their labor strategy in 1996 to limit the large turnover (better salaries, five-day week plus fringe benefits, incentives replacing a wage policy based on overtime as incentive).

8 For example, a foreign investor in a joint venture project approved by the Board of Investment (BoI) must get the Board's and its partner's approval to increase capital and gain majority ownership.

9 For example, Siam Cement started an aggressive policy as soon as the local crisis developed.

10 Similar attitudes were shown by other Thai firms that ventured into China (for example, Karat Sanitaryware sold its share to its local partner).

11 Vehicles and parts, chemicals and plastic, electronics and electrical, light industries.

References

Asia Pacific Journal of Management (1998) *Special Issue*: The Asia MNC, National University of Singapore, 15: 2 (New York: John Wiley).

Boisseau du Rocher, S. and Simon, J-C. (1998) 'Thaïlande, une crise salutaire?', *Futuribles*, 229, 5–28.

Chaponnière, J.-R. (ed.) (1994) *Analyse comparative des problèmes posés par la coopération industrielle: les entreprises allemandes et françaises en Corée et en Thaïlande* (Paris: MESR).

Chiasakul, S. and Koike, K. (eds) (1998) *Financial Crisis in Thailand: Adjustment of Local Companies* (Tokyo: Institute of Developing Economies).

Chiratiwat, S. (1998) 'Crisis and its Impact on ASEAN Economic Integration', *Workshop Paper, EU Consortium Program* (Bangkok, Chulalongkorn University).

Foy, C., Harrigan, F., and O'Connor, D. (1998) *The Future of Asia in the World Economy* (Paris: OECD).

Institute of Developing Economies (1998) *The Study on Trade and Investment Policies in Developing Countries – Thailand* (Tokyo: Institute of Developing Economies).

JETRO–IDE Joint Symposium (1998) *Can Asia Recover its Vitality ? Globalization and the Roles of Japanese and US Corporations* (Tokyo: Institute of Developing Economies).

Sakura Institute of Research (Various issues) *Pacific Business and Industries*, Tokyo.

Williamson, P.J. (1997) 'Asias's New Competitive Game,' *Harvard Business Review*, September–October, 225–48.

5

The HRM Strategies of Korean Companies in China: Localization of Management

Robert Taylor, Cho Yong-Doo and Hyun Jae Hoon

Introduction: objectives and profile of companies

Since the 1980s, in the wake of the Chinese leaders' open door policy, investment in China by foreign manufacturing companies proliferated. To date, however, much research attention has been focussed on high-profile manufacturers from Western countries in major Chinese cities and the plethora of investors from Hong Kong and Taiwan in China's south-eastern seaboard. In contrast, the focus in this chapter is on companies from a late industrializer, the Republic of Korea, having undergone a severe economic crisis, and in the decades of the 1960s and 1970s known as a low-wage economy. Undoubtedly, one of the current motivations for Korean industries in China has been the presence of cheap labor relative to that in other Asean countries. Nevertheless it will be argued in this chapter that such Korean investment in China involves wider issues and incentives, without consideration of which it is impossible for companies to develop long-term strategies crucial for profitability stemming from the successful penetration of Chinese and foreign markets.

Accordingly, the objective of this study is to examine human resource strategies in general and the localization of management in particular on the part of Korean companies, and it will be argued that effectiveness in this area is indispensable for success in competitive Chinese and international markets.

The study has been generously supported by the Asia Research Fund of the Republic of Korea, making possible two visits to China by the three authors. The findings presented are preliminary and based on research conducted by two of the authors during a trip to China in September 1998. In view of time and resource constraints, research was concentrated on interviewing in 11 companies, two in Beijing and nine in Qingdao, and located in a number of light-industrial sectors ranging across telecommunications equipment, imitation jewellery, clothing, leisure shoes, and sports equipment, with the majority in the footwear sector. Several companies were involved in original equipment manufacture (OEM) and under contract to American firms in the footwear industry. The companies were established in China in the early and mid-1990s. Initial capitalization ranged from 1 million to 9 million US$, and nearly all were wholly owned Korean ventures in China, operating largely independently of headquarters in South Korea. In most cases production was exclusively for export to, for example, the United States, the United Kingdom, France, Canada, Japan, and Korea, although, as indicated below the intention is to target the Chinese domestic market. More crucial for this chapter, however, is the employee profile; the largest companies employed 7700 and the smallest 24 employees. Figures for most companies varied from 1000 to 5000, with numbers reflecting the labor-intensive or capital-intensive nature of the industries involved. Overall, most factory workers were full-time, female and Chinese, including a number of ethnic Koreans resident in China. Statistics indicate high levels of employee satisfaction, as indicated in low rates of worker absenteeism and turnover. Access was also obtained to data concerning the localization of management, that is, the appointment of Chinese to replace Korean managers, the major focus of this chapter. Such data, collected from company records and personal interviewing through a questionnaire of senior executives will be examined under the following headings: corporate strategy; corporate structure and culture; recruitment, retention and evaluation of employees; employment of Chinese managers; progress in localization; and costs of localization. Given the commercial sensitivity of the findings, individual companies will not be named in the text. Throughout, discussion will be placed within the overall context of Chinese policy towards foreign investment.

Corporate strategy

It is argued that the most successful foreign investors in China are those who adjust to China's ongoing developmental priorities, given that since the early 1990s the Chinese leaders have, first, been placing less emphasis on investment in particular regions but more on developing the hinterland to reduce regional income inequalities and, secondly, there is greater discrimination in the approval of joint ventures, with high-technologies being favored over labor-intensive manufacturing. Evidence gathered in this study contrasts with the view that companies, especially in the labor-intensive sector, invest in China for short-term gain by exploiting cheap labor; only one company's respondent quoted low wages as a motive for investment; others spoke of rising labor costs and stressed long-term commitment to production in China. Nearly all respondents took the long-term view, as initial losses were followed, after some two years, by profits. In fact, a long strategy was deemed essential for successful operation in both Chinese and external markets; one venture's representative saw its overseas production facilities as an integral part of globalization, while the telecommunications company's directorate stressed the potential of China's domestic sales. Another interviewee envisaged five years of exports followed by a focus on the Chinese domestic market. In one case there was mention of prospective future sales in North Korea, when that country's economy was further opened. Perhaps significantly, one respondent quoted the example of Japanese investment in the Republic of Korea who had achieved sustained profit through a long-term perspective and the development of native management skills.

Additionally, the secret of investment was seen to be re-investment. Among others an interviewee in a clothing firm spoke of the initial negative factors to be overcome; preliminary studies of available infrastructure were crucial, particularly in view of unexpected high costs of utilities like water and energy and the frequent absence of immediately accessible information. Inevitably, there are lessons learned through experience but the penalties of ignorance may be avoided in the way noted above and also by keeping abreast of unexpected changes in government regulations. There was nevertheless mention of positive factors like the initial active support of government in the form of investment incentives, notably tax concessions. While central government initiatives were important it was, however, stressed again and again that local authorities could make or mar a venture. Finally, as will be shown in the following sections, national government is becoming more and more active in aspects of human resource management (HRM).

Corporate structure and culture

The majority of the companies were to some extent subject to general direction but in terms of production and HRM decisions were largely independent of headquarters in Korea. One company, for example, was guided by headquarters regarding investment but most decisions about production were taken in China. In the case of one shoe manufacturing firm, the Korean headquarters had become a center for research and development (R&D), as nearly all its production facilities had been transferred to China, with a resulting shift in decision making. This situation is generally analogous to changes in Hong Kong, where manufacturers retain service and marketing functions, while relocating production in nearby Guangdong. In fact, one respondent expressed the view that, since the onset of the recession in South Korea, the influence of the headquarters had been decreasing. In the case of the telecommunications company, a joint venture making specialized products for a personal computer network, a vice-president was seconded from the latters' headquarters but to play only a supporting role. Apart from that, there was no intervention from the Chinese parent company.

In the companies in general, the shift in decision making power to China has been reflected in a division of responsibility between senior officials. In those enterprises in several instances Korean presidents (that is, chief executive officers), have been in charge of administration, while Chinese vice-presidents have been in charge of production. There is, however, some variation in this pattern; in one shoe manufacturing company, for instance, the president was in overall charge of internal operations, while the vice-president, a local person and former government official, used his own personal connections to handle the firms' external relations effectively.

Such devolution of authority necessarily brings in its wake the localization of management. A shoe manufacturer spoke of replacing Korean by Chinese managers in the next five years, with consultation and technical skills already being imparted to potential candidates, an integral part of improving managerial quality. In another firm Chinese managers were already heavily involved in key production decisions. While the overall trend is the replacement of most Korean by Chinese managers, the former are apprehensive lest they lose influence if mutual trust between the two nationalities is not established. Even under localization it is likely that areas such as the supply of components will remain under the control of Korean nationals. Mutual trust is necessarily the key to effective HRM, and this has often proved difficult to achieve in Sino-foreign ventures. It is also infinitely easier to establish corporate structures and hierarchies, as in the case of the Korean companies under discussion, than to change existing or create new corporate culture, responsible to a new social environment.

Korean corporate cultural values and norms are not necessarily appropriate to a Chinese setting, as the management style they inform is authoritarian, hierarchical, and vertical. Korean senior executives in the companies visited perceived the legacy of the command economy within which, in spite of a traditional chain of control between the state enterprise and the central ministries, personal relationships and egalitarian norms, say in bonus distribution, remained characteristic among Chinese industrial workforces. On these terms human resource management in China must be horizontal and group oriented to a greater extent than in Korea. One shoe company respondent in fact admitted the need for greater cultural understanding. Orders from headquarters to use a Korean management style had been inappropriate. Another shoe manufacturer's executive bridled at initial cultural arrogance on the part of Korean managers who should ideally exercise authority only by virtue of superior specialist knowledge and experience. In such contexts the role of a Korean company president was said to be crucially important. One such figure, having previously served as a trading agent, had adapted Western-style horizontal management relations at the beginning, with beneficial results. In some cases ethnic Korean Chinese managers have acted as go-betweens, facilitating trust through consultation.

The central government and Chinese workers alike appear to have an ingrained suspicion that foreign ventures in China are motivated by economic exploitation. This can be overcome only by the increased use of Chinese managers but with fewer Korean colleagues in the long term. Management in such ventures will likely become a hybrid, incorporating synergies from both traditions. For the present, however, one source suggested that Chinese management will defuse immediate problems, although funding decisions will still be taken by Koreans. Such timely intervention can, of course, avert industrial action; one interviewee referred to strikes at the beginning of operations but none since 1996. In any case a sports good company has achieved a higher productivity in China in its Korean operations, while another firm's rate was 98 percent of that in its parent company. Better industrial relations may also be reflected in low labor turnover; most employees in a rubber company, established in the early 1990s, had been with the company for one or two years, indicating a high level of worker retention. Such trends, however, may also reflect rising unemployment in China in the overall context of the Asian recession. Moreover it is for these reasons that Korean employees will be able to exercise greater discernment in recruitment, the subject of the next section.

Recruitment, retention, and evaluation of employees

Most companies in the sample initially recruited with the assistance of local governments which are especially eager to attract new ventures. In one sense such a local government role is a vestige of China's command economy; high-school and university graduates were previously allocated under a system of unified assignment, regardless of the wishes of the employer and the employee. Given, however, the growing need for skilled labor and increases in unemployment, there is now a greater element of choice for both parties. Local government, according to respondents, has also assisted in the recruitment of additional labor. In one instance, a telecommunications company's Chinese venture partner sent employees, but these subsequently proved unsatisfactory and competitive recruitment was then conducted on the open market. In fact, such recruitment through the market is growing with the emergence of officially sponsored labor exchange or job centers, to which a shoe manufacturer had recourse. Lists of potential employees are sold to employers for 200 yuan; in addition, special labor markets are held twice a month. Generally, the companies have preferred to recruit local employees; one interviewee said that 90 percent of recruits fell into that category. Two companies, one in rubber products, the other in imitation jewellery, referred to the initial selection of ethnic Korean Chinese. As, however, they came from another province, it took them time to adjust to the locality. Subsequently, the number of ethnic Koreans in both companies had been reduced.

In addition, given the companies' need for more skilled and generally educated workers, the use of local labor exchanges or job centers seems set to increase. One shoe manaufacturer also spoke of direct advertising for such specialists as electricians and computer programmers, and this practice will undoubtedly play a greater role in future in the recruitment process as will its concomitant, personal interviewing of candidates.

Recruitment processes naturally bring into focus the issue of contractual status. Formerly, in China's state enterprises, managers and workers were given permanent tenure of employment. Since the 1980s, however, such enterprises have been reformed to make them more competitive on world markets, and most new employees are now being given term contracts. Additionally, foreign investment ventures with more flexible employment practices are seen as models for emulation by China's state sector. In the survey, our respondents were asked to divide employees into the categories of lifetime employment, fixed-term tenure and part-time status. Contracts varied from one- to five-year terms across the companies. A probationary period was universal: three months for those with specialist experience and one year for novices. Thus no workers were on permanent contracts. There were also very few part-time employees. The shoe manufacturing firms spoke of contacts being automatically renewed, except presumably in the case of serious incompetence, and one respondent claimed that there had only been one such dismissal in three years.

Contract renewal, however, is but one incentive for the workforce. The questionnaire enquired as to the remuneration package, in terms of basic wages, bonus and performance-related pay. Some companies also included welfare and other allowances in the package. The telecommunications company said bonuses were key incentives and these were paid at the end of June, with allocation based on a certain percentage of sales and according to the discretion of middle-level managers. Similar performance-based bonuses were awarded by a clothing company and divided among members of the work team by the shopfloor manager. An imitation jewellery company was able to provide incentives and adjust production according to market fluctuations through the use of, for example, overtime payments. Overtime at weekends was paid at 200 percent of the usual rate, with an equivalent figure of 300 percent for national holidays.

Evaluation is another method of motivation but may be punitive as well as incentive. In the survey, evaluation referred to both workers and managers although there were different procedures and criteria in the case of each category. As will be shown, evaluation processes were an avenue by which shopfloor workers could be promoted to managerial status. Assessment of the workforce, to be considered first, has been generally based on work performance and carried out by line managers initially and later by personnel officers. In a footwear company a point scale was then used to determine wage increases for the deserving. In a clothing company, after evaluation by the shopfloor managers, 5 percent of the workforce had been upgraded by two steps on the wage scale, while 3 percent received an increment equivalent to three steps. In one company a different system was in operation for evaluation and based on the following criteria: work attitude, general conduct, achievement, and additional working hours, presumably voluntary. Another respondent described how employees initially had to engage in self-evaluation and then assessment by superiors.

Promotion from the ranks of the workforce is the long-term strategy of a number of companies and integral to the localization of management, even though there are naturally external sources of potential candidates. There are, however, often cultural barriers to the institution of such an internal system; a respondent in a clothing company suggested that preferment of this kind ran against Chinese egalitarian cultural norms in the workforce and proposed promotions had been cancelled under protest. Traditionally, Chinese workers were promoted on the basis of seniority, not performance. Nevertheless the possibility of promotion is a performance incentive and likely to be accepted in the long term; a rubber company cited over 200 cases, one of which was the firm's department of international trade and had proved adept at dealing with local government. In other companies workers had been promoted to work team leadership and line management, the criteria being performance rather than seniority and recommendation from Korean technicians. Final approval lay with the president and board of directors. A sports goods company spokesman mentioned promotions to middle management from 1999. Broadly speaking, promotion from the shop floor to managerial status was based on a mixture of three criteria: education, length of service, and performance. Representatives of companies spoke of a number of instances of such promotion, with heads of department making recommendations to the company president. There are, then, other trends in internal promotion.

Selection and employment of Chinese managers

Internal promotion is one way to select Chinese managers, the other being external recruitment. A shoe manufacturer discussed the motives of such externally sourced managers who, increasingly well educated and trained abroad in business administration, seek well-paid career and advancement opportunities. Here may be noted increasing recourse to job fairs to recruit managers. In foreign companies they note higher salaries, a fresher image, opportunities for initiative and management systems vastly superior to those in Chinese native enterprises. Korean, like other foreign companies, are thus able to take advantage of such a talent pool. Our survey demonstrated that Chinese managers are increasingly being employed at all levels of the management hierarchy, although in most cases managers are initially subject to a six-month probationary period. Naturally, Chinese managers have greater cultural understanding of the workforce and interpreting skills may be at a premium when dealing with Korean managers who do not speak Chinese. Local managers are not only taking over from Koreans in lower- and middle-level technical and administrative areas but in top management as deputy heads of department and vice-directors of factories. Key roles were also noted in external relations, presumably with suppliers and customers.

Chinese managers, however, need induction into Korean corporate culture. A respondent at a clothing firm provided the most detailed account of initial and ongoing orientation of newly appointed Chinese managers. At the beginning the latter were apprised of the company's mission, its organization, and payments system as well as evaluation and promotion criteria. The uniquely Korean features of the company were stressed. This introduction is followed by monthly meetings to inform the newly appointed of the firm's current situation.

It is in the area of cultural communication and understanding that Chinese managers have an advantage in Korean companies, in terms of both internal administration and external relations. A respondent from a clothing company stated that workers were more likely to follow the instructions of Chinese than Korean production managers, and this is especially important in the area of quality control. One correspondent emphasized this Chinese role in accounting and administration. But while Chinese managers are growing in importance in production operations, long-term investment and development decision areas are as yet mainly in the hands of senior Korean management, according to a shoe manufacturer. In terms of external relations a number of respondents referred to interference in company affairs by local government, and here personal connections are of great benefit in negotiations. The vice-president of a rubber company, a Chinese, had previously worked for a local trade commission and his personal network, in addition to his language skills, proved invaluable.

Payment differentials as between Korean and Chinese managers meant employing the latter was a cost advantage, even allowing for the increasing factor of performance-related pay, sometimes including bonuses equivalent to 15 percent of basic pay, and the high salary level demanded in the capital to attract executives, an issue raised by a Beijing manufacturer.

A major objective of the Chinese leaders in encouraging foreign investment is the acquisition of managers' know-how and technological skills. For their part, Korean companies wish to retain Chinese managers who become even greater assets as the result of training, which has taken many forms among the companies surveyed. Training may be divided into three major categories: on-the-job training in-house, secondment to partner companies overseas, and instruction provided by local government departments. For example, first-line managers have been trained in practical and technical subjects relating to quality control in production and HRM on a regular basis, usually once a month, according to a respondent from a shoe manufacturing firm. Another interviewee referred to work-processing classes for line managers. Where on-the-job training was deemed insufficient, managers were seconded abroad, as in the case of the rubber company which since 1995 has been sending 20 employees per annum to its parent company in Korea. Similarly, a telecommunications company had an exchange program with an American partner in addition to a training operation in Korea. Finally, the enthusiasm of local authorities for foreign investment is demonstrated by their provision of training classes in trade, accounting, finance, statistics, and labor law during regulation sessions each year, as emphasized by a number of interviewees.

No reference was made to training in Chinese institutes of higher education. Needless to say, the employment of well-qualified managers is a *sine qua non* of localization in the long term.

Progress and localization

In general, the companies surveyed had committed themselves to a policy of localization which involves, in its fullest sense, independence from headquarters in areas like technology. Our concern, however, is with management, and here the progress of localization to date will be examined. One respondent, a shoe manufacturer, stated that Chinese were already in charge of 90 percent of operations, and the replacement of all Koreans will be achieved by 2002. It was emphatically stated that the president should be a Chinese national. A footwear firm had a similar policy, although a role was envisaged for a small number of Korean managers. In another instance a company had achieved 100 percent localization in most sectors, the exception being technological areas where the rate was 70 percent.

In the long term localization demands full integration into the community and the Chinese economy as a whole. As moves in that direction that may be cited, an imitation jewelry company's support for local services and a sports goods firms' marketing initiatives which include the establishment of 80 dealers for its products nationwide as well as an advertising campaign on China's central television over 40 days a year. The bulk of the products of the companies under consideration have to date been exported, but the lure of a huge Chinese domestic market is itself a major stimulus to localization in its fullest sense.

The costs of localization

The Chinese leaders, while encouraging foreign invested enterprises, have nevertheless shown a certain ambivalence about their future role in China's economy. On the one hand, there is wariness concerning the exploitation of China's abundant labor and natural resources for commercial gain; on the other, foreign ventures are seen as models to be emulated by Chinese state enterprises, especially in the field of welfare and social insurance. Both these attitudes on the part of Chinese officialdom entail financial costs. To prevent exploitation of local workers, the Chinese have called for the formation of trade unions in foreign enterprises. It is to be emphasized, however, that since 1949 Chinese trade unions have played a role different from their counterparts in Western market economies, being closely controlled by the government rather than representing the workforce in bargaining with management. They have nevertheless been influential in the provision of welfare and personal policies in China's state enterprises. In the foreign invested sector their role is envisaged as a counterweight to managerial power, again particularly in the welfare and personnel spheres.

It might be expected that trade union organization would exert upward pressure on wage and welfare costs in the Korean ventures under examination. The trade union presence, was, however, uneven over the company sample. In fact, an interviewee from one company stated that there was no intention to organize a trade union, even though there had been pressure from local government to form one. In a rubber company the vice-president chaired a body which played a role similar to that of a trade union. In the sample, it would seem that where a union had been set up, it was an informal consultative body, self-regulated, and without direction from the All-China Federation of Trade Unions. A consistent theme across companies was a close relationship with and support from management. A clothing manufacturer referred to union dues paid by members, with officials given leave from their everyday professional duties. In a shoe manufacturing company, for example, the trade union helped to set a general pay levels, working conditions, and welfare provision. It also cooperated with management in ensuring quality controls and levels of productivity. While admittedly our respondents were executive directors rather than workers, it is possible to conclude that trade unions in the ventures surveyed were informal and not especially militant. In the case of a clothing company, however, union officials had demanded that they be informed beforehand of any planned reduction in the number of employees. In general, the apparent low level of trade union activity may reflect working conditions and wage levels superior to those in China's state or private industrial sectors. Nevertheless in the long term the rising expectations of employees in addition to employee contributions to social insurance schemes mandated by law will increase the costs for foreign invested companies in China. It is to the latter that attention is now turned.

Traditionally, state industrial enterprises were responsible for welfare – for example, pensions to benefit their workers. But when in the 1980s the

Chinese leaders embarked on the rationalization of the state sector to make it more competitive on domestic and world markets, it was soon apparent that necessary redundancies and redeployment of labor were impeded because dismissed workers lost welfare benefits and housing as well as their employment. But a national social insurance scheme necessary to facilitate labor mobility has been slow to develop. Significantly, the foreign invested sector was used as a testing ground for the introduction of social insurance. Accordingly, since the 1980s foreign companies in China have had to contribute an amount equivalent to a certain percentage of the wage bill to a social insurance fund, managed by local city governments. The Labor Law of 1995 mandated five funds: pensions, medical, accident and disability, maternity, and unemployment, to which employers and employees are obliged to contribute. This contributory scheme was in operation among companies in our sample; an imitation jewelry venture, for example, listed deductions from salary as well as an employer's provision. One interviewee, however, resented the compulsory nature of the scheme, suggesting that a real burden had been placed on employers. Undoubtedly, the Chinese central government envisaged the expansion of social insurance funded by company contributions, and such costs will necessarily be an important factor, as the Korean firms in the sample commit themselves to a long-term presence in the Chinese market.

Summary

The purpose of this chapter has been to examine the HRM strategies in general, and the localization of management in particular, of a selected sample of Korean companies in China, located in Beijing and Qingdao, and ranging across a number of industries, including telecommunications equipment, imitation jewelry, clothing, leisure shoes, and sports equipment. Examination of the corporate strategies of these Korean companies indicated long-term commitment to China and its market, as demonstrated by the replacement of Koreans with Chinese managers. In some cases investment in China was seen as an integral part of globalization. Such a long-term strategy contrasts with that of companies which target China as a production base with cheap labor and raw materials.

Accordingly, the firms surveyed had sought to adapt corporate strategy and culture to Chinese conditions. One reflection of adaptation was independence from headquarters in Korea. Decision making, however, involved the division of responsibility between Korean and Chinese managers, with considerable delegation to the latter in areas of HRM and external relations. Korean vertical and Chinese horizontal management styles were contrasted. The adaptation of Korean corporate culture (that is, norms and values) also presented challenges, which can be addressed only through the gradual development of mutual trust. A measure of success in this area is reflected in the replacement of ethnic Koreans by Chinese managers.

Resulting productivity levels compared favorably with those in Korea. Commercial success depended on the recruitment and retention of qualified manpower. Although local government continued to assign workers, a free labor market is emerging, and a pool of managers, many trained in business administration abroad, is being attracted by higher salaries and superior conditions in foreign companies. The Chinese central government has sought to influence labor mobility in line with market fluctuations, and employees in Korean companies in our sample are subject to fixed-term contracts, usually renewable. Greater emphasis has been placed on the motivation of employees, with the use of evaluation to determine performance-related pay. Regular monitoring is also a factor in the promotion of Chinese workers to managerial status. Currently, in several companies there are instances of Chinese filling positions at all levels of management. Another aspect of localization is recourse to job fairs to recruit external candidates.

Provision is made for the induction of Chinese managers into the corporate culture through, for example, apprising them of the company mission. It was concluded that Chinese managers were of decided benefit in HRM and negotiation with local governments which sought to intervene in company policy. There were also costs advantages in employing Chinese as opposed to Korean managers. It was found that managerial training took various forms: in-house, secondment to partner companies overseas, and through the initiative of local government. Progress in localization was also assessed on the basis of the percentage of operations actually controlled by local managers. In one case localization in its fullest sense was defined as integration into the community through support for local services and targeting the domestic market through nationwide television advertizing.

Such integration into China's economic system, however, was seen to entail certain costs. The Chinese leaders in the 1980s designated foreign ventures as a testing ground for the implementation of new social insurance policies which imposed considerable cost burdens on the Korean companies. Trade unions, still not well developed and relatively quiescent, but already active in the welfare and personnel spheres, could in the long-term put upward pressure on wage levels and insurance costs, should expectations among the workforce rise. In spite of such costs, however, the Korean companies in our sample display long term commitment to the localization of management, a key element in their HRM strategy.

Bibliography

Bae, Johnseok, Rowley, C., Kim, Dong Heon and Lawler, J. J. (1997) 'Korean Industrial Relations at the Crossroads: The Recent Labour Troubles,' *Asia Pacific Business Review*, 13: 3, 148–159.

Chen, M. (1995) *Asian Management Systems* (London and New York: Routledge).

Child, J. (1994) *Management in China in the Age of Reform* (Cambridge: Cambridge University Press).

Jung, K. H. (1995) 'Changing Business–Government Relations in Korea,' *Journal of Far Eastern Business*, 1: 3, 98–112.

Kim, J. S., Kim, K. Y., and Hahn, C. K. (1994) 'Korean Manufacturing in Transition: Patterns in the Past, Current Status, and Future Challenges,' *Journal of Far Eastern Business*, 1: 2, 34–55.

Slater, J. and Strange, R. (eds.) (1997) *Business Relationships with East Asia* (London: Routledge).

Verma, A., Kochan, T. A., and Lansbury, R. D. (eds.) (1995), *Employment Relations in the Growing Asian Economies* (London: Routledge).

6

Managing Sino-French Joint Ventures in the Chinese Market: Performance Implications

Zhong-Yu Zhang

Introduction

In 1979, the Chinese government published the first law authorizing foreign direct investment (FDI) in the form of equity joint ventures.[1] Since then, other forms of foreign investment have been authorized, notably cooperative joint ventures and wholly owned foreign enterprises. The three forms of enterprises, known in China as foreign invested enterprises (FIEs) to distinguish them from their local counterparts, are widely adopted by Western companies.

FIEs are encouraged by the Chinese authorities as they facilitate the import of foreign capital, advanced technology and management know-how. For Western firms, the partnership concluded with a local firm may contribute to the shortening of the learning process and may allow them to establish a solid basis from which to develop the China market. According to Chinese statistics, FIEs in 1995 accounted for 11 percent of employment, 14 percent of GNP, and 40 percent of imports and exports.

In accordance with the census taken in 1996 by the Poste d'Expansion Economique (PEE) of Beijing, more than 400 investment contracts were achieved by French companies in China. Half of these investment contracts take the form of branch offices, whereas the other half are joint ventures or wholly owned companies. Some French companies are at the head of several joint ventures, and they can thus establish a real industrial network in the Chinese market.

Based on a recent investigation (Zhang, 1998), we found that most of the Sino-French joint ventures had an average life-span of less than four years. They had been created jointly with local partners originating either from the state-owned group or from the collective-enterprises group. The French companies in general hold the majority of capital. They seek to acquire a rapid access to the local market through association with Chinese partners. The Sino-French joint ventures are mostly small and medium-sized industrial firms (SMEs) with less than 500 employees. In terms of location, Shanghai attracts most of the French companies. Although our investigation shows that 76 percent of the joint ventures are found in the southeast provinces, we notice that 20 percent of the companies in our sample are located in the inner part of China, e.g. in the provinces of Hubei and Sichuan. Hubei is the province where Citroën has created an equity joint venture with its Chinese partner. This may contribute to the relatively strong position of the French automobile industry in this part of China.

Given the importance played by Sino-foreign joint ventures in the Chinese market, the studies of joint venture management and their performances are of great relevance. Our central idea is that the quality of the relationship between the joint venture partners seems to have an influence on the performance of Sino-foreign joint ventures in China. The aim of our study is to explore the performance of Sino-French joint ventures. We connect the performance of the joint venture with such variables as the nature of the relationship between partners on the one hand, and the independence of the joint venture with respect to human resource management (HRM) on the other. Our research is based on data collected through the medium of a postal survey conducted in 1997. In total, 51 Sino-French equity joint ventures constitute our sample; this corresponds to a response rate of approximately 32 percent.

Prior to presenting the results of our study, we will briefly review previous research on the organization and performance of international joint ventures.

Organizational characteristics and performance of international joint ventures: the conceptual framework

'An international joint venture is a separate legal organizational entity representing the partial holdings of two or several parent firms, in which the headquarter of at least one is located outside the country of operation of the joint venture. The entity is subject to the control of its parent firms, each of which is economically and legally independent of the other' (Zeira and Shenkar, 1990, p. 9). The new entity thus created can take loans, sign contracts, or engage in other activities in its own name; the consequences of its management on the legal or financial position of its parent companies are most often limited to the capital that they have invested in the joint venture (Pfeffer and Nowak, 1976).

'A joint venture pools and leverages the resources of its parents and enables them to share the risks and rewards' (Martinsons and Tseng, 1995, p. 45). It thus closely resembles a partial merger. Participants share the equity capital while committing only a part of their resources (Kent, 1991). Kent notes that this formula allows each participant to preserve its organizational autonomy, while permitting it to benefit from the joint activities. 'The joint venture represents a middle road between self-sufficiency and business merger'.[2] It is a willing and organized mode of collaboration, based on a set of financial agreements. It marks a deep commitment of the parent firms which will provide it with the necessary means for its operation. Such means include industrial and commercial assets as well as human resources transferred from the parent firms (Verna, 1998).

As underlined by Naulleau (1993), an international joint venture represents a complex world where ordinary control and coordination measures often fail. The ambiguity of objectives and power relations between the partners make it even more difficult to manage. Our knowledge of joint venture management is still scarce, and is under-developed. Shenka and Zeira (1987) observed that joint venture performance depends on the cooperation of three parts: the foreign parent, the local parent, and the joint venture itself. The relationship between joint venture partners is indeed at the heart of the alliance, and constitutes a new factor of joint venture management.

Research on joint venture organization has in particular focussed on the ownership structure of joint ventures. The analysis of such structures allows us to explore the relationship between joint venture partners, and its influence on the control and the performance of the joint venture. The published works refer in most cases to three ownership structures (Killing, 1982):

- A majority joint venture is where more than 50 percent of the equity is held by a foreign partner.
- A 50:50 joint venture involves an equal distribution of the equity between partners. In France, such joint ventures have been designated as 'filiales communes paritaires' (Brill, 1975).
- A minority joint venture is a case where the foreign partner possesses less than 50 percent of the equity.

According to Killing (1982), for example, joint ventures in developed countries are structured in such way that one parent has a dominant control. These joint ventures are more stable and have more chances of survival than those for which the control is shared between the partners. Beamish and Banks (1987), however, found a correlation between shared control between the partners, the perception of mutual long-term need between the parents, and a satisfactory performance of the joint venture.

The equity held by each partner is one of the means of obtaining the control of the joint venture, but it is not the only one. What is important is how the control is exercised and distributed (Beamish, 1992). At this point, it is worth reiterating the fact that the law in China stipulates a minimum of 25 percent for foreign capital participation in Sino-foreign joint venture contracts.[3] Friedman and Beugin (1971) suggest that the control is not an automatic result of the equity held. There are other means which will permit the acquisition of an effective control of the joint venture, for instance the right of veto, the degree of representation in the management, special technology agreements, or management transfer, etc.

Schaan and Beamish (1983) studied two types of control mechanisms: positive control mechanisms and negative control mechanisms. Positive control mechanisms are employed by the parent company to encourage a certain behavior, while negative mechanisms are measures taken to prevent the international joint venture from implementing certain activities or decisions.

According to Schaan (1988, p. 5), 'to ensure the success of a joint venture, managers have to seek a subtle balance between the need and the desire to control the venture on the one hand, and on the other hand the necessity to maintain a harmonious relationship between the partners. The inability to reach such a balance is one of the main reasons which explain the failure of the joint venture'.

Performance has been a central concept in management study. Killing (1982), for example, remarked that profitability (the traditional variable used to assess performance) is no longer a sufficient measure in the context of international joint ventures. From the viewpoint of the parents, profitability is not the only indicator of performance. The parent company resorts to multiple criteria like transfer prices, perceived returns to assets, and the cost of management incurred by the parent firm, which are not necessarily taken into account in traditional financial performance assessment. Killing thus adopted such variables as subjective assessment taken by the joint venture managers on the venture performance, the dissolution or the reorganization of a joint venture, to evaluate its success and the failure.

Chowdhury (1992) noted that several criteria of performance can be used by the different parties of the joint venture. For example, foreign partners often assess the success of the joint venture by criteria such as market access, financial performance, stability of operations, and the maintenance of management control to its own benefit. But for the government of the host country, the most important criteria are the promotion of exports, the transfer of technology, the utilization of production factors, the development of the local economy, and the increase of equity held by local partners.

A large number of performance criteria for joint ventures have been advocated, such as access to the market and stability (Killing, 1982); duration of the venture (Incuelli, 1970); realization of objectives (Schaan and Beamish, 1983), success of management (Killing, 1982; Beamish, 1988); quality of the relationship between partners (Incuelli, 1970); profitability (Tomlison, 1970) acquisition of the control by the parent (Geringer and Hebert, 1989). Performance criteria vary by venture, and they strongly reflect the reasons for which the venture was created (Anderson, 1990). Given the difficulty of assessing other criteria, a consensus seems to have been reached to measure performance by parent satisfaction (perceived performance), no matter what indicators of satisfaction have been adopted. In this study we have adopted the performance perceived by the French partners to assess the performance of the joint ventures in our sample.

Results of the study on Sino-French joint venture performance

Previous research underlines that the international joint venture is a hybrid form of organization where at least two enterprises of different nationalities put together their resources and equities to create an independent entity. How is the management of the joint venture implemented? How does the relationship between the partners influence the control and the performance of the joint venture? These are the questions that we asked for this exploratory study. This chapter presents only the results related to performance.

Based on theoretical studies presented above, completed by a series of exploratory interviews, we formulated the hypotheses as follows:

General hypothesis: *The nature of the relationship between the partners influences joint venture performance.*

H1. The quality of the relationship between the partners influences the joint venture performance.
H2. The equity held by the foreign partner influences the joint venture performance.

H3. The degree of autonomy with respect to HRM enjoyed by the joint venture influences its performance.

First, we will present the research methodology. We conducted a two-stage investigation by using two types of data: interview on the one hand, survey by the questionnaire method on the other.

Research methodology

The first-stage survey allowed us to establish a qualitative data based on face-to-face interviews with the French managers. These interviews were carried out between April and July 1996, mainly in China. They allowed us to clarify the research field and to obtain the personal opinions of the French directors on the organization, the management, and the environment of the joint ventures in China. These initial interviews provided us with information of a qualitative nature. They helped us specify our research model and formulate a questionnaire for the second stage of the research. We conducted a lexical analysis of the interviews by using the statistical software SPADT.[4] This analysis allowed us better to understand the meaning of the concepts of organization, control, and performance for the general managers of the joint ventures. Finally, a seven-page questionnaire in French was drafted, in which two pages dealt with the questions related to performance.

In order to identify the targets and the persons to interview (president, director of finance of the representative office, the French partner, and the general manager of the joint venture), we used the pamphlets and directories edited by the French Embassy in Beijing and the French Chamber of Commerce in China.[5] Our final sample was made up of French companies having created joint ventures in China at the time of the survey. According to the directory published by the French Embassy in 1996, 177 French companies had then created 270 Sino-French joint ventures in China. On this basis, we sent out our questionnaire to 142 joint ventures and 16 French representative offices in the following sectors of activity: manufacturing industry, finance, transport, wholesale trade, consultancy, and advertising agencies.

At the end of the data-collection period (e.g. in May 1997), we obtained 51 completed questionnaires. As a given firm may have set up several joint ventures in China, this corresponded to a total of 32 French firms. The statistical results concerning the perceived performance of the joint ventures are presented below.

The main results

The management of joint ventures is complex, and the probability of failure is high (Harrigan, 1992). Studies aimed at exploring the practices to improve the performance of the joint venture are strongly recommended, but these are still relatively few. In this exploratory study, we intend to identify the factors that contribute to the improvement of joint venture performance.

Assessment of the performance of Sino-French joint ventures

Given the difficulty of obtaining the financial indicators pertaining to Sino-French joint ventures performance, we chose to analyze performance in terms of the performance perceived by the French partners. The questionnaires were completed by the French managers themselves. This criterion of performance had been used in previous studies on the investment of multinational enterprises in developed and developing countries (Killing, 1982; Beamish, 1992, for example). The question that we asked was the following:

In your opinion, is the performance of the joint venture satisfactory?

not at all /_1_/_2_/_3_/_4_/_5_/_6_/_7_/ completely

More than half of the French managers in our sample (56 percent) thought that the performance of their joint venture was satisfactory. The assessment of the other managers was either negative or neutral. Compared to the analysis conducted by Beamish (1992) on 66 joint ventures in developing countries, for example, the percentage of the partners' satisfaction in our case is higher than his, since he obtained a satisfaction rate of only 39 percent.

We measured the quality of the relationship between partners using variables such as the level of cooperation, the exchange of information, and the compatibility of objectives between partners. We present the results of the correlation analysis in Table 6.1. The coefficient of correlation between the exchange of information and the satisfaction of performance is the highest (R = 0.527). This indicates the importance of regular communication between the partners in joint venture management. We also find a significant correlation at a level of 5 percent between the variable of the perceived performance by the French partners and the quality of the relationship between the partners. To our knowledge, it is the first time that such a significant correlation has been tested by an exploratory study.

Table 6.1 Correlation between performance and relationship between the partners

	Cooperation	Exchange of information	Compatibility of objectives
Satisfaction of performance	*R* = 0.4438*	*R* = 0.527*	*R* = 0.423*

Note:
*5 percent significance level.

Equity held and perceived performance

Beamish (1992), for example, found that in developing countries a more satisfactory performance is obtained by the joint venture where the multinational company holds a minority equity. The joint venture where the foreign partner holds an absolute majority equity has a less satisfactory performance than the joint venture where the foreign partner is either in a minority position or in a 50:50 venture arrangement.

We undertook the analysis of variance to test the existence of the difference in means with respect to perceived performance (Table 6.2). The difference in average perceived performance is tested for each of the different types of joint ventures classified according to the equity held by the French partners.

The results of the analysis of variance do not show a significant difference, at the 10 percent level, of the average performance perceived by the French partners among the three types of joint ventures, (that is where the French partners hold respectively more than 50 percent, 50 percent exactly, and less than 50 percent of the equity). Our analysis suggests that there is not a significant link between the perceived

Table 6.2 ANOVA

Variables	Means	Standard error	*F*	Significance
Performance/minority JV ($n = 6$)	3.83	2.04	1.020	ns
Performance/equality JV ($n = 9$)	4.89	1.36		
Performance/majority JV ($n = 35$)	4.46	1.29		

Notes:
JV = Joint venture.
ns = Not significant.

performance and the equity structure of the joint venture as, was demonstrated in the literature (Killing, 1982; Beamish, 1992), for example.

We would like to point out that in the sample of Beamish (1992, p. 16), for example, the majority (70 percent) of the foreign partners held a minority equity. By contrast, most of the French enterprises in our sample (70.6 percent) are majority partners. In China, there is no legal maximum limit on foreign equity investment in the joint venture, which is often the case for the ventures in other developing countries.

One of the reasons which might explain the discrepancy between our result and that of Beamish is the different measurement of performance used. We used performance as perceived by the French partners, whereas a satisfactory performance is not retained by Beamish only when all of the partners are satisfied. In our study, performance was assessed by using the responses returned by the French partners, since the postal survey was conducted with French managers. An evaluation of the performance perceived by both the French and Chinese partners based on larger samples may be worth carrying out in order to compare the results thus obtained.

Additionally, we have carried out several *t*-tests to examine the perceived performance in terms of life span. On the basis of these *t*-tests (see Table 6.3), we found that the joint ventures with a longer life span (in operation four years or more) are perceived to have a higher mean of performance than those with a life span which is less than four years. This result is significant at a 5 percent level. An average life span of four years has thus been identified as a cut-off point to distinguish the perceived performance of the joint ventures in our sample. Beamish (1992), for example, tested a strong instability of joint ventures in developed countries which had been in existence for less than three years. This remark is consistent with our analysis.

However, attention has to be paid to the fact that only a few joint ventures in our sample have a life-span of more than four years. This might influence the quality of the interpretation.

Table 6.3 *T*-test of perceived performance in terms of life-span

Variables	Means	Standard deviation	*T*-test (α)
Perceived performance/JV created after 1993 (n = 43)	4.26	1.36	1.9%
Perceived performance/JV created before 1993 (n = 6)	5.67	1.03	

Table 6.4 Percentage of total variance of the factors

Factors	Eigenvalue	% of variance	Cumulative (%)
1	2.830	70.742	70.742
2	0.657	16.435	87.177
3	0.387	9.681	96.855
4	0.126	3.142	100

Quality of the relationship between the partners and perceived performance: the multivariate analysis

The bivariate analysis demonstrates a significant correlation between each of the three variables measuring the 'quality of the relationship between the partners' (cooperation, exchange of information, compatibility of objectives), and 'the performance perceived by the French partners.' Based on this result, we proceed to a principal components analysis (PCA) to visualize the data related to the perceived performance and the quality of the relationship between the partners of the Sino-French joint ventures. We aim to find the links between the modalities of these variables, so as to summarize them along a number of principal dimensions.

We present in Table 6.4 the breakdown of the percentage of total variance explained by the factors.

Table 6.5 highlights the first two factors that explain 87 percent of the total variance.

The first factor explains 70.7 percent of the total variance. All the initial variables have a correlation coefficient greater than 0.5. The first factor is therefore easily interpreted. The three variables, exchange of information, cooperation, and compatibility of objectives contributed most to the constitution of the factor. Taking into account these elements, we can consider that the first factor represents the quality of the relationship between the partners of the joint ventures under study.

Table 6.5 Correlation coefficients of each variable with the first two factors

Initial variables	Factor 1: quality of the relationship between partners	Factor 2: perceived performance
Exchange of information	0.919	–0.009
Cooperation	0.919	–0.220
Compatibility of objectives	1.827	–0.254
Satisfactory performance	0.676	0.732

The second factor explains 16.4 percent of the total variance. For the second factor, only the variable of 'satisfactory performance' is known to have a correlation coefficient greater than 0.5. We may therefore consider that the second factor represents the perceived performance.

The PCA analysis allows us to describe the joint ventures of our sample along two dimensions: the quality of the relationship between the partners on the one hand, and perceived performance on the other. A visualization of the relationship between the two groups of variables is thus realized. As suggested by Tenenhaus M. (1996), it is useful to complete the graphic data representation by a typology of the individuals. For this purpose, we carried out an ascending hierarchical classification of the first factor, which accounts for the quality of the relationship between the partners (Figure 6.1).

For the first factor representing the quality of the relationship, the joint ventures are grouped into three clusters. There are 26 in the first cluster, 13 in the second cluster and nine in the third cluster. In Figure 6.1, we observe that logically the joint ventures in the first cluster are near the intersection point (that is point 0.0) with values close to 0 for the quality of the relationship between partners (axis 2). The joint ventures of the second cluster are mostly on the right-hand side of the first axis, with positive

Figure 6.1 PCA chart of perceived performance and relationship between partners

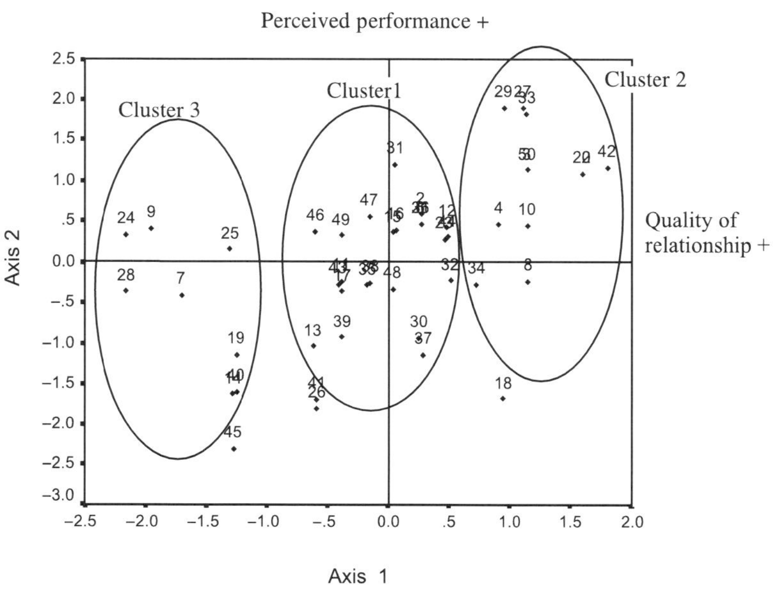

Table 6.6 Quality of relation between partners: a cluster analysis

Cluster	Number	Factor 1: quality of relation between partners
1	26	Neutral
2	13	Good
3	9	Not good

coordinates. By contrast, the joint ventures belonging to the third cluster lie in the opposite part of the chart, with respect to joint ventures of the second cluster, with negative coordinates on the first axis (Table 6.6).

We undertook the independent sample *t*-test to test if the means of the perceived performance between the three clusters of joint ventures differed from one another. We noticed that the mean of the perceived performance of the joint ventures in cluster 2 is higher than that of cluster 3. Furthermore, there is a significant difference (at a 1 percent level) of the perceived performance between the joint ventures who claim to have a good relationship with the local partners (cluster 2) and those who have problems with their local partners (cluster 3).

Similarly, there is a significant difference in the means with respect to the perceived performance between the joint ventures of cluster 2 and cluster 3 on the one hand, and the joint ventures of cluster 1 on the other hand (Table 6.7 and Table 6.A1 in Appendix 1, p. 000). This allows us to confirm our hypothesis, that the quality of the relationship between the partners of the joint venture influences the performance. A better relationship between the partners contributes to a more satisfactory performance in the viewpoint of the French partners.

Harrigan (1985, p. 376) underlines that among the factors which affect the performance of the joint venture, the relationship between the persons who manage it most influences its success. Our results corroborate this argument.

Table 6.7 *T*-test of the means of perceived performance

Variables	Mean	Standard deviation	Significance (%)
Perceived performance of cluster 2 (n = 13)	0.733	1.0396	0.5
Perceived performance of cluster 3 (n = 9)	–0.684	1.0073	

Autonomy related to HRM and perceived performance

Killing (1982) distinguished three types of joint ventures, based on the control exercised by the partners in the decision making process: a dominant joint venture where the decision making is dominated by one partner; a 50:50 joint venture where the control is rather shared among partners; and an independent joint venture where the joint venture enjoys an autonomy in terms of decision making. Such an autonomy may be given by the partners for the purpose of avoiding any interferences in the daily management of the joint venture, thereby improving its performance. According to Killing, the autonomy granted to the joint venture by the partners contributes to a more satisfactory performance compared to the joint venture where the control is shared. The presence of two parent companies may cause difficulties in joint venture management.

Inspired by the study of Killing on the links between the autonomy enjoyed by the joint venture and its performance, we studied the management of human resources in our sample. On the basis of a survey conducted by Eximbank of Japan, Delapierre M. and Milelli C. (1998) concluded that the personnel management in Sino-Japanese joint ventures was determined in China by the social considerations of the Chinese partner. According to them, 'the local authorities of the foreign partners fix, in an arbitrary manner, the employment level that they have to reach in their ventures. It is generally impossible [for the joint ventures] to engage themselves in the selection of the personnel based on the required capabilities. On the other hand, they are not free to hire and fire people' (Delapierre and Milelli, 1998, p. 63).

We intend to test the hypothesis according to which the objectives of the local partner strongly influence the human resource management (HRM) of the Sino-French joint ventures. The following questions have been suggested so as to assess the autonomy of the joint ventures with respect to HRM:

> It is said that in China the human resource management policies of joint ventures are determined by the social considerations of the Chinese partner. In your opinion, is the personnel hired mainly according to the objectives of the joint venture?
>
> Not at all/1_/2 _/3_/4_/5_/6_/7_ /completely
>
> In your opinion, is salary decided mainly according to the objectives of the joint venture?
>
> Not at all/1_/2 _/3_/4_/5_/6_/7_ / completely
>
> In your opinion, is promotion made mainly according to the objectives of the joint venture?
>
> Not at all/1_/2 _/3_/4_/5_/6_/7_/ completely

Table 6.8 PCA of HRM autonomy and perceived performance

Initial variable	**Axis 1: autonomy of HRM** $\lambda = 2.567$	**Axis 2: perceived performance** $\lambda = 0.893$
Promotion	0.935	–7.6E-02
Salary	0.893	–0.120
Employment	0.852	–0.241
Satisfactory performance	0.424	0.903

By using these questions, we aimed at understanding the degree of autonomy related to personnel management that the joint ventures in our sample enjoyed in terms of employment, salary, and promotion policies. We wished to explore the influence of autonomy with respect to HRM of the joint ventures on perceived performance.

Based on the responses to the three questions above and on those relating to the variable of perceived performance, we conducted another PCA. Two variables were retained, 'autonomy of HRM,' and 'perceived performance.' These two variables explain 86.7 percent of the total variance. The first variable explains 64.39 percent of the total variance. Except for the 'perceived performance' variable, the other initial variables have a coefficient of correlation greater than 0.5. We then consider that the first axis represents the degree of autonomy of the joint ventures related to the HRM policy. For the second axis, the perceived performance variable is the only for which the coefficient of correlation is greater than 0.5. So the second axis is taken to represent perceived performance (Table 6.8).

The projection of the variables on the factorial axes is presented in Figure 6.2. A hierarchical classification is undertaken for the factor of 'degree of autonomy related to HRM'. With the help of the software used, the joint ventures are grouped into three clusters. The first cluster, composed of nine joint ventures with positive coordinates with respect to the first axis, is in opposition with the third cluster of 10 joint ventures, which lies at the left-hand side of the axis. The second cluster of 30 joint ventures is situated near the intersection, with coordinates close to 0 with respect to the first axis (Table 6.9).

The conclusion of Delapierre and Milelli (1996), based on the survey done by the Japanese Eximbank, has to be interpreted cautiously owing to the fact that the majority of joint ventures of our sample belong to cluster 1 and cluster 2. As Table 6.10 shows, many joint ventures of our sample are perceived to have a strong autonomy in terms of HRM. This result,

Table 6.9 Degree of autonomy in relation to HRM: a cluster analysis

Cluster	Number of JVs	Axis 1: autonomy of HRM
1	9	Very autonomous
2	30	Quite autonomous
3	10	Not autonomous

Table 6.10 Mean of responses obtained, related to degree of autonomy with respect to HRM

Autonomy of HRM	Number of responses	Mean
Related to employment	44	$\mu = 5.18$
Related to salary	44	$\mu = 4.98$
Related to promotion	43	$\mu = 5.28$

although a little unexpected, indicates an interesting further research avenue.

The results of the *t*-Test show that the means of the perceived performance are significantly different at a 5 percent level between the joint ventures of cluster 1 and cluster 3. This confirms our hypothesis

Figure 6.2 Individual PCA chart on perceived performance and autonomy of HRM

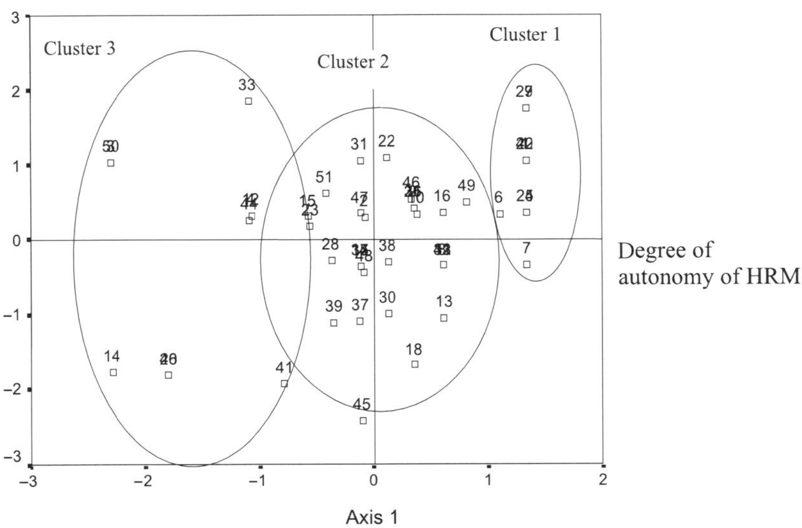

Table 6.11 *T-test* of means of perceived performance: clusters of joint ventures classified according to degree of autonomy with respect to HRM

Variables	Means	Standard deviation	Significance (%)
Perceived performance of cluster 1 ($n = 9$)	0.8228	0.702	5
Perceived performance of cluster 3 ($n = 10$)	–0.2513	1.439	

relating to the influence of autonomy with respect to HRM on the perceived performance of the joint venture (Table 6.11).

When we test the difference of the means between clusters 1 and 3, and cluster 2, we find that this difference is less significant. This is not surprising as the joint ventures of cluster 2 are mostly at the center of the chart and answered the questions cautiously (see Table 6A.2 in Appendix 2, P.000).

This analysis opens up an important field of research. A more thorough study devoted to the exploration of the links between the degree of control with respect to HRM exercised by the joint venture and its performance might bring about an important contribution to the research on international joint venture management.

Conclusion

The results of bivariate and multivariate analyses allow us to confirm the hypothesis according to which the relationship between the partners influences the performance of the joint venture. Furthermore, we noticed that a good relationship between the partners contributes to a more satisfactory performance from the viewpoint of the French partners. Besides, we found a positive correlation between the life-span of the joint venture and perceived performance. However, the link between the equity held by a partner and performance was not confirmed. We also found that the Sino-French joint ventures of our sample benefitted from a much higher degree of autonomy concerning HRM than is often believed. The hypothesis that the degree of autonomy of HRM enjoyed by the joint venture affects the perceived performance has been confirmed.

To our knowledge, this is the first time that a significant correlation between the partners' relationship and the perceived performance has been confirmed by an exploratory study, although some authors like Incuelli (1970) had already had a similar intuition. This result suggests that appropriate policies should be taken to improve the relationship between the partners. For instance, regular communication and an exchange of information between the partners have been emphasized as the means to obtain a better control of the development of the project. Such policies may help to ensure the implementation of the strategic objectives formulated by the parent companies. Promotion and remuneration policies of the locally employed personnel influence the motivation and the stability of the employees who constitute the vital factor in improving joint venture performance.

Appendix

Table 6A.1 *T*-test of means of perceived performance against clusters of joint ventures classified according to relationship between partners

Variables	Means	Standard deviation	Significance (%)
Perceived performance of cluster 1 (n = 26)	–0.1298	0.756	1
Perceived performance of cluster 3 (n = 9)	–0.6840	1.007	
Perceived performance of cluster 1 (n = 26)	–0.1298	0.756	1
Perceived performance of cluster 2 (n = 13)	0.733	1.0396	

Table 6A.2 *T*-test of means of perceived performance against clusters of joint venturres classified according to degree of autonomy with respect to HRM

Variables	Means	Standard deviation	Significance (%)
Perceived performance of cluster 1 (n = 9)	0.8228	0.702	1
Perceived performance of cluster 2 (n = 30)	–0.1631		
Perceived performance of cluster 2 (n = 30)	–0.1631	0.786	ns
Perceived performance of cluster 3 (n = 10)	–0.2513	1.438	

Note: ns: Not significant.

Notes

1 The Law of the People's Republic of China (PRC) on Chinese–Foreign Equity Joint Ventures' was published on July 1 1979.
2 Davison (1989, p. 77) cited by Martinsons and Tseng (1995).
3 Law of 1979 (see n. 1).
4 'Statistique pour l'Analyse Du Texte.'

References

Anderson, E. (1990) 'Two Firms, One Frontier: On Assessing Joint Venture Performances', *Sloan Management Review*, 32 (Winter), 19–30

Beamish, P. W. (1992) *Multinational Joint Ventures in Developing Countries* (London and New York: Routledge).

Beamish, P. W. and Banks, J. C. (1987) 'Equity Joint Venture and the Theory of the Multinational Enterprise' *Journal of International Business Studies*, Summer, 1–16.

Brill, J. P. (1975) 'La Filiale Commune,' PhD thesis, Faculté de droit et des Sciences Politiques, University of Strasbourg.

Chowdhury, J. (1992) 'Performance of International Joint Ventures and Wholly Owned Foreign Subsidiaries: A Comparative Perspective,' *Management International Review*, 32, 115–133.

Davison W. H. (1989) 'Creating and Managing Joint Ventures in China,' *California Management Review*, 29: 4, 77–94.

Delapierre, M. and Milelli, C. (1998) 'Japanese Direct Investment in China: One Bed for Two Dreams,' in S. Dzever and J. Jaussaud (eds.) *China and India, Economic Performance and Business Strategies of Firms in the Mid-1990s* (London and New York: Macmillan, 53–72.

Friedman, W. G. and Beugin, J. P. (1971) *Joint International Business Ventures in Developing Countries* (New York: Columbia University Press).

Geringer, M. J. and Hebert, L. (1989) 'Control and Performance of International Joint Ventures,' *Journal of International Business Studies*, 20, 235–54.

Harrigan, K. R. (1985) *Strategies for Joint Ventures* (Toronto: Lexington Books).

Incuelli, D. (1970) 'Management Factors and Joint Ventures: Italy, A Case Study,' PhD thesis, MIT, *Sloan School of Management*.

Kent, D. H. (1991) 'Joint Ventures vs. Non-joint Ventures: An Empirical Investigation,' *Strategic Management Journal*, 12, 387–393.

Killing, J. P. (1982) 'How to Make a Global Joint Venture Work,' *Harvard Business Review*, May–June, 120–7.

Lafaye, S. (1996) 'Les coentreprises sino-français,' French Embassy in China, *Poste d'Expansion Economique* in Beijing, July 1996; 'Les bureaux de représentation des entreprises françaises en Chine,' French Embassy in China, *Poste d'Expansion Economique* in Beijing, July 1996, Directory 1996 of French Chambre de Commerce et d'Industrie en Chine.

Martinsons, M. G. and Tseng Chou-Sin, (1995) 'Successful Joint Ventures in the Heart of the Dragon,' *Long Range Planning*, 28, 45–57.

Naulleau, G. (1993) 'La "joint venture" internationale: l'essor d'une forme complexe et instable d'entreprise,' *Problémes Economiques*, 2337, August, 6–13.

Pfeffer, J. and Nowak P. (1976) 'Joint Ventures and Interorganisational Interdependence,' *Administrative Science Quarterly*, 21, 398–418.

Schaan, J. L. (1993), 'How to Control a Joint Venture,' *Journal of General Management*,

14: 1.

Schaan, J. L. and Beamish, P. W. (1983) 'Joint Venture General Managers in LDCs,' in F. Contractor and P. Lorange (eds.), *Cooperative Strategies in International Business* (Toronto: Lexington Books), 279–99.

Shenkar, O. and Zeira, Y. (1987) 'Human Resource Management in International Joint Ventures: Direction for Research,' *Academy of Management Review*, 12: 3, 546–57.

Tenenhaus, M. (1996) *Méthodes Statistiques en Gestion* (Paris: Dunod).

Tomlinson, J. (1970) *The Joint Venture Process in International Business: India and Pakistan* (Cambridge, Mass: MIT Press).

Verna, J. (1998) 'Comment assurer le succès des filiales communes,' *Revue Française de Gestion*, 2/1017, 83–91.

Zeira, Y. and Shenkar, O. (1990) 'Interactive and Specific Parent Characteristics: Implication for Management and Human Resources,' in 'International Joint Ventures,' *Management International Review*, 30, Special Issue, 7–22.

Zhang, Zh. Y. (1998) 'Etude exploratoire sur l'organisation, le contrôle et la performance de l'entreprise conjointe franco-chinoise,' Thèse de Doctorat en Sciences de Gestion, IAE, Université de Poitiers.

Part II

The Impact of the Crisis on Industry, Labor and Finance

7
The Asian Conglomerates at a Crossroads

Christian Milelli and Pierre Grou

This chapter addresses the impact of the 1997 Asian financial crisis on the domestic business conglomerates, by questioning their future in a rapidly changing environment. It enlarges the scope of the majority of academic work, based on the financial rationale, by considering the key role of these corporate groups in the crisis: South Korea is taken as a case study.

The Asian conglomerates have reached a critical stage as internal and external factors jointly compel them to convert into more specialized groups while their vested interests are still very strong. China moves counter to this regional tendency, as the authorities are promoting the setting up of conglomerates as an element of the on-going re-structuring of the extensive public industrial sector.

The Asian conglomerates: an atypical model?

Large business groups comprising numerous subcompanies that produce a variety of unrelated products can be found in all Asian countries. Both characteristics – a high degree of concentration and a specific organization or make-up of the market – are typical of conglomerates. Hence, entrepreneurs can make substantial economies of scale and scope, and can obtain more stable earnings, by offsetting new ventures with mature activities. In this respect, there is no difference with other conglomerates found elsewhere in the world, notably with those that emerged in the United States during the 1960s. However, noteworthy differences appear when one considers either the process of development or formal and functional characteristics.

First, in the major industrial economies, mergers and acquisitions have been the motor of the enterprises groups' emergence, allowing the

Table 7.1 Local conditions and corporate features, 1960s and 1970s

Local conditions	**Corporate features**
Cloistered economy	Family controlled, with predominantly ethnic Chinese groups in Indonesia, Malaysia and Thailand
State supportive of domestic entrepreneurs	Politically connected
Poor financial structures with embryonic stock markets	High level of debt financing
	Cross-subsidization through the funneling of large sums of cash from healthy affiliates to ailing subsidiaries
	Poor accountability practices, non-existent audit reporting, and paucity of information availability
Cheap labor costs	Low technological capabilities level

Source: Grou (1988).

consolidation of the industrial structure, whereas in Asia the spread of conglomerates mainly stemmed from internal corporate growth.

Second, these groups are marked by organizational similarities around the region. Even more than legal, social or even cultural factors, which vary according to the countries, it was the pattern of economic growth termed as 'late industrialization' (Amsden, 1989) which was of great importance for corporate organization. Even in Taiwan, a country with harsh historical conditions, the importance of conglomerates in the whole economy had been rising continuously since the 1970s. The top 20 Taiwanese groups' sales represented around 20 percent of gross domestic product (GDP) in 1994 compared with 60 percent in South Korea, which is undoubtedly Asia's champion alongside Indonesia in terms of the frequency of conglomerate structures (Abe and Kawakami, 1997).

Local conditions have produced, in a rather Darwinian process, the most suitable organizational arrangements where effective political connections and debt-led diversification are the most salient features, as illustrated in Table 7.1.

The conglomerates at the heart of the 'Asian miracle'

Beside the powerful Korean groups or *chaebols*, the main driving forces behind the 'Asian miracle' have been the Astra and Salim Groups in

Indonesia, the Genting Behad and Hong Leon Group in Malaysia, the Soriano Group and Ayala Corporation in the Philippines, and the Charoen Phokphand (CP) Group in Thailand.

Diversification is the *raison d'être* of these corporate organizations. Basically, a corporation can use one of three methods to diversify: it can develop new business lines within itself, establish subsidiaries to undertake new endeavors, or buy existing enterprises or part of them after organizing and selling off unwanted activities. Each method presents advantages and disadvantages. In Asia the second method was preferred, owing chiefly to the economic developmental stage reached by the constituent countries. Hence, the owners were in a position to exercise full control over affiliates with only a minimal investment expenditure, or even with none at all. Moreover, the establishment of joint ventures with foreign investors was beneficial. The advantages were not only limited to the access to scarce resources – capital, technology, and managerial best practices – but they also offered the local partners control over the whole joint venture with a low investment of their own. In addition, the original owners were able to maintain their grip on the conglomerates either by transferring stock ownership to holding companies or by appointing family members or friends to top management positions in all major enterprises within the group.

There is strong evidence that these business arrangements have contributed to the fast growth characterizing the Asian economies during previous decades. This model of economic growth was based above all on intensive and export oriented industrialization.

In the early 1990s, diversification was nurtured by the achievement of extensive deregulation programs throughout Southeast Asia. For instance, Ayala Corporation of the Philippines entered new lines of business in the area of public infrastructure on the basis of Build-Operate-Transfer (BOT) schemes in 1992, and in the area of telecommunications in 1993.

During the same decade, the Asian conglomerates were the engines of regionalism in the South-East Asian economies through large flows of trade and investment. For example, CP Group of Thailand was the first foreign investor in Mainland China in 1997. Likewise, Daewoo, the second largest *chaebol*, was the top foreign investor in Vietnam in the same year, having made quick inroads since 1991.

The erosion of the conglomerates' foundations

During the 1980s, these corporate structures did not enjoy the same advantageous conditions as they had before. The evidence is quite clear in

Table 7.2 The South Korean corporate debt picture, 1997 (debt ratio in %)

First-tier chaebols	Debt ratio	Second-tier chaebols	Debt ratio
Hyundai	533	Anam	3 533
Daewoo	413	Haita	1 317
LG *	343	Hanjin	906
Samsung	265	Hanil	777

Note: * LG: Lucky Goldstar.
Source: *L'Usine nouvelle* 16 April 1998.

South Korea. In fact, labor costs increased dramatically as a result of tough industrial disputes: the yearly average salary increase was about 8.5 percent over the period 1980–92. In 1996, the year before the onset of the crisis, salary increases reached a full 10 percent. Furthermore, the large range of products that characterized *chaebols'* activities during the early 1990s hampered their rise to world-class level competitiveness insofar as debt-led internationalization significantly reduced their profitability. In addition, the government was no longer able to curb the stiff competition between powerful *chaebols*, which led to excess capacity at the national level: for instance, Samsung entered the automotive industry after the first movers, Hyundai and Daewoo.

The resulting lack of control worsened their indebtedness and access to borrowing became crucial for the growth sustainability of the conglomerates (Table 7.2). The access to foreign loans, either directly in the Indonesian or Thai contexts, or through domestic banks as in South Korea, owing to the strong bargaining power of the *chaebols*, combined with the de-regulation of capital markets, pushed the whole mechanism out of control (Table 7.3).

A number of warnings preceded the onset of the South Korean crisis. In January 1997, the Hanbo Group collapsed with debts reaching approx-

Table 7.3 Sources of corporate debt composition, selected Asian economies, 1996 (%)

Countries	Foreign debt	Domestic debt
Indonesia	40	60
Malaysia	43	57
Thailand	42	58
South Korea	46.5	53.5

Note: Data are derived from a sample of 5550 Asian firms.
Source: Asian Development Bank (1999) p. 27.

imately US$6 billion and in July, the Kia Group sought protection from bankruptcy. Korea First Bank, the fourth largest bank, with large outstanding loans both with Hanbo and Kia Groups as well as with some other high-risk ventures, was badly affected. During the same period the Ssangyong and Daenong Groups suffered from low activity and profitability.

There is also fragmentary evidence in other Asian countries of changes in the local conditions on which the domestic conglomerates had based their success.

The conglomerates and the economic crisis of summer 1997

The previous remarks give credit to a structural basic explanation for the Asian crisis of 1997 and highlight the real nature of the overall phenomenon. The financial hysteria revealed an exhaustion of the growth regime largely based on the conglomerates' economic rationality. Rather than relying solely on general assumptions, the analysis of a case study can be of great relevance. South Korea's dramatic experience is here an appropriate candidate.

The South Korean experience

There is little disagreement that the *chaebol* was the major actor to blame given its pivotal role in the domestic economy (Table 7.4).

In essence, the conglomerates were hugely indebted and overstretched; they started to collapse before the crisis, they dragged down the banks along with them, and finally brought the South Korean miracle to a halt.

It is worthwhile to briefly recall the entire process. In the early 1960s, the military government of Park Chung-Hee initiated, fostered, and nurtured an export oriented economic growth based on conglomerates. This pattern was similar to the Japanese one described as a 'developmental state' with long-term economic plans (Johnson, 1982). But contrary to the Japanese model, all financial resources were controlled by government bodies: for instance, there was no financial unit within the conglomerate. These arrangements were particularly efficient in the catching-up phase that rapidly decreased the gap with advanced economies. The entrepre-

Table 7.4 Total sales of top business groups, South Korea, 1994, % of GDP

Top 5	49
Top 10	60
Top 30	74

Source: Abe and Kawakami (1997).

neurs who conducted business in compliance with the government's industrial policies enjoyed a twofold benefit; first a preferential treatment regarding foreign and domestic loans for equipment expenses, and second access to export financing. Moreover, this framework was lubricated by several channels of communication facilitating the flow of information between government and private business. As the economic strength of the *chaebols* increased, they progressively adopted these practices and organized the migration of high-ranking bureaucrats from governmental bodies such as the Economic Planning Board or the Ministry of Commerce and Industry. Hence, the corporate groups were able to obtain information about decision making processes, including government priorities regarding fiscal or tax support, and they lobbied to have their industries designated as strategic ones (Hattori, 1997).

During the 1980s, this model has started to show a growing imbalance in the relationships between government and *chaebols* in favor of the latter. Moreover, domestic banks began to enter a spiral of soaring loans owing to an earlier lack of sound financial policy that resulted in the business being overcommitted.

In the following decade, the *chaebols'* overseas expansion was fueled by international loans.

In 1996, the year before the affiliation to the WTO and OECD, the Korean authorities liberalized their capital markets. Accordingly, the *chaebols* entered new lines of business through debt financing: for example, the 30 largest groups expanded the number of their subcompanies from 669 in the early 1996 to 819 in October 1997.

Finally, at the end of 1997, the South Korean government was compelled to accept a US$57 billion bail-out from the International Monetary Fund (IMF) which was mainly focussed on the sprawling *chaebols* which were forced to undergo sweeping reforms. Elections held at this time resulted in a fresh president, Kim Dae-Jung, with an urgent agenda to restructure the conglomerates, notably the top five.

The case of Indonesia

Once again, the conglomerates, even more than the privileged business arrangements, were at the heart of the national crisis. In 1997, the top 10 families controlled 50 percent of all the Jakarta Stock Exchange. The sequence was as follows: first, withdrawal of the state was confirmed in 1994 through the Sixth Economic Plan. Second, the private sector, led by conglomerates, undertook a rapid diversification. Third, as a result of the easy access to international loans at low premium risk, they increased their debt ratio. For instance, in 1999, 60 percent of the Astra debt was in foreign currency. The corporate debt culminated at US$81.5 billion at the end of March 1999, representing more than 50 percent of the whole Indonesian debt.

The issues behind the crisis

Obviously, the crisis emphasized the inefficiencies of the conglomerates that had become regarded as having traditional and inflexible structures. Nevertheless, the crisis also produced new conditions and new 'rules of the game.

A changing framework

During the 1990s, globalization emerged as a paramount driver of change. Financial deregulation and the information revolution, which are spreading all over the world at top speed, are its main features. At the industrial and corporate levels, globalization enforces new 'rules of the game': specialization of business structures is becoming the norm, and more transparency is required in transactions as corporate governance guidelines are disseminated on a worldwide basis. Behind these tendencies is a financial rationale which was clearly underlined by Chandler (1977). In a complex world of production and transactions, financial tools are the answer to the fundamental need to assess and compare numerous tasks and outcomes.

Such transformations force corporate organizations to put a premium on responsiveness to change, inasmuch as the Asian conglomerates are confronted with Western competitors, either in their domestic markets or in their overseas endeavors.

Domestic factors of change

At a country level, we encounter two salient dimensions: first, a financial aspect, as the on-going restructuring of the domestic banking system has a direct impact on debt-laden conglomerates. Banks are no longer prone to roll over loans without clear commitments from the corporations. In addition, international financial institutions are more cautious about lending, and premium risks are skyrocketing, notably for the *chaebols*. Second, legal and institutional factors are shaping the new landscape. Thus, all across Asian countries, projects are in hand with a view to:

- Abolishing fiscal restrictions which previously prevented re-organizations and corporate mergers.

Table 7.5 Asia's new bankruptcy laws, 1998 (date of introduction and contents)

	Indonesia	Thailand	South Korea
Date	April	April	February
Reforms	Judges' decisions made public Indebted companies' assets can now be confiscated	Introduced corporate restructuring Discharge can be achieved in three years instead of 10	Creditors' right strengthened

Source: Chong and Soogeun (2000).

- Relaxing or cancelling regulatory restrictions on foreign acquisitions of the stock of companies and banks. Thailand, for instance, is liberalizing foreign ownership restraints in a wide range of businesses.
- Enacting bankruptcy laws which are particularly crucial in preventing debt-laden companies with questionable viability continuing to receive loans (Table 7.5). New legislation and procedures on corporate bankruptcy have already taken effect in most crisis-hit countries where authorities are trying to bring the legal framework up to Western standards by simplifying court procedures and cutting the time required for court-ordered restructuring or liquidation. Thailand is tightening its bankruptcy law, and Malaysia, a country most resistant to changing its capital controls, established a corporate debt restructuring committee in 1998.

At a firm level, owing to public and bank pressures to slim down and focus resources, and to boost productivity, conglomerates have no other choice but to abandon non core businesses. For example, CP Group of Thailand reduced fringe or peripheral business operations and reallocated resources to the group's agri-business core.

In South Korea, the country most averse to foreign entry into its stock companies, the *chaebols* are beginning to switch to overseas partners: for instance, LG sold 50 percent of a flat panel display unit to Philips in the first half of 1999, whereas Hyundai was looking for foreign support for a similar activity. Analysts estimate at around US$40 billion the Asian acquisitions by foreigners in 1998[1], and as foreign partners are entering boardrooms, a changing management attitude and a new business mindset are gaining momentum. Henceforth, Asian entrepreneurs will be forced to disregard empire-building.

Domestic factors conducive to retaining the status quo

Once again, South Korea is a case in point as powerful business groups, notably the five largest, have been able to drag the process out for months. An analysis carried out by the Stock Exchange in 1999 on 91 listed firms of the top 10 Korean groups[2] showed that the controlling owners' average shareholding ratio jumped to 35 percent in mid-1999 from 27 percent in early 1998. To curb the conglomerates' spiraling diversification, the government in 1998 relaxed a number of restrictions on subsidiaries taking stakes in other subsidiaries. The purpose was to let companies move around some of their holdings to help shore up their shaky finances. But the *chaebols* have channeled huge sums of cash from healthy affiliates to ailing subsidiaries through mass purchases of rights issues. More dramatically, the obstructive behavior of Daewoo's president with a US$47 billion debt and 150 000 staff threatened the fragile domestic economic recovery in 1999.

Furthermore, Asia's currency devaluation, which followed the crisis, gave a one-off export price benefit to continue growth on the same basis. By doing so, the necessary upgrading of business activities could be delayed.

Towards the end of the Asian conglomerates?

There is anecdotal evidence that corporate restructuring is currently lagging behind bank restructuring owing to entrenched business customs. More generally, Mainland China, which was largely unaffected by the turmoil of the Asian crisis, is moving counter to the regional tendency of a reluctant but on-going adaptation of conglomerate structures to new constraints and 'rules of the game.' There is evidence that the transition from a command-style to a market-based economy has recently been based on the constitution of conglomerates as world-class competitors[3] together with the re-structuring, the sales, and mergers of the ailing state-owned enterprises (SOEs). In fact, China is securing suitable foundations for successful conglomerates. First, labor costs are cheap compared with other Asian countries (Table 7.6). Second, authorities at national or regional levels are strongly supporting domestic entrepreneurs. Third, the economy is still protected with heavy regulatory restrictions on capital and trade flows (Delapierre and Milelli, 1999).

But China has learned from South Korea's painful experience that the new business groups need to have solid financial foundations and not too many non core business subsidiaries.

Table 7.6 Manufacturing monthly wages, including bonuses and allowances, selected Asian countries, 1996 (US dollars)

Countries	Factory workers	Engineers	Factory managers
Malaysia	257	798	2351
Thailand	256	614	2460
Philippines	210	320	1285
Indonesia	133	342	1685
China	94	156	449

Source: *The Current State of Japanese Affiliated Manufacturers in Asia* (JETRO, 1997).

On a lesser scale, the behavior in 1999 of Petronas, the Malaysian state-owned oil and gas company, rushing to rescue key domestic companies (in property development and car-making, among other activities) is clearly a conglomerate strategy, insofar as these endeavors are based on a lack of transparency.

Finally, the financial Asian crisis of summer 1997 emphasized the crucial role played by the conglomerates before and during the crisis and the necessary adaptation to new practices which are being enforced by globalization, notably core business focus and high profitability. In this respect, the stakes are particularly high for South Korea and Indonesia, the previous Asian champions of conglomerate models.

Notes

1 KPMG Corporate Finance 1999.
2 Hyundai, Daewoo, Samsung, LG, SK, Hanjin, Ssangyong, Hanwha, Kumho, and Lotte.
3 'The Bigger, the Better: China is Set on Building its Best State-Owned Enterprises into Conglomerates that can Compete Globally,' *Far Eastern Economic Review*, May 21 1998.

References

Abe, M. and Kawakami, M. (1997) 'A Distributive Comparison of Enterprise Size in Korea and Taiwan,' *The Developing Economies*, 35: 4, 382–400.

Amsden, A. (1989) *Asia's Next Giant: South Korea and Late Industrialization* (New York: Oxford University Press).

Asian Development Bank (1999) Asian Development Outlook (Oxford: Oxford University Press).

Chandler, A. D. (1977) *The Visible Hand: The Managerial Revolution in American Business* (Cambridge, Mass.: Harvard University Press).

Chong, N. I., and Soogeun, O. (2000) 'Asian Insolvency Regimes from a Comparative Perspective: Problems and Issues for Reform,' Unpublished Manuscript (Paris: OECD and Seoul: Korea Development Institute).

Delapierre, M. and Milelli, C. (1999) 'Japanese Direct Investment in China,' in S. Dzever and J. Jaussaud (eds), *China and India: Economic Performance and Business Strategies of Firms in the Mid-1990s* (London: Macmillan).
Grou, P. (1988) *L'émergence des géants du Tiers-Monde* (Paris: Editions Publisud).
Hattori, T. (1997) '*Chaebol*-style Enterprise Development in Korea', *The Developing Economies*, 35: 4, 341–57.
Johnson, C. (1982) *MITI and the Japanese Miracle, 1925–1975* (Stanford: Stanford University Press).

8

The Impact of Structural Reforms and De-Regulation Measures on FDI in East Asia

Guy Faure

Introduction: the effects of Asia's economic crisis on its high-speed reform processes

One consequence of the Asian crisis has been the adoption by potential investors of a whole range of new strategic approaches to the issue of foreign direct investment (FDI) in that part of the world. Investors' attitudes have varied according to the way in which they have interpreted the changes that have occurred as a result of the region's recent economic crisis. The economic typhoon in the Far East caused a number of major transformations. The most urgent of these were the structural reforms and the de-regulation measures that the International Monetary Fund (IMF) strongly recommended to the three main victims of the crisis, South Korea, Thailand, and Indonesia.

However, this general trend towards reform and de-regulation can be observed even in those Asian countries that have not been among the crisis' principal victims. In reality, most countries in Asia had been trying for a number of years to implement a process of reform, albeit to varying degrees, and for a variety of reasons. For example, both China and Vietnam, each at its own pace, had been trying to make the transition from state capitalism to a market economy. Japan, a pioneer in the field of structural reforms, was on the cusp of a structural 'Big Bang,' the result of its long-standing and permanent drive towards de-regulation.

Did the Asian crisis simply serve as a catalyst for a reform movement that was already under-way? To answer this fundamental question, we should consider the multiple aspects of this historical event. The crisis, which broke out in July 1997, was initially sparked by a monetary crisis (the collapse of the Thai baht), followed by a cascade of competitive devaluations that initially involved most of the currencies in South-East

Asia, spreading to the Korean won a few months later. Within a very short period of time, the Asian monetary crisis had lead to a severe financial crisis, as financial institutions' foreign liabilities caused a dramatic deterioration in their cash positions (the service of the debt being amplified as a result of the local currencies' falling parity against the dollar). It was clear that the Asian financial authorities were at least partially responsible for this critical state of affairs, either because they tolerated it – or, in some cases, because their actions were a contributing factor. Asian authorities had been exercising insufficient control over their financial institutions, thus enabling speculation and inappropriate investment to take place. As such, none were in a position to take the measures that the situation called for, and certainly not within an appropriate time frame. In fact, this lack of control over financial and monetary institutions was symptomatic of a more serious dysfunction existing at the very core of the Asian countries' political institutions, especially with regard to the complex relationship that existed between the state and the business world. As such, the crisis worked like an 'electroshock' on the institutions that it affected, and it served to accelerate the reforms and de-regulation policies that were already being introduced all across Asia. In Japan, for instance, reform and de-regulation processes had been initiated two decades prior to the crisis, but their implementation has been very slow. The country has now reached the point where any further delay in the move towards reform would cause immediate damage. For this reason, Japan should be re-introduced into the framework of our analysis, especially since it has been experiencing, as a result of its deregulatory measures, a sea change in its attitudes towards foreign investors.

The present chapter addresses three separate issues:

1. The various approaches that Korea, Malaysia, Thailand, and Vietnam have taken with respect to the issue of reform (with reference to Japan).
2. A comparison of the immediate effects that these reform processes have had on their respective business environments.
3. The trends in these countries' FDI flows.

Our initial objective was to enrich our presentation with a comparison of foreign (American, European, and Japanese) investors' attitudes, and with a study of their regional mergers and acquisitions (M&A) strategies. However, to study Asia's multiple reform programs in any great detail, we need to limit the scope of the present chapter to a single question: in general, do Asian reforms help to improve the business environment in such a way as to benefit FDI and market liberalization?

A panorama of Asian reforms

At first glance, Japan, with its painstakingly slow plans for reform and extremely fastidious process of de-regulation, does not seem like a reliable model for other Asian governments seeking to further their own national programs of reform. Moreover, Japan is itself a victim of its past attitudes towards foreign investors on at least two levels. On the one hand, the very low levels of FDI into Japan translate the fact that foreign affiliates have made little or no contribution to job creation. On the other hand, owing to its lack of domestic competition, Japan has not really been able to benefit from the latest managerial know-how – a good example being the country's financial sector, in which foreign banks were restricted to a mere 3 percent of the market throughout the 1990s.

In recent years, Asian countries have been reluctant to use Japan as a point of reference for their own policy making. Yet this is exactly what Malaysia's Prime Minister Mahathir did during the 1980s with his notorious 'Look East Policy'. According to his strategy, ASEAN countries should have adopted the Japanese *modus operandi* of combining unequivocal declarations in favor of free trade and investment liberalization with a persistent and deep-seated economic nationalism. Furthermore, this tendency to replicate the Japanese model survived, at least to a certain degree. An example is the way in which both the Japanese and the Korean Finance Ministries were reorganized. Each country has created an independent body to supervise the finances of its local banking sector. It should be noted that these steps were taken after each Ministry had already been blamed for its perceived lack of rigor, and for having exerted insufficient control over its local banks (an institutional failure common throughout Asia, and which is in fact a key component of any thorough analysis of the origins of the financial crisis).

Japan was the first Asian country to decide to remedy this situation as much as possible, by cutting the number of governmental ministries (from 21 to 12). Subsequently, in February 1998, the new Korean administration of President Kim Dae-jung announced that it would implement a similar package of reforms. This proposal foreshadowed a reorganization of the Korean administration, as well as a reduction in the number of ministries (from 23 to 17 or 16). Indeed, this 'small-government' approach can also be found in China, which has a plan for downsizing the number of its ministries and government committees (from 40 to 29). In sum, administrative reforms have been carried out in parallel with economic restructuring (*chaebols* in Korea, *keiretsu* in Japan and privatization of state-owned enterprises (SOEs) in China).

Many Asian countries have followed a philosophy of reform similar to that of Japan's. However, this does not necessarily mean that Japan has been the inspiration behind its neighbors' reform policies – at least, not all of them. After all, as our study of Malaysia, Korea, Vietnam, and Thailand will demonstrate, not every Asian country has felt the same need to introduce urgent and drastic institutional and structural reforms. Each country operates in a specific political environment. The only real common denominator is that each country has been promoting a business environment that is new, and that is designed to attract FDI.

Malaysia and Mahathir's inwardly focussed economic policies

Malaysia has been following its very personal trajectory. It turned down IMF funding, it strongly denounced the role of foreign speculators, especially American pension funds, and sometimes resorted to racist assertions while vilifying the international speculator George Soros. In the aftermath of the Asian crisis, this country, which had been one of the most stable in the region, found itself politically destabilized by its leaders' total disagreement as to the political orientations that could best surmount the effects of the crisis. Mohamad Mahathir, Malaysia's prime minister, overruling his deputy prime minister and his finance minister, sought to enforce exchange controls in order to stop the flight of capital. Although FDI is still welcome in Malaysia, the country now considers FDI as a threat to national security, as foreign interests take a total or a partial stake in a Malaysian firm. Moreover, the crisis is now generally deemed to have been an external problem rather than a domestic issue. The government's policy has therefore been to cushion the country from the various waves of international market deregulation – an example being Mahathir's disagreement with his deputy prime minister Anwar Ibrahim (Pomonti, 1998a), who had been in favor of austerity policies. Ibrahim was accused by the head of the government of advocating IMF-type measures, even in the absence of direct intervention by the IMF. With an external debt reaching $35 billion and with $22 billion in reserves, the financial situation in Malaysia is not as critical as in neighboring Thailand or Indonesia. Nevertheless, Mahathir felt compelled to assert, in a September 1998 interview, that 'it is obvious that we cannot continue to operate within the structures of the so-called free market system' – and shortly thereafter measures aimed at curbing speculation via the restriction of offshore ringgit deposits were announced:

- foreign portfolio investments could be repatriated only after a 12-months period.
- Nonresidents had to pay for Malaysian securities in ringgits, or else by debiting a nonresident account that was domiciled in Malaysia.
- Exports had to be paid for in foreign currency.
- Ringgits held outside of the country became worthless after 30 September 1998.
- Exchange controls were implemented whereby resident travelers could not bring in or take out more than 10 000 ringgits, nor take out more than10 000 ringgits' worth of foreign currency.
- Central bank approval became mandatory for: (a) all transfers between nonresident accounts and between nonresident and resident accounts, (b) investments abroad for amounts exceeding 10 000 ringgits, (c) investments abroad in foreign currency.

In an open letter to Mahathir, Paul Krugman warned that controls should be viewed as an aid rather than as an alternative to reform (Keenan, 1998a). The American economist suggested that in order to avoid certain negative side-effects of this policy (i.e. the creation of a black market, corruption through the falsification of trade documentation, and, worse of all, a collapse in new FDI flows), the controls should be dismantled within three years at the very most. As far as control policies were concerned, Malaysia's path was diametrically opposed to Thailand's. Some Western businessmen were so unsettled by the climate of uncertainty in Malaysia that they openly expressed their fear that all foreign investment into the country could soon end.

However, the Malaysian strategy of economic isolationism (Pomonti, 1998b) had been based on an incorrect assumption. The country's economic recovery could not take place without substantial inflows of foreign capital – and, indeed, one of the immediate effects of Mahathir's policy was a 27 percent decline in FDI inflows to Malaysia between 1997 and 1998 (UNCTAD, 1999). As a result, Mahathir removed many of these controls in September 1999, exactly one year after he had first put them in place – despite the fact that, in retrospect, Malaysia's economic performance in 1999 was relatively good. Fears of investors' boycott were greatly exaggerated, and a total of $1 billion was invested in the country during this period. In fact, from February to September 1999, investors applied for a total of $1.8 billion in investment (compared to a total of $3.2 billion for the whole of 1998). Moreover, although Malaysia's capital control policy initially received, with the notable exception of Paul Krugman, a chilly response from Western economists, it now receives a grudging respect from most political commentators. Recent IMF praise for Malaysia's actions demonstrates the ongoing nature of this shift towards more flexible policies of economic aid and restructuring.

Thailand's preference for quick and efficient reforms

Thailand, the first country to be affected by the Asian crisis, has since gained a reputation as the IMF's model pupil. Despite its relatively high unemployment rate and numerous business bankruptcies, Thailand's economic situation improved greatly. This relatively quick recovery was the result of the extremely comprehensive reform program (Thailand's Economic Rehabilitation Program) that the Thai authorities implemented in the immediate aftermath of the crisis. A synopsis of this program is as follows (Ministry of Foreign Affairs, 1998):

(a) *Financial sector reforms* to date (above and beyond the suspension of 58 finance firms):

- financial institutions are now required to hold adequate levels of reserves for bad debts;
- two new agencies have been set up with the purpose of easing the Bank of Thailand's task of rebuilding the country's financial system: the Financial Sector Restructuring Agency (whose mandate is to develop a comprehensive package of financial restructuring), and the Asset Management Corporation (responsible for purchasing the troubled assets of the 58 financial companies that were shut down, and for putting these assets up for auction);
- the country's bankruptcy laws were amended in the immediate aftermath of the crisis;
- a general strengthening of the financial sector became an explicit objective of government policy over the medium and long term (from 1998 onwards). This was to be achieved by changing the Banking Act, thus bringing Thailand's banks into line with international norms by the year 2000.

(b) *Monetary and fiscal policies* aimed at facilitating a return to macroeconomic stability, thus ensuring economic growth:

- the baht was devalued and left to float;
- VAT was increased from 7 percent to 10 percent;
- the current account deficit was reduced from 7.9 percent to 3.9 percent.

(c) *Bureaucratic reforms*:

- subsidies to state-run enterprises were ended;
- the privatization of state-run enterprises was accelerated,

- a performance-based public administration was created, and the administrative process modernized;
- the state's operating costs were cut through a downsizing of the civil service (at least 20 percent over the 1998–2002 years).

Other measures were also taken with the help of the World Bank. These policies purported to minimize the social impact of the economic crisis, that is its impact on the labor market, on education, and on health care. As a result, foreign investment flows into Thailand in 1998 showed a sharp increase over the preceding year.

Vietnam and its low-speed transition policy

The side-effects of the Asian crisis were immediately felt in Vietnam. The country had first opened up to foreign investment in 1986; between 1986 and 1997, two-thirds of its FDI inflows came from Asian sources. By the end of this period, foreign investment had created 300 000 jobs in Vietnam, and it represented the equivalent of 8.6 percent of its GNP. Then the Asian crisis broke out, and foreign investments recorded a year-on-year drop of 50 percent (1997: $4.4 billion, 1996: $8.8 billion), a trend which, by any measure, continued well into 1998. The Korean *chaebols*, for example, who had previously been amongst the most active investors in Vietnam, canceled projects that had already been agreed with the Vietnamese authorities. This also happened with the country's other main foreign investors (including Japan, Malaysia, Thailand, Singapore, and Hong Kong). In such an environment, it is no surprise that foreign investors wanted to keep a close watch on the evolution of the Vietnamese reform program.

In the early part of 1998, the Vietnamese Communist Party (VCP) published a report containing its new development strategy (Keenan, 1998b). The resolutions outlined in this report stated that the country should start planning the following reforms:

- labor-intensive industries were to be developed in those sectors where Vietnam has a comparative advantage
- privately held companies were to be granted permission to engage in direct export activities
- small and unprofitable state firms were to be sold, merged, or liquidated
- schedules for reducing import tariffs were to be published
- special economic zones (SEZs) were to be set up, albeit on a trial basis

- foreigners were to be allowed to buy shares in some local firms
- tax policies, and prices for services, were to be standardized
- farmers were to be given permission to trade land-use rights (the goal being the creation of larger holdings and thus the possibility of increased mechanization).

Many local and foreign investors were reassured by the fact that the VCP, at the very least, was staying on the reform bandwagon. However, the Communist Party's report failed to convey any sense of urgency in dealing with the immediate impact of the Asian downturn on the Vietnamese economy, and many experts called for measures that were even more radical than the ones being proposed. Yet the situation, both present and future, is not without threat for the VCP. After all, the greater the reforms it implements, the less power it conserves. As such, the party is divided over the major issues that would be at stake in any accelerated reform of Vietnam's state-run firms and banking system. Moreover, even though the party conservatives may be generally unwilling to show flexibility on economic matters, there is a chance that they would be ready to consider small administrative reforms in an effort to assuage the country's discontented rural populations. In any event, many VCP members are not convinced that it is in Vietnam's interest to follow the Chinese model of rapid market liberalization. It should finally be noted that the industrial production of the private sector in Vietnam provides only 2.4 percent of the country's GNP.

Korea's fast-track liberalization

The Korean path to trade and capital liberalization has been similar to that of Japan's, in that the process of total liberalization was postponed for as long as possible, with a protectionist attitude being maintained in certain key sectors. For the authorities in Korea, as in Japan, FDI promotion has been a relatively new policy – and it is noteworthy that both countries have transformed their respective trade promotion agencies, JETRO and KOTRA, into instruments for the promotion of foreign investment. Until recently, the Korean market still had the reputation of being unfriendly to foreign business initiatives. The best example of this closed system is Korea's automobile market, in which foreign car makers have a negligible share (less than 0.5 percent). Yet, ironically, if Korea is to further stimulate its economic recovery, it badly needs FDI inflows. Towards this end, the country enacted in 1998 a new liberalization package – legislation that was in fact a simple extension of a similar plan that had first been agreed in 1993. Before 1995, total yearly foreign investment in Korea fluctuated between 1 billion and 2 billion dollars. In February 1997, a new law (the Foreign Direct Investment – Foreign Capital Inducement Act) was passed, resulting in an improvement in the scope of the country's FDI-related legislation. The policy was very successful in that it resulted in a sharp increase in FDI over 1995 levels. FDI peaked in 1997 at $6.9 billion (up 1 percent on a yearly basis). New investment plummetted by 24 percent over the first half of 1998, but most of this fall occurred in the months of January and February, after which time the investment growth rate slowly rose back to the previous year's level. In 1998, a new law, The Foreign Investment Promotion Act, further improved upon previous legislation. Its measures included the opening up of new sectors to foreign investors, other measures that were designed to loosen administrative constraints, and a new regulation in the area of mergers and acquisitions.

Sectors that have been recently opened to foreigners

In order to qualify for OECD membership, Korea was required between 1993 and 1997 to liberalize a large number of its sectors of activity. At present, 1117 of the 1148 sectors in the Korean Standard Industrial Classification (SIC) have been entirely opened up to foreign investment. Another 13 sectors remain totally closed, including agricultural products, cattle, seafood products, TV broadcasting, and insurance. Of the 18 partially opened sectors, some will be liberalized in the near future. These include alcoholic spirits, which will be totally opened by the year 2000, and energy and other utilities (water). In these latter two sectors, private firms have been completely opened up to foreign investors, but foreign participation in public sector companies is still restricted to less than 50 percent.

The liberalization of regulations related to mergers and acquisitions

As a result of the February 1997 legislation, there are fewer restrictions on foreign takeovers of a firm in Korea than in most other industrial countries. The concept of foreign acquisition has progressively become an acceptable outcome in Korea. Yet this is a country that had once implemented a system so protective that hostile takeovers were virtually impossible. This was both because of the draconian regulatory environment (no more than 10 percent of a company's shares could be acquired without the approval of the Board of Directors), and because such takeovers required the prior consent of the Korean Ministry of Finance.

The Foreign Investment Promotion Act

In June 1998, the Korean government came out with new FDI legislation designed to facilitate the establishment of foreign firms in the country. This law is expected to have the following main effects:

- new sectors such as communications and media will be opened to foreign stakeholding
- tax cuts will be extended to high-tech ventures, or to firms settled in Free Investment Zones (FIZs)
- foreign investors located in industrial parks will benefit from low leasing rates
- local authority efforts to encourage FDI in the provinces will be supported by state incentives
- leasing terms will be extended from 20 to 50 years in sectors that are to be determined by a Committee for Foreign Investment (i.e. in sectors other than hi-tech)
- The Korean Trade Organization (KOTRA) is to be reorganized, reinforcing its role in the overseas promotion of Korea, and allowing it to better assist foreign investors with domestic formalities
- Investment zones with special fiscal and land tax exemptions for foreign firms are to be created.

By 1999, the situation had clearly begun to improve. In September, the South Korean Ministry of Commerce, Industry, and Energy announced that foreign investments had risen dramatically, primarily in the services sectors. There was a 90 percent year-on-year increase over the period running from January to August 1999, with investments reaching $7.7 billion. German, Dutch, and Belgian investments showed the greatest increase, though US investment did decline.

The authorities will continue pushing for corporate re-structuring, and for a further opening of the Korean market – a process of liberalization that is clearly tied into Korea's desire to be admitted to the OECD. The Asian economic crisis clearly accelerated this process; it has also given further impetus to Korea's drive for economic restructuring (a policy that has already met with a good deal of success, at least as far as foreign investment is concerned). South Korea represents a test case – more than any other country; it has been diligently trying to implement the IMF notion that new macroeconomic programs must be accompanied by structural reforms. Even so, Korea's liberalization program is not always as it seems. The Korean authorities severely restrict ownership in the country's financial sector, and this continues to put a damper on capital inflows (*Financial Times*, 1999).

Conclusion: the effects of the Asian reform fever

With the advent of large-scale reforms throughout Asia, markets in this part of the world are more open than ever before. Yet it is too early to assume, as did a former minister from Chile, that Asia represents the equivalent of a second fall of the Berlin Wall. According to this viewpoint, the ultimate demise of state capitalism is near, and what we are witnessing today is the triumph of ultra-liberal Anglo-Saxon principles (e.g. less state intervention and little regulation). Even though the Asian environment is particularly exposed to American pressures in favor of liberalization, the fact remains that the main conduit for external influence has been the IMF, an international organization that has been promoting 'liberal de-regulation' trends throughout the world. In any event, the reform process has become indispensable at both the national and international levels. It constitutes a strong signal to foreign and domestic investors. This is particularly significant given Asia's need for FDI to fuel its economic recovery.

To revert to the three issues raised in the introduction, summarized by the following question, 'Do Asian reforms generally help improve the business environment in such a way as to encourage FDI and market liberalization?,' we can now assert that despite the uncertainties experienced during 1998, reform and de-regulation policies have made a positive contribution to the investment climate in this part of the world. (Johnson *et al.*, 1999). Asian governments have at last chosen effective political remedies for turning Asia, once again, into an attractive region for international capital.

References

Financial Times (1999) 'Asian models,' June 9.

Johnson, B., Holmes, K. and Kirkpatrick, M. (1999) *Index of Economic Freedom*, The Heritage Foundation.

Keenan, F. (1998a) 'Desperate Measures,' *Far Eastern Economic Review*, September 10, 10–13.

Keenan, F. (1998b) 'Half Measures, Hanoi Says it's Okay to Get Rich, but How?,' *Far Eastern Economic Review*, February 12, 10–13.

Pomonti, J. C. (1998a) 'Le limogeage du vice-premier ministre malaisien ouvre un conflit politique face à la crise financière' (The Ousting of Malaysia's Deputy Prime Minister Causes Political Conflict in a Time of Financial Crisis), *Le Monde*, September 4.

Pomonti, J. C. (1998b), 'La Malaisie parie sur son isolement économique' (Malaysia Bets on Economic Isolation), *Le Monde*, October 6.

Ministry of Foreign Affairs, (1998) *Ambassador's Digest*, Ministry of Foreign Affairs, Thailand, 1: 6,.4–5.

UNCTAD, (1999) *World Investment Report*, Washington, DC September.

9
The Korean Financial Crisis and NFDI

*Kyoo Kim and Charles R. Chittle**

With the spread of the Asian financial crisis, Korea has been hit by its worst economic depression since 1970. Industrial production declined, plant operation rates nose-dived, and unemployment soared to 1.5 million at the end of May 1998. Facility investment declined 8.7 percent in 1997 and 38.5 percent in 1998. Such investment had been increasing before the crisis at an average annual rate of over 10 percent for some years. Korean GDP for the first time decreased at an annual rate of 5.5 percent in 1998. One of the causes of the slump was a loss of confidence by foreign investors. The Korean economy has since recovered rapidly. According to IMF sources, the growth in real GDP is expected to have reached 9 percent in 1999 (IMF, 1999). Industrial production increased by 22.5 percent in 1999; this is the highest rate of increase recorded since 1980.

In this chapter, we investigate the flow of Korean net foreign investment. Net foreign investment can be decomposed into two components: net foreign portfolio investment (NFPI) and net foreign direct investment (NFDI). We investigate these two parts in detail before and after the beginning of the current Asian economic crisis. Despite the Korean economic liberalization measures in the 1980s, Foreign Direct Investment (FDI) into Korea has had a much wider variation than other components of investment. An initial increase in FDI flows into Korea in the 1980s was followed by a slowdown in the late 1980s. FDI inflows returned to a more normal trend in the 1990s. Following an interruption associated with the financial crisis, the inflow of FDI was nearly $9 billion in 1998, a 27 percent increase over the previous year.

We relate the theory of international capital movements to the Korean financial crisis. Government policies and their role in the financial turbulence are addressed. The effects of the financial crisis on European economies and businesses will receive some scrutiny. The crisis directly affects foreign trade, interest rates, inflation, and financial flows. Profits and investment opportunities of businesses are also affected. Indirect effects are related to the impact of the crisis on third countries, as growth rates and economic policies feel the effects of Asian developments. Changes in government economic policy in response to the crisis and the involvement of the IMF have implications for European and foreign firms. For example, the financial sector is undergoing reform, capital inflows are being liberalized, and changes in labor laws have resulted in a more flexible labor market. The pampering of the *chaebols* by the government is being reduced and these large conglomerates will feel pressure to become more efficient (see Chapter 7).

The flow of FDI into Korea now originates from Europe more than from Japan. Japan's domination of FDI in Korea has ended. In 1997 Japan's share was only 18.6 percent while Europe and the United States, respectively, accounted for 36.3 percent and 41.3 percent of the total FDI flow into Korea. What will happen to this composition in the future? Re-structuring the Korean financial sector with the changes in corporate governance and government policies will have a significant impact on Korean–European bilateral trade. The chapter concludes with some perspectives on the post-crisis Euro–Korean relationship.

A macroeconomic model of Korean capital flows

In an open economy, net exports (*NX*) are equal to net foreign investment (*NFI*). *NFI* is the link between the market for loanable funds and the market for foreign currency. In the loanable funds market, national saving (*S*) represents the supply of funds (which consists of private and public saving), while *NFI* and domestic investment (*I*) represent the demand for loanable funds (Froot and Stein, 1991). The interest rate is determined by the balance of supply and demand in the loanable funds market. In the foreign currency market, *NFI* represents the supply of domestic currency and *NX* constitutes the demand for domestic currency. *NX* and *NFI* thus determine the equilibrium exchange rate.

The loanable funds market

In the loanable funds market, the simultaneous nature of the above three economic factors (*NFI*, *I*, and *S*) allows us to use the simultaneous equation model to detect the effect of NFI, domestic investment, and national saving on the Korean real interest rate (*R*). The model is specified as follows:

$$NFI = \beta_1 + \beta_2^* R + \beta_3^* R1 \quad (6.1)$$
$$I = \delta_1 + \delta_2^* R + \delta_3^* GDP \quad (6.2)$$
$$S = \gamma_1 + \gamma_2^* R + \gamma_3^* \mathit{Income} \quad (6.3)$$
$$S = I + NFI \quad (6.4)$$

where
NFI = NFI of Korea
I = Domestic investment of Korea
S = National saving of Korea
R = Domestic real interest rate of Korea
*R*1 = US real interest rate
GDP = GDP of Korea
Income = Gross national income

The first three structural equations, (6.1)–(6.3) are the behavioral representation of NFI, domestic investment, and national saving, and the fourth equation, (6.4), is the equilibrium condition for the loanable funds market. Each equation has one endogenous variable of the domestic real interest rate. Every behavioral equation has one exogenous variable (*R*1, *GDP*, and *Income,* respectively) on the right-hand side.[1] We can use the two-stage least square (2SLS) procedure to estimate each of the coefficients of the equation system. The time-series data (see below) contains a first-order auto-correlation in the implied functions in (6.1) and (6.2). The Cochrane–Orcutt procedure has been used to transform the data of the above two functions in the second-stage estimation in order to correct auto-correlation.

The data used in the regression are quarterly data from 1980 to 1997, just before the Asian financial crisis. All the data of Korea come from the web site of the Korean central bank, Bank of Korea <http://www.bok.or.kr>. The US data come from the web site of the Federal Reserve Bank of St. Louis <http://www.stls.frb.org/fred>. All variables are in real terms (in 1990 prices).

The interest rates used in the regression are the real interest rates of Korea and the United States (as a proxy for the foreign interest rate for Korea), which are calculated by subtracting the expected inflation rate from the nominal interest rate in each country. The real rate is the nominal rate minus the expected inflation rate.[2] The CPI (consumer price Index) is used to measure the inflation rates in each country. The data for Korean nominal interest rates are from the money market rate of Korea. The nominal interest rates of the United States are the federal fund rates. NFI is the sum of the net foreign direct investment and net foreign portfolio investment. National saving is calculated by subtracting government consumption and private consumption from GDP, all in nominal terms. Then, we use the quarterly GDP deflator to transform the nominal values into real ones. The units of *NFI, I, GDP, S,* and income are in million US dollars.

The result of the two-stage linear regression estimation is shown below:

$$NFI = 4.52.075 - 325.838^{*}R + 203.378^{*}R1 \quad (6.1')$$
$$(1.662) \quad (-5.424) \quad (3.762)$$
$$R^2 = 0.343$$

$$I = -1265.557 - 271.168^{*}R + 0.408^{*}GDP \quad (6.2')$$
$$(-2.525) \quad (-1.547) \quad (23.77)$$
$$R^2 = 0.941$$

$$S = -4.995.78 + 409.98^{*}R + 0.395^{*}Income \quad (6.3')$$
$$(-6.249) \quad (2.126) \quad (22.909)$$
$$R^2 = 0.951$$

(*T-statistics in parenthesis*)

We hypothesize that the Korean interest rate, *R*, has a negative relationship, and the foreign interest rate, *R1*, has a positive relationship with Korean NFI. The higher the rate of interest in a country, the more attractive are the assets in that country. The above result in (6.1′) shows clearly that the signs of the coefficients of the independent variables meet our expectation, and both of them are statistically significant at the 5 percent level. If the domestic interest rate increases by 1 percentage point, net foreign investment will decrease by about $326 million. If the foreign interest rate increases by 1 percentage point, net foreign investment will increase by $203 million.

In (6.2′) the sign of the coefficient of the domestic interest rate is negative, which means that a higher domestic interest rate will lead to a decrease in domestic investment. A 1 percentage point increase of the domestic interest rate will lead to a $271 million decrease in domestic investment. The sign of the coefficient of *GDP* is positive as expected, and a $1 million increase of GDP leads to an increase of domestic investment of $0.41 million. The coefficient of the interest rate is not significant at the 5 percent level.

In (6.3′), the sign of the real interest rate is positive. A higher domestic interest rate is associated with an increase in national saving. A 1 percentage point increase of the domestic interest rate results in an increase of domestic saving by $410 million. The high value of the coefficient of interest rate, larger than in the investment of (6.2′), is consistent with the high saving rate in most Asian countries. The sign of the coefficient of *Income* is positive as expected, and a $1 million increase in national income leads to a $0.4 million increase in national saving.

The foreign exchange market

The nominal exchange rate and the price level in Korea and the United States influence net exports. In the foreign currency market, *NFI* represents the supply of domestic currency and *NX* represents the demand for domestic currency. Both *NX* and *NFI* thus determine the equilibrium real exchange rate. Because of the simultaneous nature of net exports and the foreign exchange rate, we again use the simultaneous equation model to detect the effect of foreign exchange rate on net exports of Korea. The model is specified as follows:

$$NX = \alpha_1 + \alpha_2^* EX + \alpha_3^* T \tag{6.5}$$

$$NX = NFI(Fixed) \tag{6.6}$$

Where
NX = Net exports of Korea
NFI = *NFI* of Korea
EX = Real exchange rate of Korean won against the US dollar
T = Average tariff rate of Korea

Equation (6.5) is a representation of the behavior of net exports. The demand for currency comes from net exports which, for example, are stimulated by a lower real exchange rate. Since NFI is determined completely in the loanable funds market, NFI is assumed fixed in the foreign exchange market, representing the supply of the currency. Consequently there is no behavioral equation of NFI in this system illustrating the foreign exchange market. Equation (6.6) is the equilibrium condition for the foreign exchange market. We again use the two-stage least squares (2SLS) to estimate each coefficient in the equation of the system. There is no auto-correlation in this function.

The estimation result is as follows:

$$NX = 14235.05 - 11651780.8^* EX + 256.86^* T \tag{6.5'}$$

$$(1.761) \qquad (-2.351) \qquad (.722)$$

$$R^2 = 0.206$$

(*T-statistics in parenthesis*)

We expect to find a negative sign for the real exchange rate and a positive sign for the tariff rate of Korea. An increase of the real exchange rate is associated with an appreciation of the Korean currency (won), which will lead to a decrease in net exports of Korea. An increase of the tariff rate will decrease the imports of Korea, resulting in an increase of Korean net exports. If the real exchange rate of the won increases by 0.01 cents (equivalent to a 16 percent appreciation of the won), net exports will decrease by $1.16 billion. An increase in the tariff rate will decrease Korean imports, raising net exports. The result of our regression shows that net exports will increase by $256 million if the tariff rate increases by 1 percentage point, which is equal to at least a 20 percent increase in the tariff rate. The result in (6.5′) meets our expectation, the real exchange rate is statistically significant at the 5 percent percent level. But the tariff rate is not. The reason for the insignificance of the tariff rate is that it is usually stable over several years. So the quarterly data may not be appropriate to detect the tariff rate's influence on net exports in the short run.

The data used in this regression are quarterly data from 1980 to 1997. The ratio of the tariff revenue to total imports of Korea is used as a proxy for the Korean tariff rate. Net exports are the balance of goods and services from the balance of payments accounts of Korea. The GDP deflator of Korea and the United States, respectively, is used as a proxy for the price level of Korea and the United States to calculate the real exchange rate.

Decomposition of NFI

The estimated NFI function for Korea sheds an interesting light on how important the role of NFI is for the growth of the Korean economy. In 1997, for instance, NFI for Korea was $–12 690.1 million. So Koreans brought in more capital from abroad than they invested abroad. The main concern of the policy makers in Korea is that they want to stabilize the Korean economy from the current recession by aggressively bringing foreign capital into Korea. Such infusion of capital will invigorate production and restart the growth engine of Korea, raising the growth rate to the previous high positive level from the current negative growth. The question is how relevant NFI is to the growth rate for Korea. It appears that foreign capital is more important than the dire domestic capital. It will shift out the production possibility curve (PPC), both by closing the gap of the investment need that can not be satisfied only with domestic capital and by generating positive externalities and learning effects from the technology diffusion coming with the foreign investment.

Our estimates above address this issue. Suppose the Korean government wants to raise the growth rate by 1 percent. How much of NFDI out of NFI should be generated to accomplish this task?[3] Given $303.77 billion as the 1997 real GDP (1990 base year) and 1 percent of GDP growth requiring about a \$3 billion increase in GDP, we can calculate the necessary increment of NFDI by solving the first four equations. That is

$$\Delta \mathbf{NFI} = \left[\frac{(\beta_2 \cdot \delta_3)}{(\gamma_2 - \delta_2 - \beta_2)}\right] \Delta \mathbf{GDP} \tag{6.7}$$

The bracketed term on the right-hand side of (6.7) turns out to be roughly –0.132, which indicates that a \$1 increase in GDP requires a 13.2 percent increase in FDI. Thus a \$3 billion increase in GDP requires a \$396 million increase in FDI.

We now turn to the composition of NFI in Korea (Figure 9.1). Here we look at both direct foreign investment (DFI) and foreign portfolio investment (FPI).

In Figure 9.1, the positive numbers mean that Koreans invested more capital in foreign countries than foreigners invested in Korea. The ratio between NFPI and NFDI is calculated by using their absolute values. FPI can be considered as a short-term investment, while FDI is long-term. If a country has more short-term investment, it will be more vulnerable to a financial crisis. It can be seen from Figure 9.2 that short-term foreign investment increased dramatically in Korea from 1990 to 1997, reaching a peak in 1996, just one year before the crisis. The average ratio of NFPI to NFDI in the 1990s (7.82) was almost twice as large as that of the 1980s (4.31).

Why was Korean direct investment abroad greater than FDI in Korea during the 1990s? Why was there a surge of short-term portfolio investment in Korea during the same period before the crisis? One explanation comes from Krugman (1998). Krugman argues that effective financial supervision is the most efficient way of protecting the financial system, but most Asian countries including Korea resorted to overprotection of their banking institutions, thus creating moral hazard and leaving too much room for the banks to make excessive loans to businesses.

Government protection enabled banking institutions to make excessive investments, which in turn created massive bubbles. Domestic firms can borrow with implicit guarantees by the government, thus willing to pay higher prices than foreign investors, despite their lower expected returns. As a result foreign firms will be crowded out of the domestic market (Krugman, 1998). The bursting of the bubbles led to a devaluation and aggravation of the quality of the banks' assets. The chain reaction caused a contraction in the credit supply and economic recession and the eventual collapse of the banking institutions. And the transfer of ownership from domestic firms to foreign investors became inevitable.

Therefore, empirically we want to see how strong is the moral hazard explanation that Korean FDIs are crowded out of the domestic market

Figure 9.1 NFI, NFPI, and NFDI, Korea 1980–97

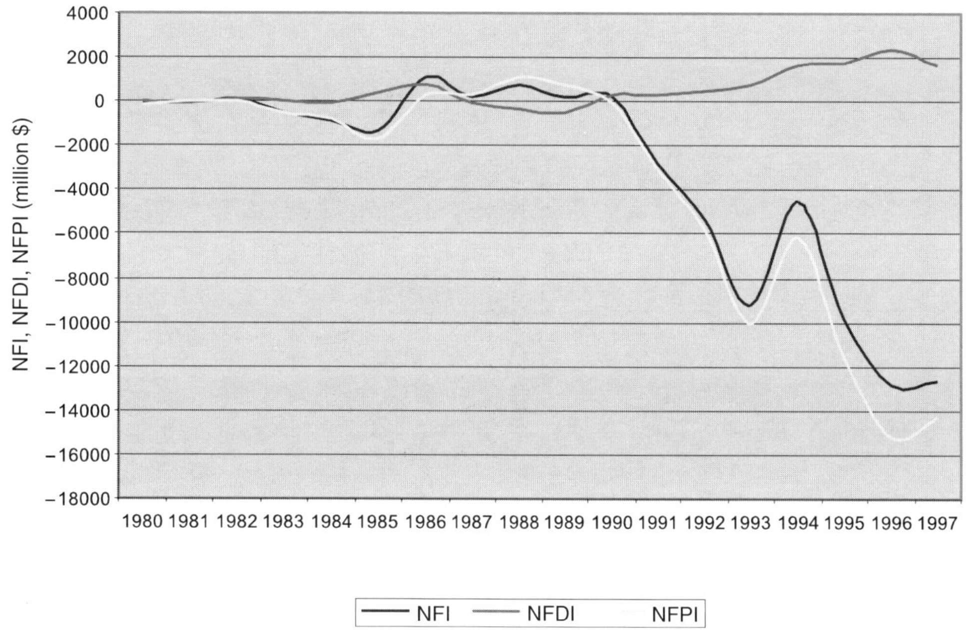

Notes: NFI: Net Foreign Investment; NFDI: Net Foreign Direct Investment NFPI: Net Foreign Portfolio Investment.

Figure 9.2 Average ratio of NFPI to NFDI, Korea, 1980–97

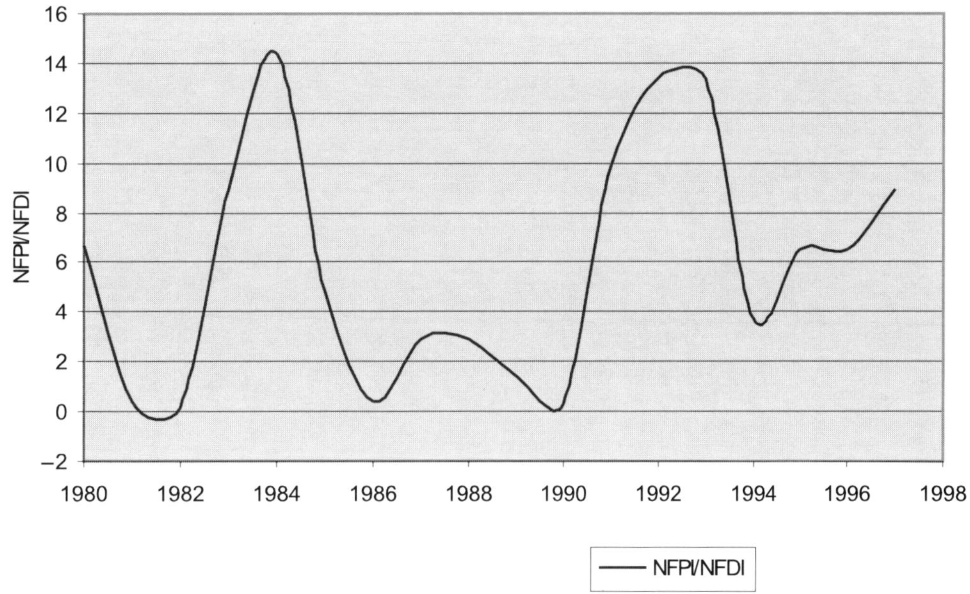

Note: NFDI: Net Foreign Direct Investment NFPI: Net Foreign Portfolio Investment.

before the crisis. We want to examine the hypothesis of the moral hazard explanation for the financial crisis by setting up a model to show the crowding effect in the domestic investment market of Korea.

The crux of the moral hazard argument is that the presence of foreign buyers will limit the actual fall in domestic asset prices. Foreign acquisitions prevent domestic asset prices from decreasing as much as they would without the acquisitions. Therefore, first, we want to see the effect of domestic asset prices in Korea on foreign investment. Domestic total loans as a proxy measure domestic asset prices. We use the ratio of the growth rate of domestic total loans in Korea (L) to the growth rate of GDP (G), which we call L/G, to measure the change in domestic asset prices in Korea. The growth rates of GDP and total loans are, respectively, the annual percentage changes. Second, we investigate which part of the total domestic assets is attributable to foreign sources. To do so, we focus on the effect of credit expansion from abroad on foreign investment into Korea. We look at the liabilities side of the 'balance sheet' to select and use the annual percentage changes of the ratio of foreign liabilities (F) to total liabilities (T), which we call F/T, to measure the credit expansion from abroad. For the dependent variable we use FDI (long-term) and foreign net stock investment (NSI) as a proxy for FPI (short-term), because stock investment is the most important component of FPI in the financial markets. We run the OLS regression of FDI and NSI on the above two variables, L/G and F/T, respectively.

To verify the moral hazard effect, we hope to find negative coefficients of independent variables in the four OLS regressions. If L grows faster than needed to support the economy's growth rate, G, then the ratio L/G will be larger than one. The larger this ratio is, the more the crowding-out effect is to diminish the need for FDI flow. Similarly this is true for the other side of the 'balance sheet' item, foreign liabilities F. F/T measures the portion of the domestic asset prices attributable to foreign sources. The larger the F/T is, the easier it is for domestic firms and banks to borrow short-term capital from abroad to finance risky projects. Thus the foreign firms' investment opportunities will be diminished and FDI into Korea will be crowded out.

The data for the liabilities are from the Monetary Survey table issued by the Bank of Korea. The loan data are from the Deposits & Loans information issued by the Bank of Korea. The value of FDI and NSI are both from the balance of payments data of Korea. The loan data are quarterly data from 1981 to 1997. The data for FDI and liabilities are both quarterly data from 1980 to 1997. We have quarterly data for NSI only from 1992 to 1997.

The results of the regression are presented in Table 9.1. The first column reports the dependent variable – the type of investment. The second

Table 9.1 Estimation results of regressions (OLS and Cochrane–Orcutt procedure)

Investment	L/G	F/T	R^2	D–W	DF
FDI	−1.209				
	(−0.432)		0.177		68
		−13.67			
		(−2.7)	0.304		72
NSI	−113.908				
	(−0.858)		0.032	1.936	24
		−106.7			
		(−1.065)	0.049	2.084	24

Notes: *L/G*: Loan growth rate/GDP growth rate; *F/T*: Foreign liability/Total liability (percent); NSI: Net foreign stock investment in Korea.
(*T*-statistics in parenthesis).

column shows the independent variable, measuring the change in domestic asset prices. The third column shows the independent variables measuring the expansion of foreign credit to Korea. The OLS was used to estimate the coefficients. There is auto-correlation in the regression of FDI. The Cochrane–Orcutt procedure has been used to correct auto-correlation in the regressions on FDI. After the correction, it is not appropriate to show the Durbin–Watson statistics value in the first two regressions. We show DW statistics only in the regressions on NSI.

From the results, we can see that each foreign investment is negatively correlated with the corresponding explanatory variable. One interpretation is that if domestic firms in Korea can easily get loans from the domestic and international capital markets and their assets are bloated in prices, they expand their investment excessively and crowd out foreign investment. The *T*-statistics values of the two regressions within each investment function reveal that the coefficient of *F/T* in the regression on FDI is the only significant value. That means that domestic firms crowd out more FDI from the domestic market if they can borrow more capital from the international financial market. This outcome is consistent with the implication of Krugman's moral hazard for FDI. From these results, the financial crisis in Korea can be explained by the moral hazard behavior of the domestic firms, banks, and government.[4]

Korean government policies concerning foreign capital, and their impact on Europe

Korea historically has not been very receptive to FDI. The focus of economic growth in the initial stage was on the growth of indigenous industries. The Foreign Capital Inducement Act of 1960 focussed on controlling and restricting rather than on encouraging FDI. The amount of FDI was miniscule. In the early 1990s, because of expansion of Korean companies in offshore markets and Korea's trading partners' reciprocal rights to invest in Korea, the Korean government changed its policy regarding FDI and gradually liberalized its capital market. By early 1997, the Foreign Capital Inducement Act was amended to be more consistent with standards set in the capital movement code of the OECD, of which Korea is a member.

To further liberalize its capital market, the Korean government in July 1998 took the following five steps. First, the ceiling on foreign equity investment in domestic companies was raised to 55 percent and was abolished by the end of 1998. Large foreign corporations are also now allowed to list on the Korean stock market. Therefore, all industrial sectors except national security and culturally sensitive ones are now open to foreign investment, as is land. Second, in the bond market, small and medium sized foreign enterprises can issue guaranteed bonds and large firms can issue non-guaranteed bonds. Third, deferred payments for imports and advanced receipts for exports are being progressively eased. Fourth, both friendly and hostile mergers and acquisitions of Korean companies by foreigners are being made easier. Finally, in the foreign exchange market, the requirement for prior approval of transactions has been repealed.

In addition, in order to promote FDI in Korea, the Foreign Investment Promotion Act (FIPA) was passed in the National Assembly and put into effect in November 1998. Let us take a look at this legislation in detail. The major points of the act can be summarized in three points given below.

- First, for the first time in Korean history, the central government intends to delegate the initiation and administration of economic policy from Seoul to local governments. Greater autonomy in the areas of tax reduction or exemption and rent reduction for FDI will be given to local governments.
- Second, FIPA will streamline all bureaucratic red tape in the regulation and administration of FDI so as to focus on promoting and supporting FDI activities with simplification and transparency. As a process, FIPA will use the Korea Trade Investment Promotion Agency (KOTRA) as a clearing-house to provide a one-stop service for FDI.
- Finally, FIPA will create a Foreign Investment Zone (FIZ) to induce large-scale FDI. The location of the FIZ will be determined at the request of foreign investors. Various tax exemption and reduction plus

Table 9.2 FDI, selected developing countries, 1996

	Inflow (US$ billion)	Inflow (% of GDP) (a)	Outflow (US $billion)	Outflow (% of GDP) (b)	Difference (%) ((a)–(b))
Singapore	9.44	10.0	4.80	5.1	4.9
China	42.30	6.1	2.20	0.3	5.8
Indonesia	7.96	3.5	0.51	0.2	3.3
Mexico	7.54	2.3	0.55	0.2	2.1
Hong Kong	2.50	1.6	27.00	17.4	–15.8
Thailand	2.43	1.5	1.74	1.0	0.5
Brazil	9.50	1.3	0.97	0.1	1.2
Korea	2.31	0.5	4.19	0.9	–0.4
Taiwan	1.40	0.5	3.10	1.1	–0.6

Source: UNCTAD (1997).

low rental facilities and infrastructure will be provided to foreign firms in the FIZ. This appears similar to the Special Economic Zones (SEZs) used by China to attract FDI in the 1980s.

With this reform, will Korea get its 'share' of FDI? Table 9.2 shows the FDI flow into some developing countries.

Singapore, China, Indonesia, Hong Kong, and Thailand are among the countries in Asia that attracted more FDI in relation to GDP inflow than Korea. In particular FDI as a percentage of GDP was 10 percent in Singapore, compared to a meager 0.5 percent in Korea. Existing foreign companies cite the major stumbling blocks to FDI in Korea as the 'complex approval procedures for investment,' and 'export–import/tax procedures'. Hopefully, the new legislation mentioned above could rectify these problems. However, unless the Korean people understand the mutual benefits of international trade and FDI, there will not be a significant change in the FDI statistics.

In the next section we consider how these changes in FDI policies will affect Europe.

Implications for the European economy

As pointed out earlier, and demonstrated in Table 9.3, Europe accounted for 36.3 percent of FDI in Korea in 1997, a share that was exceeded only by North America. The FDI share of the Union was 34.4 percent, which was second to the 41.1 percent of the United States. This ranking was reversed in 1996: the share of Europe has been rising since 1995. The policy changes outlined above should provide a stimulus to FDI in Korea from

Table 9.3 FDI, Korea, by country share, 1990–7 (%)

Country of origin	1990	1991	1992	1993	1994	1995	1996	1997*
America	**41.8**	**22.3**	**48.5**	**32.9**	**24.6**	**34.3**	**28.9**	**45.0**
United States	39.6	21.2	42.4	32.6	23.6	33.2	27.4	41.1
Asia	**32.1**	**17.8**	**19.0**	**37.5**	**43.2**	**40.7**	**38.0**	**18.6**
Japan	29.4	16.2	17.3	27.4	32.5	21.5	7.9	4.2
Europe	**25.8**	**59.1**	**31.6**	**29.4**	**30.9**	**24.5**	**33.0**	**36.3**
EU	23.4	53.7	27.1	28.7	29.8	23.8	27.9	34.4

Notes: * Through November only; shares in bold add up to 100 percent.
Source: Ministry of Finance and Economy (1998).

Europe and North America. The state of the economies in other regions is such that FDI from them is more problematic.

Europe is in a good position to maintain its leading position as a foreign direct investor in Korea. In 1997, it had a current account surplus of over $120 billion. In 1998, it was close to a $100 billion surplus, while the United States was experiencing enormous and rising current account deficits. And NFI is the counterpart of the current account balance. Thus Europe is experiencing positive NFI, while the US position is negative. The implication is that Europe is in a more favorable financial position to invest abroad. Of course global foreign investment, portfolio as well as direct, in Korea, from Europe as well as North America, will likely decline in the face of unattractive economic conditions. In fact, the Institute for International Finance (IFI) estimates that Korea, Indonesia, Malaysia, Thailand and the Philippines have experienced a decline in net private capital inflows from $93 800 million in 1996, to a net outflow of $24 600 million in 1998. Equity investment appears to be less affected than portfolio investment. This decline may contribute to lower European interest rates and more rapid economic growth as well as greater imports, with a resulting positive effect on the Korean economy and other economies.

Exports from Korea and other Asian countries can be expected to rise. However, the impact of this expansion should not be overemphasized. No European country received as much as 5 percent of its total imports from Korea and the four other Asian countries most affected by the Asian crisis (Indonesia, Malaysia, the Philippines, and Thailand). The share of these five countries in EU imports and exports was 2.5 percent in 1996. Thus a major increase in exports would not be expected to have a significant effect on the trade or current account balance. Export growth is to be affected positively by currency devaluation and rising excess capacity and negatively by liquidity problems and higher costs of imported inputs. (WTO, 1998)

Owing to the serious liquidity crunch that has existed since the onset of the IMF bail-out at the end of 1997, an increasing number of cash-strapped Korean businesses have been turning to foreign investors, in particular Europeans, for an inflow of much-needed funds. For example Norske Skog of Norway has taken over production facilities and related assets from Korean Hansol Paper Co. The local seed industry has been bought out by Norvatis Seeds, Inc. of Switzerland. Hanwha Chemical Corporation sold its hydrogen peroxide business to Kemira Chemicals OY of Finland, while Hanwa BASF Urethane Co. and Hyosung BASF Co. were taken over by their former German partner BASF. Samsung Heavy Industries Co. sold its heavy equipment division to Sweden's Volvo conglomerate, the Hanwha Group sold off its 50 percent equity interest in Hanwha BASF Urethane Co. to BASF, Hansol Paper Co. established a joint venture with Norske Skog in May 1998, Interbrew SA purchased 50 percent of Oriental Brewery Co., and Newbridge Capital agreed to acquire 51 percent of Korea First Bank.

At the end of the 1990s, because of concern over the potential fallout from the global financial crunch stemming from the Russian economic turmoil, the speed of FDI into Korea appears to have slowed down. But as the international financial jitters are easing, FDI into Korea will rebound and Europe can play a key role. This is especially apparent from the passage of the 1998 Foreign Investment Law, which provides various incentives.

Conclusion

International capital flows have increased tremendously since the 1980s as barriers to international capital movements have come down and firms and investors have become more globally oriented. Changes in capital flows have been cited as contributing to the recent economic and financial crises in several countries, especially in Asia. The major focus of this chapter is on Korean capital inflows and outflows. Europe and North America are the major providers of FDI in Korea. With its current account surplus, the European Union is a net provider of foreign investment to the rest of the world, while the United States, with its large and growing current account deficit, is a net absorber of international capital flows.

Korea has experienced a large increase in net inflows of FPI in the 1990s. NPI is positive and of a much greater magnitude than NFDI, which was negative during the 1990s. FPI, especially of the short-term type, tends to be more volatile than FDI. An obvious implication is that the nature of foreign investment has increased the vulnerability of Korea to financial crises. We use data on Korean foreign investment to test the moral hazard model as an explanation of the financial crisis in Korea. The results of the empirical test lend support to this explanation.

Policies of the Korean government to liberalize foreign investment, especially FDI, are outlined. Korea has lagged behind other countries in the region in attracting FDI when related to the size of GDP. The chapter also shows the importance of FDI to the economic growth of Korea.

We are optimistic that the Union will remain a major player in terms of FDI in Korea, its current account surplus and recent examples of such investment lend support to this view. When indirect as well as direct effects of the economic and financial crisis in Korea and several other Asian countries are considered, Europe does not appear to be vulnerable to any significant extent.

Appendix

In the 1990s Korean firm invested huge amounts of capital in foreign markets and the inflow of foreign portfolia investment in Korea also increased dramatically. Might it not be possible that Korean firm use short-term foreign capital to invest abroad (long-term). When the crisis happened, foreign banks or financial institutions lost confident in Korean firms and wanted to withdraw their capital before the investment project became mature to produce profits. In this situation, the Korean firms under the crisis had less liquidity and had to transfer the control of firms to foreign investors who can borrow enough capital at lower cost.

In order to verify this hypothesis, we ran a simple OLS regression of the FDI outflow on the inflow of foreign portfolio investment. The inflow of foreign portfolio investment is the independent variable in this model.

The data for outflow FDI and inflow portfolio investment are monthly data from January 1990 to August 1998. The source of the data is the balance of payment of Korea on the website of the bank of Korea <http://www.bok.or.kr>.

We lagged the nominal exchange rate for 1 month in the regression. The regression results are shown below.

$$\text{Outflow FDI} = \underset{(9.588)}{176.274} + \underset{(3.44)}{0.0541}{*}\text{Inflow FPI}$$

R square = 0.104, *t*-statistic in parenthesis.

From the result, we find that an increase of the inflow of foreign portfolio investment is associated with an increase of the outflow of foreign direct investment of the Korean firms. Thus, our hypothesis of the positive relationship between the FDI outflow and the FPI inflow is verified.

Notes

* We appreciate Jerry Chen's statistical help and comments of Jerry Auten and Mark Wheeler.

1 Invoking the small-country assumption, we treat the world interest rate, *R*1, as exogenous for Korea .

2 We have used the actual inflation rate as a proxy for the expected inflation rate, assuming rational expectations.

3 Of course, the impact of NFDI could be different from that of NFPI.

4 The *chaebols'* risky investment overseas were also tested under the assumption that much of the FPI was used to finance the projects overseas. See the Appendix (p. 000).

In order to verify that foreign buyers limit the actual fall in domestic asset prices, we ran another regression of FDI on the price index of the real estate and rental sector. The data of FDI are monthly data from January 1995 to August 1998, while the data for price index of the real estate and rental sector are from February 1995 to September 1998. The source of the data comes from the web site of the Bank of Korea <http://www.bok.or.kr>. We lagged the price index for one month in our regression. The coefficient of FDI in this regression is 0.011, which is significant at the 5 percent level (*t*-statistic = 2.865). This correlation is consistent with Krugman's argument.

References

Froot, K. A. and J. C. Stein (1991) 'Exchange Rates and Foreign Direct Investment: An Imperfect Capital Markets Approach,' *The Quarterly Journal of Economics*, 106: 4, 1191–217.

IMF (1998), *IMF concludes Article IV consultation with Korea* (Washington, DC: IMF External Relations Department.

10
The Japanese Model of HRM in Crisis

Jacques Jaussaud

Background

The Japanese model of human resources management (HRM) has gone through a serious crisis since the 1990s. Faced with a comprehensive industrial reorganization program and the vanished possibilities of sustained economic growth, the viability of the Japanese model has suddenly been thrown into question. The model, as it is generally understood, is based primarily on the assumption of stable employment relations.

As a result of the collapse of the stock and property markets in the early 1990s, industrial production in Japan contracted significantly between 1991 and 1993 (index 101.7 and 91.2 respectively). Appropriate steps were immediately taken by the government to address the problems. Five economic plans were implemented, at a cost of 70 000 billion yen between August 1992 and September 1995. As a result, the situation improved somewhat between 1995 and 1996, giving rise to GNP growth of 2.2 and 2.8 percent, respectively. Weakened, however, by the increase in the value added tax (VAT) rate in April 1997 (from 3.5 percent to 5.5 percent), economic growth slowed significantly once again, aggravated this time by the financial crisis in Asia. Thus, the significant expansion programs of 1997–8 seemed only to further damage public finances at the end of 1999.

Confronted with increasing negative results, companies were forced to put into place drastic cost-cutting measures – such as, for example, incentive plans for early departure of employees over 40, and transfer of manpower to subsidiaries, suppliers, and other associated companies. Most significantly, however, efforts were made, for the first time, to modify workers' employment contracts from permanent employment to temporary positions (Japan Airlines and All Nippon Airways in particular).

The extent of these programs and the diversity and profiles of the companies involved signaled the beginning of the end of the Japanese model of HRM.

The prevailing literature on the model seems to emphasize the significance of industrial reorganization in the 1990s and its dramatic implications for the Japanese employment system. However, as we shall see, our analysis of the situation seems to paint a different picture and, indeed, helps us better to understand the cogency of the model in terms of incentives. The chapter then goes on to emphasize that, in the context of the 1990s, companies simply intensified their recourse to the HRM methods which are an integral part of the model rather than a departure from it. It is also important to note that HRM systems in Japan are under significant pressure as a result of industrial reorganization as well as the dramatic changes taking place in the Japanese socio-economic environment (durable low growth, ageing of the population, etc.). The question that seems inevitable is whether the Japanese model will continue to remain a major point of reference when addressing these issues in general, and even within the context of the Japanese work environment.

What is the Japanese model of HRM?

The Japanese model of HRM, as a number of authors have indicated (Abegglen and Stalk, 1985; Aoki, 1988; Ujihara, 1991; Uemura and Ebizuka; 1994, etc.), relies primarily on three fundamental characteristics: stable employment relations (the so-called 'life-time employment'), the use of seniority as a major criterion for wage increases, and the system of company-based trade unions. That said, it should be added that the model is subject to at least two different interpretations: one based on a cultural approach and the other on an incentive mechanism. These interpretations are addressed in greater detail below.

The cultural approach

Recruited as they leave school or university, Japanese wage-earners are supposed to carry out their entire careers in the same company, and, except under extenuating circumstances, their remuneration and career progress in the company is based mainly on seniority. When they leave the company, the employees receive an accumulated compensation calculated proportionately to their wages, number of years with the company, and reason for departure. The lump sum is significant when employees take their retirement at the normal retirement age, but much smaller if they leave the company in the course of their career for personal reasons. Thus, not being concerned with possible skills drainage, the employer does not hesitate to invest in the training of his employees. In return for job security and the prospect of promotion which are offered to him, employees are expected to be honest, loyal, and hard working.

Therefore, the Japanese company seems like a real community. The enterprise-based trade union is an additional element of cohesion since it will, naturally, take more account of the constraints placed on the organization than if it were some other form of trade union.

Presented in this way, however, the model appears to leave unsolved the problem of the 'moral hazard' underlined by agency theory (Uemura and Ebizuka, 1994). Within the framework of a system protecting the employee so much, what mechanisms prevent the appearance of opportunistic behavior, consisting in reducing personal effort? What mechanisms prevent the generalization of such behavior, which would affect the company, and, at a broader level, Japanese society as a whole? The explanation often provided, within the framework of this first presentation of the model, goes back to the theme of cultural identities (Abegglen and Stalk, 1985, Nakane, 1970): group dependence, respect for hierarchy and elders, etc., all of which appear to be attributes inherited from Confucian philosophy. For simplicity of exposition and tradition this interpretation of the model appears to be more readily accepted in the literature and is strongly anchored in the perceptions that Japanese employees of large companies have had until recently about employment relationships (Louart, 1995).

Seen from this perspective, therefore, it can be said that the reorganizations of the 1990s marked a dramatic change in the model. Companies implementing programs for early departure of older employees no longer emphasize attributes such as loyalty, honesty, experience, etc. which were generally associated with Japan's economic success. The ageing of the working population, in the context of the forecast long-term slow growth, seems to put in danger the principle of remuneration based on seniority, as companies can no longer afford the high costs associated with it.

From the point of view of management research, this approach seems to pose a number of questions: to start with, it relies largely on an explanation which appears to be far removed from the field of management itself – the argument of cultural identity. Furthermore, it is rooted in an *a priori* reasoning which, to the best of our knowledge, is yet to be sufficiently addressed. Our prolonged professional experience in Japan leads us to question this argument. Without denying the existence of a certain cultural identity, it seems to us rather excessive to build a whole theory of implication (and more broadly that of social relations) on the basis of this one argument.

Our empirical observation of HRM in several companies in Japan (Toshiba in 1983, Kirin in 1987, Toppan in 1995, to name but a few) (Jaussaud, 1996), as well as our studies of the strategies of large Japanese companies in different industries (cars, distribution, shipbuilding, and textile, see Jaussaud, 1991, 1992, 1993) have led us to highlight systematic practices which seem to be in contradiction with the model as has been outlined in the preceding discussion. We refer here to the wide use of precarious forms of employment, and to the methods of performance review and promotion of wage-earners throughout their career. This leads us to prefer a second presentation of the model, in the perspective of the agency theory, and from the point of view of, for example, Aoki (1988), Koike (1994a, 1994b) and Uemura and Ebizuka (1994).

A presentation based on agency theory

Large Japanese companies generally distinguish between two types of workers: 1. permanent employees (*seishain* or 'true employees') and temporary employees (Jaussaud, 1996). Workers belonging to the first category enjoy a stable employment relation, effective career-advancement opportunities, welfare benefits, and training. They are thus managed in accordance with the principles of life-time employment (job security, remuneration in relation to seniority, affiliation with the enterprise trade union, etc.). The second category of workers are generally less well paid, have less social protection, and may at any time lose their jobs. They are commonly called *pâto* in Japanese (derived from the English 'part-time') and have relatively fewer working hours a week. These workers are not regarded as a part of the company's 'real' manpower and the majority of professional directories, for instance, do not take them into account.

The Labor Standards Law (*Rôdô Kijun Hô*) requires companies with at least 10 employees to write 'rules of employment' specifying working conditions, remuneration, etc. Different rules apply to different workers (i.e. permanent and temporary workers) belonging to the same organization. This is in line with the requirements of the employment law which was introduced in 1993. In this sense one could say that dualism is, in effect, ratified by Japanese labor law (Hanami, 1994).

Workers with non-permanent employment status are generally hired on the basis of part-time employment contracts (35 hours or fewer a week), the duration of which is generally limited to six months and tacitly renewable. In the French labor law, for example, a contract of limited employment duration can be signed only under certain conditions (e.g. replacement of an employee on leave of absence, momentary overloads in activity, etc.), and can be renewed only under special conditions. The Japanese law, on the other hand, does not impose any such conditions with respect to employment contracts of limited duration (Hanami, 1994). As a result, many workers with limited employment contracts, including in large companies, have their job for several years. In the event of difficulties, however, they are the first to be laid off.

Determining the number of workers with flexible employment status poses many methodological problems. Statistics most commonly used generally employ nomenclatures which do not coincide with the distinction between permanent and temporary employees as outlined above. This is the case, for example, with the Labor Force Survey (*Rôdô Ryoku Chôsa*) compiled by the statistical services of the Japanese government and widely used by the majority of scholars in the field of labor research in Japan (for a synthesis on this, see Aoki, 1988). There is, however, another investigation published each year by the same services which divides the employees according to the distinction permanent/temporary employment contracts. It is the (bilingual) Report on the Special Survey of the Labor Force Survey. This Report is not often used by Japanese scholars (and by Western ones as well), presumably because it covers less phenomena than other sources. It, however, has the merit of taking into account the above distinction which is of particular interest to us in the present chapter. Outside the agricultural and public services sectors, there were approximately, 2 040 000 employees in February 1997 who had temporary contract arrangements in companies of more than 500 people, that is to say 15.84 percent of their total labor force (see Table 10.1).

Temporary employment helps in reducing wage costs and in adjusting the quantity of labor to the workload requirements without affecting the group of permanent employees.

Permanent employees enjoy good prospects of growth in their remuneration and job security. The company benefits as a result from their loyalty and honesty. Here one finds the general outline of efficiency wage theory, especially when one considers the device of incentives not based upon wages perceived on a given date but rather on the whole development of the career and wage prospects (Gazier, 1992, p. 240). Job security and career advancement opportunities help companies to face adverse recruitment problems, giving them the means of attracting the best potential workers. Employees' turnover is also reduced, as are the

Table 10.1 Employees outside agricultural sector and public service, Japan, by nature of contract, February, 1994 and 1997

	Companies with 1–499 employees		Companies with 500 employees or more	
	1994	**1997**	**1994**	**1997**
Executives	3 440 000	3 640 000	170 000	190 000
Other permanent employees	22 520 000	23 090 000	11 120 000	10 650 000
Employees with contracts of limited duration	7 350 000	8 620 000	1 610 000	2 040 000

Source: Based on *The Report of the Special Survey of the Labor Force Survey*, Tokyo: Management and Coordination Agency, 1994 and 1997 edn.

related costs. As Gordon (1988) points out, it was with this aim that Japanese companies introduced the rules of stable or nonflexible employment in the 1920s, and then reinforced them in the 1950s and 1960s.

Flexible employment, in times of economic difficulties, allows the possibility of not disturbing the career of the permanent employees, and thus seems a necessary condition for the stable employment offered to them. The Quantitative flexibility that nonpermanent employees offer makes it possible to guarantee continuity in the application of the rules of management of the permanent employees. Otherwise, the mechanisms of this incentive would not be possible.

Permanent employees, moreover, are subjected, throughout their career, to a process of evaluation and of selection, which has been more fully described by authors such as Cole (1971) and Dore (1973), and, more recently, Aoki (1988) and Koike (1994a, 1994b). The company is thus protected from 'moral hazard' and, as a result, supports the development of its human resources. The principle is that of rotating younger employees to different work responsibilities irrespective of position and primary responsibility (i.e. blue-collar, white-collar or executive). They can thus acquire an overall vision of the production processes, increase their experience and skills, and be evaluated by different superiors. During the early years there is very little differentiation in terms of promotion in each of these three work categories, thereafter the accumulation of evaluations results in opening the range of career-advancement opportunities. According to Koike (1994a, 1994b), one of the characteristics of the

Japanese system is that it offers the blue-collar worker the possibilities of promotion throughout their career in parity with their white-collar counterpart. It is important to note that this situation does not appear to be the case in Europe or the United States. The promotion process in Japan is not based on a hierarchy of job positions or functions, even though to reach such functions as that of foreman, for example, one needs to have climbed a given number of levels. The Japanese workmen are consequently encouraged to enrich their skills and experiences even if they know that they may not have the possibility of promotion to the position of foreman. This situation is very much unlike that of the American workman (Cole, 1971) or his British counterpart (Dore, 1973) who appears to be traditionally locked in his field of specialization, with little or no prospect of change.

In Japan, employees who suffer from repeated poor evaluations are frequently transferred to a subsidiary, a supplier, or a smaller company (Aoki, 1988; Uemura and Ebizuka, 1994). Judging therefore from this development, we can say that the model does not appear to require any more cultural explanations to be achieved by the process of evaluation/selection.

Aoki (1988) insists on the high degree of centralization of the HRM function which this process of training/evaluation/selection requires. The operational units should not be able to oppose the rotation of permanent employees, in spite of the disturbances which it may generate. In addition, the reduced impact of the evaluation of a given employee by each operational unit, because of these rotations, lessens the risk of subjectivity which would undermine the whole system. Aoki suggests that the HRM function holds more power and mobilizes more means in Japan than in other industrialized countries, a point which, in our view, needs to be further researched. The enterprise-based trade union is generally informed of the outcome during the whole process of evaluation. It is associated with the decisions of transfer of workers towards outside firms, particularly in the case of reorganizations, which reduces the risk of a dispute occurring as a result of the decision taken.

The expression 'enterprise union' should not be misleading, as there are in Japan powerful federations of trade unions in every industry organized in national confederations (Garanto, 1993, 1994). The so-called 'Spring offensive' as regards annual wage negotiations shows that Japanese employees can coordinate their action beyond the borders of the company or the branch of activity when useful. But the great strikes which followed the Second World War and those of the 1950s led employers and workers to measure the high costs of such confrontations

(Gordon, 1988). As a result, negotiations organized at company level of the company were gradually promoted. From a comparative analysis of the situation in the United States and Japan, Lincoln and Kalleberg (1996) note that the enterprise-based trade union in Japan promotes both the attachment (reduction of turnover) and the identification of employees to their organizations.

This second presentation of the model provides a more precise picture than the first. It is no longer necessary to resort to the argument of cultural 'specificity', raising the possibility of universality of the model. The question that remains to be answered, however, is to what extent it can withstand all the turbulence currently facing Japanese companies.

The Japanese model under pressure

In the short term, the model has been put to the test by the reorganizations of firms undertaken since the beginning of the 1990s. In the long term, the prospects of a durable slow growth coupled with the problem of ageing population does not seem to provide the right basis for the model to remain the principal point of reference when discussing HRM in this environment.

Reorganization of firms in the 1990s

The plans which were implemented during the first half of the 1990s, including massive transfers of personnel towards other companies and incentives for those in excess of 40 to leave, led many observers to envisage the end of the model. These plans were regarded as a rupture of the moral contract which bound the company to its employees, as well as questioning the value of age and experience.

During the 1990s, Japanese companies in difficulties implemented some very aggressive cost-cutting measures. They dismissed workers on temporary contracts, intensified the programs of transfer of workers to other firms within the group and also put into place a new program of incentives aimed at encouraging early retirement (Table 10.2).

None of these measures are really new but since the 1950s they have never been implemented all at once and on such a massive scale. Even within the framework of the Japanese model each of these measures has been commonly used, although at a much lower extent, in order to adjust for economic fluctuations as well as the implementation of various incentive mechanisms.

Table 10.2 Adaptation of labor force in large Japanese firms: examples and measures taken

• Reduction of overtime	Japanese labor law allows a massive recourse to overtime (360 hours a year per worker), which helps to adapt the quantity of work to the fluctuations of the economic situation
Reduction of manpower with temporary work contracts	In the event of layoff, the courts make sure that the company first dismissed workers with temporary status (Hanami, 1994)
Transfers of employees to other firms	Specificities in the relations between companies in Japan, suppliers, and customers, as within the horizontal *keiretsu* groups (Mitsubishi, Mitsui groups, etc.) help in implementing such transfers. Nissan, 2500 people, Mazda, 1500 people in 1993–4; Mitsubishi Electric, 1000 people in 1993, Nippon Steel, 15 000 people over several years from 1994, etc. massive transfers were been implemented following the collapse of Yamaichi Shôken in 1997 (41 percent of its 7694 employees) and the reorganization of Nissan in 1999 after Renault took over 36.8 percent of its capital (Nissan will reduce its workforce in Japan by 17 000 people in the next few years).
Incentive plans for early departures	Pioneer, Fujisawa Pharmaceutical, Renown (textile), NKK (iron and steel industry), NTT (Telecoms), Mitsui & Co. (trading company), Iwatsu (electronics), etc.

Source: *Labor Issues Quarterly* and *Japan Labor Bulletin* (Tokyo: Japan Institute of Labor) various issues; Hanami (1994).

However, the reorganizations of firms in the 1990s dealt a serious blow to the notion of symbolic representation (Louart, 1995) which some Japanese employees had regarding their relationship to their companies (long-term commitment, solidarity, valorization of age and experience, etc.). This loss of confidence may, in turn, affect the working of the mechanisms of incentives developed above. If they do not have confidence in the future that the company reserves for them, some employees are likely to decide between what the company offers to them now and what they can get from their skills elsewhere. This may damage the traditional process of development of human resources within the Japanese company. On a longer perspective, the prospects of a long-term slow growth and the ageing of the population also pose serious challenges to the Japanese model.

Socio-economic challenges

The mechanism of selection developed above was efficient in motivating workers owing to its provision with regard to promotion based on effort. The growth of the company, year after year, resulted in increasing the number of people required at all levels of the hierarchy, thus creating new promotion opportunities. Final transfers towards other companies could be restricted primarily to the worse-performing or less cooperative employees.

In the context of long-term slow growth, the majority of companies will have to reinforce the mechanisms of selection. The implication that employees are no longer guaranteed promotion, means that individual strategies are likely to evolve. A growing number of employees, when they see their chances of promotion decrease, will reduce the amount of effort they make on behalf of the company in order to prepare their transfers before it is imposed upon them.

Another dimension of socio-economic maturity, the ageing of the Japanese population, poses problems at various levels. On the one hand, companies must manage the evolution of the age pyramid of their workforce, which is not easy, as we have just seen. They must also face the swelling of social contributions aimed at financing the welfare payments of retirement and health. Indeed, while 1 out of 7.7 Japanese were 65 years old or more in 1992, the ratio was 1 out of 5.9 in the year 2000, and 1 out of 3.9 in 2025, according to the projections of the Japanese Ministry of Health. The compulsory contribution of old-age insurance, almost half paid by the companies, was increased from 14.5 percent to 16.5 percent of the basic wage in October 1994, and 17.35 percent in October 1996. This is to be gradually raised to 29.8 percent in 2025 according to the same source. That still increases the cost of employment of the older, better-paid workers. Moreover, the share of the wage cost that an employee will directly receive will regress as in Europe, for instance, and consequently the contribution of the wage cost to the mechanism of incentive will be reduced.

The need for reinforcing promotion mechanisms while guaranteeing their objectivity, and for finding new bases for the mechanisms of incentive, raises the outstanding question of evaluation and remuneration based on merit rather than on seniority. In the 1960s, the employers' confederation *Nikkeiren* underlined the fact that the principle of remuneration based on seniority was a threat to companies. In fact, at that time, a significant share of the wage was calculated on the basis of merit, as incorporated into the process of performance review/promotion outlined above and testified by many case studies (Cole, 1971; Dore, 1973; Nohara, 1985; Aoki, 1988; Gordon, 1988; Hanada, 1994, etc). The frequent highlighting of a strong correlation between wages and age in Japanese companies (Suzuki, 1994, for example) does not show that wages are based on age and seniority. In our view, it expresses above all the effectiveness of the mechanisms of performance review implemented by the company throughout the career of the employee.

However, these systems are now being revised and reinforced. In 1995, Toyota, for example, announced a project to increase the share of remuneration based on merit although it accounted for, as of that date, 65 percent of the total amount (The *Nikkei Weekly*, December 4, 1995). Asahi Beer announced that it would raise this share from 45 percent to 60 percent (*The Nikkei Weekly*, May 1, 1996). Sony, Matsushita, Takeda Chemical, and many other companies have since announced an evolution in the same direction.

That is frequently done by transforming posts of general operatives, whose individual performances are difficult to evaluate over short periods, to posts of specialists with more precise and quantifiable objectives. Fuji Film, for example, transferred 580 general operatives to positions of specialists, and adapted the system of remuneration (*The Nikkei Weekly*, January 20, 1996). The company did not expect a cut in the wage bill, but a better relation between remuneration and individual performances so that the productivity of administrative work would eventually increase.

More definitive studies have not been undertaken with respect to these new systems. Igalens and Roussel (1996) underline, from the French case, that the various components of remuneration have different effects on job satisfaction and motivation with regard to work. It would be appropriate at this point to analyze more precisely how the systems of remuneration in the larger Japanese companies are revised. Trade union representatives and managers in charge of human resources in Japan are anxious concerning this question. Taking into account merit or results, the short term is likely to run counter to the expectations of workers or, to use the words of Pierre Louart (1995), to the symbolic representations which they carry in their relation to the company. This concern is further confirmed by the investigation of Lincoln and Kalleberg (1996) noted above.

We should finally mention the decision of some of Japan's large companies, including Toyota since 1994, to recruit more mid-career specialists, which does not appear to fit the Japanese model of HRM as presented above. These employees, well paid, are recruited on contracts of limited duration, one year generally, possibly renewable. Companies argue that for certain specialized tasks, the training of in-house employees would be too long and expensive; it is thus better to recruit outside. The recent increase of the number of such unemployed specialists on the labor market, because either they lost their employment, or did not find permanent employment at the end of their studies, encourages these companies to develop this form of employment. Table 10.3 suggests the extent of this practice, which has been too often presented as entirely new

Recruitment of mid-career specialists poses two fundamental problems in relation to the Japanese model: it is likely to disturb the incentive mechanism referred to earlier as certain positions which before would have been offered to promoted permanent employees are likely henceforth to be fulfilled by the recruitment of external candidates. The increased variety of nonpermanent posts poses a further problem: how to benefit from these differences while at the same time supporting collaboration between these groups of employees (Louart, 1994).

Table 10.3 Rate of company plans to recruit mid-career specialists, 1995 (%)

	Management	Clerical	Technical
Total	28.2	37.5	44.1
Over 5000 employees	13.7	24.3	26.0
1000–4999 employees	16.6	25.2	26.1
300–999 employees	23.0	32.7	33.0
100–299 employees	26.9	36.5	39.9
30–99 employees	29.5	38.6	47.0

Source: 'Survey on Employment Management, Ministry of Labor, 1995,' in *Labor Situation in Japan 1999* (Tokyo: Japan Institute of Labor).

Concluding remarks

A superficial reading of the Japanese model of HRM results in the conclusion that it is, in the current context, condemned to disappear. Japanese companies seem forced to adopt a more general model, nearer to that of their Western counterparts. A better understanding of the model results, on the contrary, in a more relative representation of its specific features, without claiming their demise. The upheavals of the 1990s seem important adjustments which indeed put the system to the test without bringing about a complete rupture. However, these adjustments, in the Japanese mature socio-economic environment, may gradually change the systems of HRM in the country.

Nikkeiren (The Japan Federation of Employers' Associations) released a report in 1995 entitled 'New Japanese style of Management System: Concrete Measures for Challenge', which suggested how Japanese companies should reorganize their workforce. This includes dividing it into three different groups: the core group of long-term employees (which would benefit the traditional HRM model), the sophisticated specialist group of workers (often recruited mid-career), and the flexible workforce. It appears that this vision is now gradually becoming a reality in the Japanese work environment. However, the rapidly decreasing number of the young cohort of workers (owing to the structure of the age pyramid in Japan) appears to put another constraint on Japanese companies in implementing this new scheme. How can one recruit sophisticated specialists in the coming years if they do not benefit from some kinds of long-term future within the company? Once more, redesigning HRM principles should not be done on too short-term a basis.

References

Abegglen, J. C. and Stalk, G. (1985), *Kaisha, The Japanese Corporation* (New York: Basic Books).

Aoki, M. (1988) *Information, Incentives, and Bargaining in the Japanese Economy* (Cambridge: Cambridge University Press).

Cole, R. (1971) *Japanese Blue Collar, The Changing Tradition* (Berkley: University of California Press).

Dore, R. (1973) *British Factory – Japanese Factory, The Origins of National Diversity in Industrial Relations* (Berkeley: University of California Press).

Garanto, A. (1993) 'Existe-t-il un modèle japonais des ressources humaines?,' *Cahiers Français*, 262, 95–109.

Garanto, A. (1994) 'Le Mouvement Syndical Japonais,' *Pouvoirs*, 71, 73–90.

Gazier, B. (1992) *Economie du Travail et de l'Emploi* (Paris: Précis Dalloz).

Gordon, A. (1998) *The Evolution of Labor relations in Japan, Heavy Industry, 1853–1955* (Cambridge, Mass.: Harvard University Press).

Hanada, M. (1994) 'Modalités de la Fixation des Salaires au Japon et en France: Etude du bulletin de paye de Nissan et Peugeot,' *Japon in Extenso*, 31 , 23–41.

Hanami, T. (1994) *Managing Japanese Workers, Personnel Management – Law and Practices in Japan* (Tokyo: The Japan Institute of Labour).

Igalens, J. and Roussel, P. (1996) 'Etude comparative des liaisons entre rémunération, motivation et satisfaction des cadres et des non cadres,' *Revue de Gestion des Ressources Humaines*, 19, 19–36.

Japan Institute Of Labour (1996) *Labour Situation in Japan 1999*, (Tokyo).

Japan Institute Of Labour (various issues) *Labour Issues Quarterly*.

Japan Institute Of Labour (monthly), *Japan Labor Bulletin*.

Jaussaud J. (1991) 'Le Japon, premier constructeur automobile mondial,' *Japon in Extenso*, 22, 2–21.

Jaussaud, J. (1992) 'La distribution à l'heure de la déréglementation,' *Revue Française de Gestion*, 91, 35–42.

Jaussaud, J. (1993) 'Statuts des travailleurs et réduction des effectifs dans les industries en crise au Japon,' Problèmes Economiques, 2321, 20–24.

Jaussaud, J, (1996) 'Gestion des ressources humaines: l'adaptation des effectifs dans la grande entreprise japonaise,' *Ebisu*, 12, (1996) (Tokyo: Maison Franco-Japonaise), 7–41.

Lincoln, J. R. and Kalleberg, A. K. (1996) 'Commitment, Quits and Work Organization in Japanese and US Plants,' *Industrial and Labor Relations Review*, 50:1, 39–59.

Louart, P. (1994) 'La GRH à l'heure des segmentations et des particularismes,' *Revue Française de Gestion*, 98, 79–94.

Louart, P. (1995) *Succès de l'Intervention en Gestion des Ressources Humaines* (Paris: Editions Liaisons.

Koike, K. (1994) 'Intellectual Skills and Long-Term Competition,' in K. Imai and R. Komiya(eds.) *Business Enterprise in Japan* (Cambridge, Mass.: MIT Press), 261–274.

Koike, K. (1994b) 'Learning and Incentive Systems in Japanese Industry,' in M. Aoki and R. Dore (eds.), *The Japanese Firm, Sources of Competitive Strength* (Oxford: Oxford University Press), 41–65.

Management & Coordination Agency (1994, 1996) *Report on the Special Survey of the Labor Force Survey* (Tokoyo: Management & Coordination Agency).

Nakane, C. (1970) *Japanese Society* (Tokyo: Charles E. Tuttle).

Nohara, H. (1985) 'Les nouvelles politiques salariales des entreprises japonaises,' *Revue Française de Gestion*, 51

Suzuki, H. (1994) 'Pay Classifications in Japan,' *Waseda Business & Economic Studies*, 30, Waseda University.

Uemura, H. and Ebizuka, A. (1994) 'Incentives and Flexibility in the Hierarchical Market-Firm Nexus: A Prelude to the Analysis of Productivity Regimes in Japan,' *Japon in Extenso*, 31, 53–68.

Ujihara, Shojiro (1991) 'Essai sur la transformation historique des pratiques d'emploi et des relations professionnelles au Japon,' *Sociologie du Travail*, 33: 1, 19–25.

11
Thailand's Industrialization: Overcoming Structural Obstacles?

Doryane Kermel-Torrès and Philippe Schar

Thailand reached a crisis point in 1997, after a decade of vigorous growth. In various analyses of the situation, the emphasis is generally placed on economic factors and their financial and monetary dimensions, without devoting much attention to the structural roots of the problem. Even before the alarm bells started ringing, a number of structural effects relating to the country's growth model could be felt, especially in the manufacturing sector, but these went largely unheeded in political and economic circles (Boisseau and Simon, 1998; Raillon, 1998; Schwab and Nguyen, 1998).

At the beginning of the 1980s, the policy of industrialization was firmly geared towards external markets and was founded on two basic principles: a cheap labor force, and participation by foreign investors (Akrasanee, 1991; Lim, 1994; Samudavanija, 1995; War and Nidhiprabha, 1996). This was strongly supported by public policies that rapidly tried to reconcile the imperatives of national growth with those of regional development. A myriad of tax benefits combined with the introduction of wage legislation helped investors to set up their firms in the peripheral regions of Thailand (i.e. north-east, south, and north) or to move firms away from the central region, traditionally the most industrialized area of the country (Simon, 1996; Kermel-Torrès and Schar, 1997a). Whether it was due to the attractive nature of these measures, to a rejection of the central region, or to other reasons, favorable responses to this decentralization policy began to take shape at the end of the 1980s (Parnwell, 1992; Dhiratayakinant, 1995). Industrial development started to accelerate in the peripheral areas, while maintaining at all costs the two basic factors underlying the growth process listed above. We shall analyze these phenomena through two key factors in the overall economic picture: industrial production and the labor force. Some of the weaknesses that can be observed in the peripheral regions are perhaps more pronounced than in the central region, but they serve only to demonstrate even more clearly that a breaking point had been reached in the model of industrialization then being implemented.

The analyses that follow are based on surveys carried out on employers and production workers (laborers, technicians, and supervisors) in a number of manufacturing firms in the north-east and south of Thailand. Employers were surveyed in 72 industrial units and more than 400 employees were surveyed in 30 units. In determining the selection process for the firms, we deliberately selected a large proportion of firms that had benefited from the advantageous conditions offered by the Board of Investment (BOI) to companies setting up in the peripheral regions. This was done in order to take into account the major regional industrial trends relating to the production sectors, the market, the nationality of the investment, and the size of the business. In relation to firms' size, the sample was broken down as follows: 40 percent of firms had between 500 and 1000 employees; 42 percent, between 100 and 500, and 18 percent had fewer than 100 employees.

The structure of industrial production

The study and analysis of the firms' structure, their supply strategies, as well as their markets, are useful for determining the constraints and strengths of the internal dynamics within the peripheral regions. In doing so, the invitation extended to foreign businesses and investors, the role of Thai businesses and investment, their interaction, and the impact of their supply and market strategies must all be taken into account.

Structure of industrial businesses

Geographical origin

The local employers hold important positions in their respective regions, either independently (about 40 percent of firms), in association with other Thai businesses (almost 14 percent), or in alliance with foreign businesses (more than 8 percent). This emphasizes the region's dynamism. The emergence of entrepreneurs from the north-east and south has been encouraged by the opening up of regional markets. The regions have also benefitted from the experience gained in firms located in the Bangkok Metropolitan Region by employees who subsequently set up a business in their own region, either on their own account and/or on the account of a national or foreign group. Returning to their own region is also one of the reasons for the relocation and expansion of firms from the central region into peripheral areas. Firms with Thai or foreign participation also represent a considerable opportunity for regional employers to broaden their base, to penetrate foreign markets, and to diversify their production. They have also been able to benefit from BOI aid (almost 60 percent of their firms receive aid) even though social and family reasons would justify their location in their region of origin (Table 11.1).

A little less than 30 percent of all firms surveyed in the two regions are owned by sole proprietors originating from the central region. Another 18 percent are owned by entrepreneurs from the central region in partnership with other businesses, especially foreign. The share of BOI-assisted firms is greater among employers originating from the central region (more than 63 percent) than it is among local and regional businesses. The firms owned by entrepreneurs originating from the central region are more export oriented, although regional resources play, at least for some of them, an important part in their procurement strategy for raw materials. The proportion of businesses owned entirely by foreign investors is about 10 percent, whereas 20 percent of firms have a partnership with foreign investors. In both instances, BOI firms (about 90 percent and 80 percent respectively), represent without question the highest proportion in all categories. In the case of the first group, this highlights the very clearly defined export orientation of firms, with feeble backward linkages in terms of locally sourced raw materials. However, the second case does show a high degree of interrelations between domestic and foreign markets, with a moderate reliance on regionally based supplies. Whereas joint ventures enable Thai industrialists to gain access to foreign markets, they also enable foreigners to penetrate the domestic market, at regional as well as national levels.

Foreign investment has an important role in the regional dynamics. At the end of the 1980s, it undoubtedly contributed to the acceleration of the industrialization process, especially through the relocation of manufacturing production units from other East Asian countries. The south region took advantage of its proximity to Malaysia to attract industries keen to exploit the region's natural resources and manpower. The North-east region was a major recipient of foreign investment, especially from Japan and Taiwan. Conversely, it is indisputable that foreign companies have tended to favor these regions because of their industrial characteristics, consisting of Sino-Thai entrepreneurs, a favorable environment in terms of infrastructure and services, and social and political stability. Despite this degree of foreign direct investment (FDI), Thai capital has played, and still continues to play, a vital role. Ironically, foreign firms were expected to generate substantial spillover effects in the economy, especially through advanced technology transfer to Thai firms, a phenomenon that

Table 11.1 Geographical origin of industrial businesses, Thailand[a]

	Local/Regional			Central region			Association of Thais			Association with foreigners			Foreigners			Total
	BOI	Non BOI	Total	BOI	Non BOI	Total	BOI	non BOI	Total	BOI	non BOI	Total	BOI	non BOI	Total	
Agri-food	5	6	11	5	3	8	1		1	5	2	7	1	1	2	29
Textile and associated	2	1	3	1	2	3		1	1				2		2	9
Rubber and associated	1	2	3	2	1	3				2	1	3				9
Wood and associated	1	5	1		1				1		1				7	
Chemical/Plastic/ Petroleum	2		2	2		2				2		2	1		1	7
Non-metallic	1	1	2													2
Mechanical Products	1		1		1	1										2
Vehicle assembly										1		1				1
Electrical/Electronics													2		2	2
Other	1		1	2	1	3										4
Total	**17**	**11**	**28**	**13**	**8**	**21**	**1**	**1**	**2**	**11**	**3**	**14**	**6**	**1**	**7**	**72**

Note:
[a] 'industrial businesses' refers to individuals as well as companies.
Source: Personal surveys.

has been very limited so far. Legal restrictions relating to foreign participation in registered share capital allow the granting of exceptions to the general rule of a maximum of 49 percent foreign participation. These exemptions are granted on the basis of the type of market – priority is given to exports – and of the production sectors – volume of investment capital in the 'protected' sectors of agri-food, mining, and services. The realization that technological upgrading was needed led also to the relaxing of legal formalities in the case of manufacturing production involving technological development. Foreign firms tend to be concentrated in the agri-food sector, with varying degrees of advanced technology. Their presence tends to be predominant, if not exclusive, in those production sectors that are relatively new in Thailand – for example, vehicle assembly, electronics, and electrical industries. In these capital- and labor-intensive industries, most of the technological developments are carried out outside Thailand.

Sources of capital

Two types of capital were considered, based on their share in the total investment package. The first is when the investment represents the entire capital sum, be it foreign, from family origin or from profits made by Thai businesses. The second is where investment from one main investor is added to several minor sources of funds. This overview takes into account initial or start-up capital for businesses, as well as additional capital required for later developments (Table 11.2).

Table 11.2 Sources of capital (% of firms)

	Capital 100 % family or Thai business	Main complementary funding			100 % foreign capital	Non determined
		Institutional credit	Foreign capital	Share capital		
Agri-food	10	41	21	7	7	14
Textile and associated	22	44	0	0	22	11
Rubber and associated	33	33	33	0	0	0
Wood and associated	0	71	0	14	0	14
Chemical/Plastics/ Petroleum	0	57	0	29	14	0
Non-metallic	0	100	0	0	0	0
Mechanical	0	100	0	0	0	0
Vehicle assembly	0	100	0	0	0	0
Electrical/Electronics	0	0	0	0	100	0
Others	0	100	0	0	0	0

Source: Personal surveys.

Besides the range of sources of capital, one of the salient features of Table 11.2 is the importance of contributions by combinations of capital source, since 70 percent of all firms complement their principal funding from other sources. A little over 11 percent use funding that is entirely from a family source or else from Thai companies; this appears to be limited generally to start-up investment, whereas for the expansion or modernization of their production process, the firms tend to draw on other sources. These businesses are also usually limited to only a few sectors. About 10 percent of firms rely entirely on foreign capital, in line with their direct control by foreign companies. For more than 12 percent of firms, foreign capital represents the main source of investment and in other cases it is a complementary source, even minor, with other investments, institutional credit or share capital. Therefore, there appears to be a close cooperation between foreign capital and Thai sources of investment in any arrangements regarding funding.

More than 50 percent of firms make use of institutional credit. This is negotiated through Thai bodies and covers loans at high current rates of interest or at rates fixed under special conditions in the context of public support programs for the industrial sector and under the BIBF[1], which directs foreign capital towards Thai businesses. The use of institutional credit, in terms of the number of firms and of the sectors concerned, can only confirm the vulnerability of the industrial sector when confronted with the financial crisis in Asia. Share capital is not negligible as a funding source, involving almost 7 percent of firms, but it is limited to a few major Thai groups or to groups with foreign participation, and operates in a few specific sectors. Foreign capital definitely plays a rather more important role than that indicated by FDI shown in Table 11.2, by granting short-term loans (7 percent of firms have combined a commercial loan with a loan through the BIBF), and through the stock market: but even there, the combination of Thai and foreign capital clearly demonstrates the synergy of internal and external initiatives.

Market and procurement strategies

The analysis of market and procurement strategies has to be viewed in conjunction with other factors in order to understand the industrialization process in the peripheral regions, and the industrial location strategies. We can thus appreciate the state of inter-industrial relations and the degree to which they have become internalized. Procurement or supply areas, and market areas, were separated into 11 levels, according to the combinations observed, and for each of the three categories, the

Table 11.3 Sources of supply and markets (% of firms)

	Raw materials	Intermediate products	Markets
100% Regional	65	6	11
100% other Thai national	2	32	1
100% foreign	5	8	50
Predominantly regional	21	6	7
Predominantly other Thai national	0	27	4
Predominantly foreign	7	13	10
Other Thai national + Regional = 100%	0	0	6
Foreign = Regional + other Thai national	0	0	6
Foreign = other Thai national	0	5	3
Predominantly regional + other Thai national	0	0	1
Foreign = regional	0	3	1

Source: Personal surveys.

proportion of firms was calculated according to the total number of units concerned (Table 11.3).

Table 11.3 shows that there are three main levels that either account for 100 percent of the total sources of supply or markets, or predominate. These are: the regional level, the domestic other than regional level, and the foreign level. These three levels combined provide 100 percent of raw materials, 90 percent of intermediate products and 83 percent of markets The balance is derived from five other combinations of the three main levels. The trend towards the export of industrial goods produced in the peripheral regions is clearly confirmed, as 60 percent of the industrial units produce either exclusively or mainly for external markets, owing, in particular, to the large proportion of BOI-aided firms. The fact that 30 percent of production units, especially those that are non-BOI-granted, have turned towards the domestic market, especially the regional markets, is in response to a demand that has been stimulated and diversified by the improvement of the population's standard of living, with the setting up of import substitution regional units. Firms whose market is foreign and domestic in equal proportions represent 10 percent of the total.

The regional source provides the greatest proportion of raw materials, with the foreign source overtaking the domestic (nonregional) source. The main reasons for this are the fact that the stock of certain raw materials has been exhausted, and that industrial behavior can now be seen as being geared towards export strategies. The regional source ranks third, behind the foreign source, with regard to the supply of intermediate products. The majority of firms buy their intermediate products domestically. A few examples drawn from different sectors are given below. This is the result of both complex strategies on the part of the industrialists, and of the import substitution process through the strengthening of the heavy industry base which is still under way in the metropolitan region, as well as in the petrochemical and steel making complexes in south-east Thailand. The weak incidence of inter-firm relations at the regional level reflects the low degree of integration within the regional industrial framework, which itself is poorly diversified into the upstream levels of the production process. In sectors such as electronics and motor vehicles, the technical division of labor between units of the same group – involving for Thai firms the domestic, regional, and foreign levels –, leads to a subordination of regional units to firms located in the metropolitan area and in other parts of Asia. These different factors help also explain the fairly similar behavior between BOI-granted firms and other firms.

The analysis of a few production sectors will shed some light on the interdependence between sources of supply and markets. The export orientation of production can be observed in all sectors with varying degrees of intensity, with the exception of motor-vehicle assembly and mechanical engineering. The industrial exploitation of regional natural resources and its inter-relatedness with the other supply levels and markets, varies with the nature of the production sector. For example, the increasing value added derived from rubber-based products provides this sector, through the strategy of diversification, with export outlets as well as openings in national and regional markets, depending on the position of the firms in the supply chain. In the agri-food sector, 82 percent of firms buy their inputs exclusively or essentially at the regional level, but only 10 percent of these firms sell their products exclusively in the same region. In the north-east, the diversification of agricultural products, stimulated by the demand from industry, has made it possible to extend the range of agri-industrial products, whereas value added gains made some products, such as cassava, more profitable and worth deploying in foreign markets. The overexploitation of marine resources in the south has forced companies to resort to importing raw materials from abroad, as much as 100 percent in some cases. This represents a considerable handicap for the industrialization process of this region. The wood sector is, to some extent, handicapped in the same way. This is particularly true for the north-east region, where some industrial units have gradually been compelled to resort to buying intermediate products from other Thai regions, or even from abroad. Despite being highly fragmented internally between different types of production, the textile sector generally uses regionally sourced raw materials to a lesser extent than before. The garment industry is one of the best examples of just-in-time (JIT) production, which is almost exclusively geared to foreign markets, and the specifications of which give rise to imports of intermediate products. This is an industry where regional comparative advantages, in terms of labor costs, are crucial.

The example of industries using petrochemical products is a final illustration of why the domestic level (excluding the regional level) plays such a significant role in the supply of intermediate products to regionally based firms. Because there is, within the domestic economy, a wider and more varied availability of certain chemical components (continuous import substitution and increased number of importers), the regional firms' strategies consist in not favoring any single supply channel. By contrast, they use various available channels, depending on the price and the quality of intermediate products, as well as the market for finished products, thus dictating their margin of maneuver in terms of competitiveness. Although of comparable quality to those found abroad, these types of intermediate products are more expensive than on the foreign market. However, the savings made in terms of foreign exchange and inventory are seen as a considerable advantage by those producing for the domestic market.

The analysis of the composition of businesses and of procurement strategies leads us to highlight the very close inter-relatedness between the different types of industry, the geographical origin of investment, and the procurement areas and markets. The internalization of inter-industry transactions, or the reliance of the regional industry on foreign economies, according to which viewpoint one adopts, has to be modulated not only according to the sector of industrial production but also of the regions. It has to be seen in the context of business strategies where in any case low labor costs are an essential factor in the industrial framework.

Social behavior

While the supposed abundance of labor in the peripheral regions, and its low cost, may have been regarded as a considerable advantage by policy makers and firms alike, its social characteristics today represent a major obstacle to the continuation of the industrialization process, according to the model followed so far (Hewison and Brown, 1994). The behavior of workers and the responses it has generated on the part of entrepreneurial circles have slowed down the re-orientation of the economy towards a more capital-intensive industrialization model (Kermel-Torrès and Schar,

1997b). This would improve productivity considerably, improvements made necessary by the gradual erosion of the competitiveness of Thai industries.

The industrial labor force and the behavior of workers

As in Thailand in general, the population of workers is young and poorly educated. More than 80 percent of those surveyed in the firms were under 35 years of age. There was a noticeable difference between women and men in the 15–25 age-bracket. The men appear to join their companies a little later. This tendency is accentuated further by the fact that women are more likely to leave their job for reasons associated with changes in their family situation, as we observed in surveys carried out on the active population of the villages situated in the catchment area of the firms investigated. Typically, they quit their job after the birth of their children, or else to take care of ageing parents (Table 11.4).

The majority of the workers surveyed left school after the primary level, that is at about 12 years of age in the normal school system. Nearly 80 percent of all those surveyed had an educational level at best equivalent to the first degree of the secondary school level, which is normally reached at the age of about 15. We should also note that few among the employees had had any form of technical education: these represented less than 15 percent of the total sample, and these were mainly men (Table 11.5).

Most of the labor force is of rural origin and the nature of the links kept with the agricultural sector has significant consequences, both in relation to their behavior as workers and from the point of view of the managers. Nearly 70 percent of the population interviewed had parents who were currently active in the agricultural sector. The rural origin of the labor force is in fact even more marked when we consider that the replies recorded relate only to principal occupation and therefore exclude heads of families who still work in agriculture on a part-time and secondary basis. This multiplicity of jobs is a widespread phenomenon in rural Thailand. In contrast, less than 4 percent had parents employed in the manufacturing sector. If we consider the occupation of spouses, the majority (54 percent) work in the manufacturing sector compared with less than 12 percent in agriculture (Table 11.6).

We are clearly dealing here with the first generation of industrial workers, a young generation with little tradition of working for a company, and who still maintain important links with an agriculturally based family background. These links are not only social ones. Indeed, one-third of the industrial workers surveyed in the south region declared that they worked regularly, occasionally, or seasonally on the family land

Table 11.4 Sample population, according to age and sex

	Aged <25 years	25–34 years	35–44 years	45–54 years	>54 years	Total
Women	106	85	28	1	3	223
%	47.53	38.12	12.56	0.45	1.34	100
Men	53	94	29	9	1	186
%	28.49	50.54	15.59	4.84	0.54	100
Total	**159**	**179**	**57**	**10**	**4**	**409**
%	**38.88**	**43.76**	**13.94**	**2.44**	**0.98**	**100**

Source: Personal surveys.

Table 11.5 Level of education of employees (%)

	Illiterate	Primary		Secondary		Vocational training		>Degree
		Level 1	Level 2	Level 1	Level 2	Level 1	Level 2	
Women	0	10.76	56.05	20.18	6.73	3.14	2.24	0.90
Men	0.54	9.14	34.95	15.59	12.90	12.37	11.83	2.69
Total	**0.24**	**10.02**	**46.45**	**18.09**	**9.54**	**7.33**	**6.60**	**1.71**

Source: Personal surveys.

Table 11.6 Main occupation of parent (%)

	Agriculture	Commerce	Construction	Industry	Public Sector	Services	Non-defined
Women	70.85	6.28	5.38	3.59	3.59	7.17	3.14
Men	65.59	5.91	2.15	4.30	12.37	3.76	5.91
Total	**68.46**	**6.11**	**3.91**	**3.91**	**7.58**	**5.62**	**4.40**

Source: Personal surveys.

holding. For the total south/north-east sample, 18 percent admitted that they sometimes left work for a few days, for this same reason. Among the different forms of absenteeism noted in the firms, the highest rates occurred at peak times of the rice-growing season. As well as the work carried out directly, there is also the contribution from the workers' salary, often handed over by children to their farming parents, and which helps in some cases to keep the farms in business or to fund agricultural business plans. Another strong reason for the continuity of these ties is the fact that the family land-holding often plays the role of 'social safety net' during periods of illness or unemployment from the firms; this is a form of protection that manufacturing employment cannot provide.

Despite their young age, most of the workers have already had one or several professional experiences, usually outside the manufacturing sector, before starting their present job. In fact, starting work for the first time in a manufacturing plant is not the most common route. It must be stressed that the agricultural job is of considerable importance. It is not simply a brief period spent helping the family on the agricultural holding, between the end of schooling and the entry into working life. If we were to simplify the professional routes that we encountered, then agricultural work is typically followed by work experience in the construction sector or in the retail sector. This type of work usually enables the young person to maintain a secondary occupation, at least in the short term, in the agricultural sector. This transition between agriculture and industry facilitates the gradual move towards more financial independence, and allows a certain distancing between the worker and the constraints of the family circle. Manufacturing work experience brings in a regular income, but this is not necessarily much better paid than in other sectors. The economic criterion is not the only one to be considered in choosing a job: there is also the social prestige attached to the job, the professional and social environment, the location of work and residence, and the tediousness of the job. All these factors have to be taken into consideration and in a context of full employment they all strengthen the mobility between sectors of activity or between firms (Table 11.7).

The length of service of industrial workers in the same firm is generally not very prolonged, yet this cannot be attributed entirely to the youth of the population surveyed or to the age of the firms. More than 60 percent of employees had been in their present employment for less than six years, and more than one-third less than three years. The mobility between firms is even more pronounced if we consider previous manufacturing jobs. These concern mainly the younger population and these seldom exceed three years. Apart from the wage level, it would seem that these young employees are concerned particularly with the general atmosphere in the company, the presence of friends, the organization of work, or the relations with management. The perception that the workers have of their own manufacturing job underlines even more this idea of instability. Paid work in a firm is often considered as a temporary situation, designed either to provide cash for a specific purpose (the purchase of durable consumer goods, children's education, etc.) or to build up enough capital to become self-employed.

Signs of tension in the labor market and the employers' responses

At the beginning of the period of rapid industrialization in the peripheral regions, the abundance of cheap labor enabled the employers to maintain wages (that is, basic wage plus bonuses) at around the legal minimum level, to be selective in choosing their employees, to adapt quickly to market fluctuations, or to exploit the flexibility of the bonus system so that workers could be forced to leave of their own accord. Some very strong tensions soon began to emerge in the labor market, owing to a number of factors:

- The long underestimated propensity of the agricultural sector to retain a large proportion of the working population originating from the rural areas.

Table 11.7 Length of service in same firm (%)

Age (years)	<6 months	6–12 months	1–3 years	3–6 years	6–8 years	8–11 years	11–14 years	14–20 years	20 years
15–24	20.13	9.43	31.45	33.96	2.52	2.52			
24–34	4.47	2.79	16.20	30.73	24.58	16.20	3.35	1.68	
34–44		1.75	8.77	24.56	19.30	19.30	5.26	14.04	7.02
44–54				20	10			50	20
>54 years							25	25	50
Total	**9.78**	**5.13**	**20.54**	**30.56**	**14.67**	**10.76**	**2.44**	**4.16**	**1.96**

Source: Personal surveys.

- The major expansion across all sectors of economic activity in regional urban centers.
- The continuing migration into the capital city or abroad, which the processes of regional industrialization were not able to halt.

As well as not being able to find sufficiently qualified or semi-qualified workers, the manufacturing sector also had difficulties in satisfying its needs in the area of low-skilled or unskilled posts.

For the firms, the most obvious sign of tension persisting in the labor market was felt at the level of workers' recruitment, turnover, and absenteeism. The importance and the consequences of these phenomena vary from company to company, depending on their sector of activity, their location and their ability to anticipate and react to the situation. It is particularly difficult to recruit workers in areas where firms are clustered, such as in the industrial estates, and this hampers the expansion of some businesses or their ability to work to full capacity. Even when this is technically possible, an increase in mechanical operations is confronted with a lack of qualified employees in sufficient numbers. Therefore, the firms had to be less demanding in terms of some of the hiring conditions they had originally laid down, such as the level of education or the age limit, as well as their preference for recruiting women, who are seen as more serious workers and more easily controlled.

Annual labor force turnover rates of about 30 percent are commonplace, mainly because of the attraction exercised by the fact of changing jobs, for reasons that are not always pay-related. However, this represents a major disincentive to train in-house workers in the technical areas when their general level of education is very low, and this in turn limits the possibility of bringing mechanization into the production process. Whenever possible, it is not uncommon for employers to try to resort to excess personnel strategies as a means of coping with absenteeism. The repercussions of seasonal absences vary according to the proportion of workers who have kept close contacts with their families in the countryside. They also depend on the possibility of including contract workers in the production process, of being able to distribute production to other parts of a network of businesses so as to fulfil orders, and being able to defer delivery, and build up stocks.

There is no concerted agreement between regional employers as to the best responses to the problems of recruitment and of labor force turnover. Reactions are many and varied, though there is agreement on one point: employers should maintain a wide variety of forms of pay and employment status, and should maintain wages at their lowest possible level. The strategy of buying the loyalty of the labor force through increased basic wages has its own limitations, owing to the constraints of production costs and the imperative to be competitive. It is thus limited to those businesses that supply most of their production to the domestic market, or to some sectors that have the benefit of some major advantages when they export, apart from that of the labor force. Beyond the very real constraints in terms of competitiveness, the firms that have experienced major growth over the last 10 years, are now unwilling to see a lowering of the profit margins that they have been enjoying until now.

The strategies of industrial labor force management cover an entire spectrum, ranging from paternalism to a type of management that is very similar to that used by Western capitalist businesses. To the basic wage, which is scarcely more than the minimum set by the government for unqualified workers or for those with minimum qualifications, have been added a number of social or financial benefits. The calculation of wages, using extremely complicated scales, varies from one firm to another. Special bonuses (employee loyalty to the factory, punctuality and regular attendance, attitude to work or to management, etc.) have been introduced alongside the traditional productivity or work-quality bonuses. These financial incentives can amount to more than 30 percent of the basic wage and allow the employer a degree of flexibility in adjusting wages to match firms' profits.

The different forms of employment status (monthly, daily, contractual, and seasonal) represent a scale graduating the integration of workers in the firm. They govern the way their pay is calculated, the level of their pay, and also their access to social advantages and bonuses. For the majority of workers, pay is calculated on a daily basis. It is equivalent to, or slightly higher, than the legal minimum wage, with a strong tendency to generalize the calculation based on returns, at least for the jobs where this is applicable. Overtime work is widely encouraged; this is seen as a stabilizing factor in the firm as the workers are then able to increase their income. The modes of payments are so complex that newly recruited workers never know how much they can effectively expect to earn. In contrast with the desired effect, this would seem to contribute to maintaining the rapid turnover of employees, as the workers tend to try several jobs in several different firms before coming to a final and permanent decision.

Another alternative solution to keep labor costs as low as possible is to mobilize new pools of workers. In some of the sectors where this happens, we note the emergence of different types of subcontracting, based on home-based work. Some industrial groups are also extending their activity into the creation of new production units in those rural areas that have so far been little affected by industrialization and where the amount paid in bonuses and the range of social advantages can be considerably reduced. However, this trend is limited, given that it depends on access to infrastructure. In this attempt to redeploy spatially business activities, we should also note that there is a trend towards the relocation of some activities into neighboring countries (Southern China, Burma), as well as a declared will to strengthen this trend with the opening up of other Asian markets.

The wish to maintain wages at a low level represents a technological choice that has until now been very little challenged in Thailand. However, the transition to an industry with more autonomous and innovative techniques is confronted with a number of obstacles. These are: the speed of regional industrialization and of the emergence of international competition; inadequate technology transfer; a low level of professional experience on the part of Thai employers; and poor qualifications on the part of the very mobile labor force.

Conclusion

The competitiveness of Thai industries in world markets has gradually been eroded when compared with the country's Asian, European, or American competitors. This is owing to a considerable increase in labor costs, linked among things to the growing scarcity of workers. The structure of the country's industrial system, the social behavior of the principal actors, and the fact that the choice of labor-intensive production techniques has never been challenged are all factors that represent obstacles to the necessary changes. These changes would enable a moving up the scale of industrial value added, and would result in increased productivity in the workplace.

The lack of a qualified labor force can to some extent be connected with the well-known inadequacies embodied in the Thai educational system. Nevertheless, it is also the result of the firms' very low level of investment in professional training, and only a willingly government policy can change this *état de fait*. In Thailand, there is a high degree of inter-connection between the business community, politicians, and technocrats. The influence of the business world in defining the country's economic policy has been steadily strengthened since the 1980s. Company heads have played an active role in redirecting industrial policy towards exports; they now play a prominent role in the process of democratic transition that began in 1992. Most of the solutions that have been suggested or implemented in relation to the problem of the gradual erosion of Thai industry's competitiveness have tended to favor maintaining the low-wage policy. This has taken the form of employing foreign workers, or of creating special investment zones where Thai labor laws are not applicable.

The quest for short-term profit, the lobbying exercised by the business community, and the ambivalent relationship between this community and the corridors of power have not been able to redirect public action quickly enough. The financial rescue and adjustment packages proposed by international institutions may make it possible to erase the most obvious effects of the crisis. However, if they also fail to challenge the industrial development pattern itself, then their supposed benefits will be very short-lived.

Note

1 Bangkok International Banking Facilities, introduced during the financial liberalization set in motion in 1992.

References

Akranasee, N. (1991) 'Thailand's Export Led Growth: Retrospect and Prospects,' Thailand Development Research Institute (Bangkok), *Policy Study*, 3.

Boisseau, S. and Simon, J-C. (1998) 'Thaïlande, une crise salutaire?,' *Futuribles*, 229, 5–28.

Dhiratayakinant, K. (1995) 'Public–Private Sector Partnership in Industrialization,' in M. Krongkaew (ed.), *Thailand's Industrialization and its Consequences* (London: Macmillan), 99–115.

Hewison, K. and Brown, A. (1994) 'Labour and Union in an Industrialising Thailand,' *Journal of Contemporary Asia*, 24–4, 483–513.

Kermel-Torrès, D. and Schar, P. (1997a) 'Croissance industrielle et redéploiement spatial en Thaïlande,' *Autrepart*, 3, 45–64.

Kermel-Torrès, D. and Schar, P. (1997b) 'L'industrialisation thaïlandaise confrontée à la mobilité de la main d'ceuvre,' *Informations et Commentaires*, 99, 33–9.

Lim, D. (1994) 'Explaining the Growth Performances of Asian Developing Economies,' *Economic Development and Cultural Change*, 42: 4, 829–44.

Parnwell, M. (1992) 'Confronting Uneven Development in Thailand: The Potential Role of Rural Industries,' *Malaysian Journal of Tropical Geography*, 22: 1, 51–62.

Raillon, F. (1998) 'La crise asiatique, une victoire pour l'Amérique?,' *Futuribles*, 231, 61–74.

Samudavanija, C.-A. (1995) 'Economic Development and Democracy,' in M. Krongkaew (ed.), *Thailand's Industrialization and its Consequences* (London: Macmillan), 235–50.

Schwab, L. and Nguyen, T. M. D. (1998) 'La crise financière en Asie,' *Futuribles*, 227, 15–20.

Simon, J.-C. (1996) 'The Thai Manufacturing Sector: New Patterns of Expansion,' in: J. G. Parnwell (ed.), *Uneven Development in Thailand* (Aldershot: Edward Elgar), 82–108.

War, P., and Nidhiprabha, B. (1996) *Thailand's Macroeconomic Miracle: Stable Adjustment and Sustained Growth* (Washington D.C.: World Bank).

12

The Evolution of China's Industrial Structure 1990–6: Implications for China's Future Development

Yong He and Xiaolin Pei[*]

It is generally accepted that China will be a great competitor to the Western industrialized countries in the twenty-first century. Is this a reasonable opinion? Is it true that China's size and growth rate are important in measuring its potential as a competitor? Two questions should be considered. First, is the growth rate of the Chinese economy based on productivity gains? If economic growth is sustained only by an increase in inputs, it will be short-lived (Krugman, 1994). Second, is the high growth rate being followed by a rationalization of the Chinese industrial structure?

The most important element of this rationalization process is a tendency towards of increasing rates of concentration in most industrial sectors. Two arguments justify this tendency. First, according to the transaction cost theory, the minimization of transaction costs makes modern firms increasingly larger and integrated (Williamson, 1985). Second, modern industries are also characterized by their large potentialities in terms of scale and scope economies, and large-sized firms are more capable of exploiting these potentialities (Chandler, 1990).

Following these arguments, we will study the tendency of concentration trend of China's industrial structure between 1990 and 1996. We believe that an increasing level of concentration should be a natural result of industrial development. This tendency can be easily found in the experiences of all the industrialized and newly industrialized economies (NIEs). From this point of view, it will be shown that the efficiency of China's industrial system did not increase between 1990 and 1996. If this trend persists, China will not remain the growth champion in the new century.

Table 12.1 Production share of different-sized firms, China, 1990 and 1996

	1990		1996	
	Number	% of industrial production	Number	% of industrial production
Large-sized firms	3 965	34.83	7 057	39.41
Middle-sized firms	9 450	19.77	16 870	15.22
Small-sized firms	403 667	45.41	482 518	45.37

Source: *China Statistical Yearbook* (1991, 1997).

In what follows, we will present some general indicators of China's industrial structure, and we will introduce the sectoral analysis framework. This will be followed by the estimation of results, their explanation, and some conclusions.

China's industrial structure: some general indicators

From Table 12.1,[1] we can see that the level of concentration of China's industry has been decreasing over the 1990–6 period. In 1990, the 3965 large-sized firms accounted for 34.83 percent of industrial production. In 1996, the number of large-sized firms increased by 3092 (an increase of 78 percent).[2] Nevertheless, their share in the industrial production was 39.41 percent (an increase of 13 percent). If we consider only the first 3965 large firms, their share in the industrial production was undoubtedly less than 34.83 percent in 1996.[3]

According to the *China Industrial Statistical Yearbook* 1995, China's 500 largest firms accounted for only 18.51 percent of industrial production in 1994, which was much lower than some NIEs.[4]

The industrial analysis framework

The purpose of this section is to analyze the evolution of China's industrial structure at the industrial level.

The sample

We examine 33 industries, six of which are mining, petroleum, and wood industries; two are public utilities (electricity and water production); 10 are raw materials industries; 11 are consumer goods industries, and five correspond to equipment goods and durable consumer goods industries.

Hypotheses

In what follows, the following hypothesis is tested: the profitability of industries affects the structure of the market through two mechanisms that operate in opposite directions: (i) On the one hand, the increase in profits encourages the entry and prevents the exit of firms at the margin of the point of entry or exit. If entry barriers are low, new entry will slow down the concentration trend. (ii) On the other hand, dominant or large firms tend to engage in many anti-competitive pricing and nonpricing strategies, such as the building up of excess capacity. With excess capacity, large firms can expand production instantaneously in order to bar entry. As a result, their profitability will improve and the concentration trend will accelerate.

Second, market demand affects the structure of the market. Its variation has two effects similar to that of profitability on market structure. (i) The increase in demand supports firms at the margin who will either remain in the market or enter it. (ii) The change in demand affects the large firms more because of their larger market share. All these depend on which effect is more important at the time.

Third, the industry's level of capital intensity influences market structure. In general, a higher level of initial capital is a requirement in the capital-intensive sectors. Thus small firms are likely to be excluded from this industry, and these firms should display a larger average size of firms and a higher level of concentration.

Fourth, the property-right nature of firms also affects market structure. In China, the larger firms of most industrial sectors are state-owned enterprises (SOEs). However, their share in the national total industrial output has decreased gradually since the beginning of the economic reforms. If there were no entry of large firms with their own specific property rights (for example, foreign invested enterprises or FIEs), the level of concentration would increase.

The model

With the above hypotheses, we specify the model as follows:

$$C = \alpha_1 + \alpha_2(D) + \alpha_3(\pi) + \alpha_4(K) + \alpha_5(PR) + \alpha_6(S) + \varepsilon$$

C represents the dependent variables reflecting the level of concentration and its evolution. C is composed of three variables: Varsize90–96, *Concentration96* ,and *Varconcentration90–96*. We will define all the variables in the following section.

D re-groups the three explanatory variables, reflecting market demand for the production of sectors. The π variable refers to three explanatory variables reflecting the profitability of industries. K represents two explanatory variables reflecting the capital intensity of sectors. *PR* is composed of three explanatory variables reflecting the property-right nature of the firms in the sector, and finally *S* re-groups the dummy variables reflecting sector differences.

In each estimating model, we do not utilize all the variables but we choose only one or two variables among them that can be substituted for each other.

The variables

The variables reflecting the industrial structure and its evolution

(1) *Varsize90–96*

This is the variation of the average firm size of the sector in terms of turnover between 1990 and 1996. The turnover amount for 1996 is re-adjusted with the comparable wholesale price of each sector.

(2) *Concentration96*

China lacks data about industrial concentration. It was in 1994 that the turnover of the 500 largest Chinese firms was published for the first time. However, data on the average size of SOEs can provide some information on the level of concentration between 1990 and 1996. We find that in 1990, the average size of the state-owned enterprises was 9.44 times larger than that of 'the others' in terms of turnover. In 1996, this ratio was 5.02. The FIEs in 1996 should be regarded as large firms since their share in industrial production increased from 4.67 percent in 1990 to 19.08 percent in 1996, and they were 4.4 times larger than 'the others' in terms of turnover. With this observation in mind, we consider the SOEs and the FIEs as being large firms, and the others as being small companies in 1996.[5] In 1990, the industrial share of FIEs was very low; therefore we consider only the SOEs as being large firms; the others are small firms. We use the following equation to measure the level of concentration:[6]

$$\frac{n \times |x - \bar{x}| + N \times (x_j - \bar{x})}{Q}$$

where

n is the number of large firms (SOEs in the case of 1990 figures, and SOEs plus FIEs for 1996 figures)

N is the number of small firms

$\bar{x}$ is the average firm size of the industry

x_i is the average size of the large firms of the industry and x_j is the average firm size of the small firms of the industry

Q is the total production of the industry

With the help of this equation, we get a coefficient varying between 0 and 2. It approaches the value of 0 when the sizes of all firms are the same. It is close to 2 when one large firm realizes 99 percent of production, and when the remaining 1 percent is shared by a large number of small firms.

(3) *Varconcentration90–96* This is the difference between the 1996 and 1990 coefficients of concentration for a given industry. It is positive (negative) when the level of concentration increases (decreases).

The variables reflecting the market demand for the sector

(4) *Rtexport96* This is the export rate of the industry in 1996.
(5) *Varrtexport90–96* This is the difference of the export rates between 1990 and 1996.
(6) *Varmarket90–96*
The market size of the industry is measured by (production + import – export). Its variation is defined as the difference between that of 1996 and of 1990.

The variables reflecting the profitability of the industry

(7) *Rtprofit96* This is the rate of profit measured by the value of profits (before tax) divided by the total capital of the sector.
(8) *Vartrtprofit90–96* This is the difference of the profit rates between 1990 and 1996.
(9) *Rtprofitjv96* This is the profit rate of the foreign capital firms of the industry.

The variables reflecting the capital intensity of the industry

(10) *Capitalperhead96* This is calculated by the total capital divided by the number of employees of the industry.
(11) *Sharestateproduction90* This is the share of the SOEs in the total production of the industry in 1990. It also reflects the capital intensity of the industry, because in China this share tends to be higher in more capital intensive sectors.

The variables reflecting the firms' property right nature of the industry

(12) *Varcapitalstateshare90–96* This is the difference of the share of SOEs in total capital between 1990 and 1996.
(13) *Capitalsizejv/state96* This is the ratio between the average firm size of the FIEs and SOEs of the industry in 1996. It reflects the size difference between them.
(14) *Capitalsizestate/all* This is the ratio of the average size of the state enterprises relative to the industry's average firm size.

Table 12.2 Firm size, concentration, and evolution, 1990 and 1996

	Size in 1996 (million yuan)	Difference from 1990 (%)	Concentration level in 1996	Difference from 1990
Average	6.10	+39.29	0.6155	–0.1258
Standard deviation	21.29	57.93	0.2655	0.2470
Minimum	0.32	–78.48	0.2361	–0.5096
Maximum	123.25	+163.45	1.3887	0.6072

Source: Authors' calculations.

The variables reflecting the sectors' difference

(15) The sectors
We distinguish three broad classes of sectors: production of raw materials, consumer goods industries, and equipment and durable consumer goods industries. These are dummy variables (0 or 1).

Results and analysis

The Results

From Table 12.2, we note that the average size of firms at the total industrial level increased by 39.29 percent between 1990 and 1996. On the other hand, the concentration ratio decreased by 0.1258 points, that is a reduction of 16.97 percent during this same period.

From Table 12.3, it can be seen that four industries, petroleum and gas extraction, tobacco, petro-chemical products, and chemical fibers, have the largest average firm size. It is also true that the concentration levels are highest in the exploitation and production of raw materials industries (petro-chemical products, coal mining, and steel).[7]

The industries with higher increases in average firm size between 1990 and 1996 were all consumer goods industries (furniture, cultural and educational goods, timber, and leather). The reason was that the massive entry of Hong Kong and Taiwanese capital made the small average firm size of these sectors increase significantly during this period. We can see that the variations in the levels of concentration followed the same trend. By contrast, in the case of industries of exploitation and production of raw materials, the average firm size and the level of concentration decreased during the same period.[8] The food sector also saw a decrease in its level of concentration. The reason was that the firms in the 'others' category were very small before 1990, except for some of the SOEs. In 1996, the small firms saw their size increase significantly, whereas the SOEs progressed very slowly.

Table 12.3 Levels of size, concentration, and evolution, by sectors, 1990 and 1996

	Size 96 (million yuan)		Varsize 90–96 (%)		Concentration 96		Varconcent 90–96	
The highest	Exploitation petroleum	123.25	Furniture	163.45	Petro-chemical products	1.389	Exploitation petroleum	0.6072
	Tobacco	28.90	Cultural and educational goods	153.27	Coal mining	1.153	Furniture	0.2493
	Petrol chemical	8.47	Timber	136.92	Metallurgy	1.116	Timber	0.2195
	Chemical fiber	5.84	Leather	103.15	Electricity	1.0003	Printing	0.1646
The lowest	Furniture	0.32	Exploitation petroleum	–78.48	Chemical fiber	0.236	Ferrous metal mining	–0.5096
	Timber	0.34	Metallurgy	–35.81	Pharmaceutical	0.252	Non ferrous metal smelting	–0.4019
	Printing	0.35	Metal products	–35.37	Exploitation non metal mining	0.3216	Non ferrous metal mining	–0.3981
	Non-metal exploitation	0.40	Nonferrous metals mining	–32.85	Garment	0.351	Food	–0.3937

Source: Authors' calculations.

As shown in Table 12.4, the average firm size of the equipment and durable consumer goods sector was relatively small. The smallest was the consumer goods sector (if tobacco was removed, it was 1.05 million yuan). Between 1990 and 1996, the increase in the average firm size was highest in the equipment goods sector. By contrast, the exploitation of mining products, electricity and water production saw a decrease in average firm size. Regarding the level of concentration, the most concentrated industries were mining, electricity, and water production, followed by the raw material sector. The least concentrated was the consumer goods sector. All concentration ratios decreased between 1990 and 1996, with equipment goods and the production of raw materials decreasing most rapidly. An important explanatory factor was that the shares of the SOEs in these industries were much higher than in other sectors, but then decreased significantly during the period.

It can be seen in Table 12.5 that, first of all, profit rates have a positive impact on concentration levels. In the sectors with a higher rate of profits, the absolute level and the evolution of the concentration rate are higher. Second, demand conditions, home market size and export rates have a limited impact on the level of concentration, except that home market size has a strong effect on the evolution of average firm size of the sectors. Third, the raw materials and equipment goods sectors have a higher absolute level of concentration. The average firm size of the equipment goods sector has increased significantly. Fourth, the capital-intensive level of the sectors also has an impact on average firm size and on concentration rates. In the sectors with a higher level of capital per head, average firm size fell significantly between 1990 and 1996. Finally, property-rights factors do matter. In the sectors traditionally dominated by SOEs (the criteria being their share in the total production, and their firm size relative to the sector's average firm size), the rates of concentration decrease more significantly, though their level of concentration remains higher than that of other sectors. Further, in the sectors where the capital shares of the SOEs have declined less substantially, the concentration ratios have been reduced less too. In the sectors where the profitability of the FIEs is higher, the concentration ratio is lower, and both the concentration ratio and the average firm size decrease more (or increase less) as well. In the sectors where the average size of the FIEs is relatively larger than that of the SOEs, the absolute level of concentration is higher, and the average firm size increases, too.

The reasons for the decrease in concentration levels

Why is there no tendency for the level of concentration to increase? The first reason is that the financial state of China's enterprises has

Table 12.4 Firm size and concentration, by broad category of sector, 1990 and 1996

Sectors	**Number**	**Size 96 (million yuan)**	**Varsize 90–96 (%)**	**Concentration 96**	**Varconcent 90–96**
Mining, electricity and water	8	16.3	–6.32	0.7093	–0.0757
Raw materials production	10	2.8.4	+27.39	0.6692	–0.1679
Consumer goods	11	3.58 (1.05)	+63.97	0.4924	–0.0933
Equipment goods	5	1.83	+81.78	0.6286	–0.1933

Source: Authors' calculations.

Table 12.5 Multi-regression results (OLS)

Independent variable	Dependent variable Concentration 96	Dependent variable Varconcent 90–96	Dependent variable Varsize90–96
Constant	–0.4437	0.2750	–0.7051
	*(–2.4)***	*(1.96)***	*(–2.33)***
Rtprofit 96	2.6072	3.9192	4.7988
	*(2.61)***	*(4.28)***	*(2.50)***
Vartrtprofit 90–96	1.4710	2.1620	–1.4936
	*(2.53)***	(4.51)**	*(–1.20)*
Varmarket 90–96			0.3203
			(5.61)**
Rtexport 96	0.5869	0.3564	
	*(1.82)**	*(1.29)*	
Varrtexport 90–96	–0.4092	–0.5204	0.8862
	(–1.04)	*(–1.71)**	*(1.53)*
Rtprofitjv 96	–2.5864	–2.0289	–3.3138
	*(–2.53)***	*(–2.40)***	*(–1.85)**
Capitalsize jv/state 96	0.0850	–0.0938	0.2013
	*(2.08)***	*(–2.43)***	*(2.65)***
Share state production 90	0.8717	–0.4040	
	*(5.97)***	*(–2.97)***	
Capital per head 96		0.0062	–0.0259
		(1.40)	*(–3.09)***
Capital size state/all	0.110	–0.0591	–0.0731
	*(3.97)***	*(–2.69)***	*(–1.53)*
Var capital state share 90–96	0.5805	0.7325	1.0826
	(1.42)	*(2.19)***	*(1.48)*
Sector: raw materials	0.1910		0.1352
	*(2.05)***		*(0.85)*
Sector: consumption goods	0.1590		0.2913
	(1.47)		*(1.52)*
Sector: equipment goods	0.2340		0.6151
	*(2.14)***		*(3.16)***
Sample size	34	34	34
R^2 (adjusted)	0.6497	0.7012	0.7698
Durbin–Watson	2.16	2.26	1.83

Note:
* Significant at 10 percent level; ** Significant at 5 percent level.

deteriorated. As shown in Table 12.6, the reduction of the average profit rate was 4.78 percent between 1990 and 1996.

The second reason is that although market demand increases rapidly everywhere in China, supply remains localized by the policy of regional

Table 12.6 Profitability of Chinese industrial sectors, 1990 and 1996

	Profit rate in 1996 (%)	**Difference with 1990 (%)**
Average	6.67	–4.78
Standard deviation	3.53	6.28
Minimum	1.36	–15.6
Maximum	16.75	15.89

Note: The tobacco industry is not included because its profit rate and variation are too high relative to those of other industries. Its profit rate was 133.9 percent in 1990 and 60.35 percent in 1996, a reduction of 73.55 percent.
Source: Authors' calculations.

governments. Decentralization brought about by the Chinese reforms gives local governments more power; some of these powers are used to stop imports from other provinces. This creates very low entry barriers for local new enterprises, and even the smallest enterprises with the highest production costs can manage to survive during a boom period. In fact, local governments support the entry of such firms, because the governments' aim is to develop local production capacity so as to increase local fiscal and financial revenue. On the other hand, the exit barriers are extremely high. Different levels of government often support the state and collective enterprises that find themselves in financial difficulties, and there are many policies against bankruptcy.

The third reason is that the large firms in China are mostly SOEs, and are basically found in the heavy industries sector. However, the market oriented reforms in China have made the heavy industries relatively weak in contrast with the development of consumer goods industries. This leads to a decrease in the level of concentration. This decrease has not been compensated by the reinforcement of the private sector, because the heavy industries require a large amount of investment and have a lower level of profit, at least at the beginning of their operation. All these factors prevent the entry of private firms. The entry of FIEs may substantially affect the level of concentration in the long run. However, it is only in the suite recent past that foreign-invested firms have entered the SOEs, and therefore their entry does not change the trend in the short term.

Conclusion

Despite Chinese industry's unprecedented growth, the level of concentration has decreased, particularly in the industries that produce raw materials and equipment goods. This seems to reflect the fact that the development of Chinese industry is based mainly on an extensive mode of production; that is, it depends on the increase of inputs, rather than on productivity improvements and economies of scale. One of the reasons for the decrease in the level of concentration is that the large firms are mainly SOEs found in the heavy industry sector; the market oriented reforms have left them largely weakened. Moreover, entry barriers are relatively low but exit barriers are very high. Indeed, the Chinese industrial system will need a profound structural reform, without which reform, China's industrial growth will not last. From this point of view, the future of Chinese industry is not as promising as is generally believed. In fact, the structural problem will be a real challenge for China in the twenty-first century.

Notes

1 In Table 12.1, the firms were classified as having independent accounting systems. Below them, there were 7 million Township and Village Enterprises (TVEs) that represented 25.29 percent and 39.59 percent of the total industrial production in 1990 and 1995, respectively. Most of the TVEs were small, except for 212 large and 1414 middle-sized firms in 1995 that produced less than 5 percent of the industrial output of this group. They were also classified as having independent accounting systems, but they are not included in Table 12.1.

2 In China, the classification of firms according to their size is based on the capacity of production. The criterion is specific to each sector.

3 Data sources in this paper are from *China Statistical Yearbook*, unless otherwise specified.

4 For example, the turnover of the 101 largest Taiwanese industrial groups was equivalent to 35.32 percent of Taiwan's GNP in 1992. In South Korea, this proportion was even higher.

5 Where the average size of the FIEs in some industries is not larger than the average firm size of the industry, we consider only the SOEs as being large firms.

6 This method is certainly rather limited to reflect the exact concentration ratio. Among SOEs, there are also middle-sized and small firms. These should be classified in the 'others' category as well. The ideal way is to find data on the relative importance of different sizes of enterprises. However, such data are not available. What we know clearly is that 80 percent of the large-sized enterprises fall, with all probability, in the category of 'State enterprises' and only 20 percent of them in the 'others' category. Therefore, by SOEs we mean 'large enterprises', whereas middle and small firms fall in the 'others' category.

7 Two exceptions were the chemical fiber and pharmaceutical sectors industries, for which the average firm sizes were among the largest, but their levels of concentration among the lowest. This was because there was no significant size difference between those classified as small firms and those as large firms.

8 An exception was the petroleum and gas extraction sector in which the average firm size decreased but the rate of concentration increased significantly. The reason was that the firm number of the sector increased from 33 to 133 during this period, and the new companies seemed to be of an auxiliary type and of small size, so the size difference was increased.

References

Chandler, A. D. (1990) *Scale and Scope: The Dynamics of Industrial Capitalism* (London: Harvard University Press).

China Statistical Yearbook (1990–1997, annual issues), (Beijing: China Statistical Press).

Krugman, P. (1994) 'The Myth of Asia's Miracle,' *Foreign Affairs,* November–December 62–78.

Williamson, O. E. (1985) *The Economic Institutions of Capitalism* (New York: Free Press).

13
The Impact of Foreign Trade on the Economic Growth of Shanghai

Hua Wang

The role of international trade in the process of economic development has long interested economists.[1] Numerous empirical studies have been conducted to determine this relationship, but little has been said about the exact contribution of international trade to economic growth in the case of the People's Republic of China (PRC).

Since the government opened the economy to the outside world in 1978, the modern economic experience of China has been equivalent to a virtual economic miracle. A significantly strong correlation has been found between open door policy (measured by exports and foreign direct investment or FDI) and GDP growth (Wei, 1995). The objective of this chapter is to show the exact contribution of foreign trade to GDP. Various Chinese researchers have tried to address this issue, using Denison's method, but their work remains incomplete.[2] In this chapter, we have made some modifications to the classification of economic growth in Denison's model (Denison, 1962, 1967, 1971 and 1972), and we have applied it to the case of Shanghai as the first step towards a nation-level study.

The characteristics of Shanghai's foreign trade are reviewed in a first section. Different theoretical contributions on the relationship between export growth and GDP growth are then presented, and the reasons for choosing Denison's model for its application to the Chinese case are given. The following section reports the empirical results. Besides foreign trade, it includes some other factors. Finally, we present the summary and conclusions of the study.

Characteristics of Shanghai foreign trade

Fast expansion after Deng's open door policy

In 1979, China carried out Deng Xiaoping's reform program, with the open door policy being its most important component. The average annual growth rate of inflation-adjusted GDP for China was 9.5 percent between 1980 and 1990. The average annual growth rate of foreign trade was 13.3 percent during the same period. As Krugman and Obstfeld (1991, p. 247) noted, Chinese economic growth in the 1980s 'amounted to a virtual economic miracle – and a classical demonstration of the potential of export-oriented industrialization'.

Shanghai, one of the most important cities in China, recorded a progressive expansion of foreign trade. Exports rose from US$2.89 billion in 1978 to US$11.58 billion in 1995. Between 1978 and 1980, the average annual growth rates of foreign trade, exports, and imports was 24.9 percent, 24.5 percent, and 34.6 percent, respectively. However, in the 1980–5 period, the average annual growth rate for exports dropped to 5.4 percent. The main reason was the reform of the foreign trade policy in China.[3] After 1986, the growth rate of exports rose continuously. From 1990 to 1995, total foreign trade growth rate was above 20 percent; this was 5 percentage points higher than that of GDP in the same period (Table 13.1).

Large fluctuations in economic development

The above description has partially revealed a situation of large fluctuations. Through a review of China's and Shanghai's foreign trade history, we can observe 10-year cycles with peak periods noticeable in the 1950s, 1970s, and 1990s and periods of economic downturn during the 1960s and 1980s (Table 13.2). The 1950s represented the first period of the establishment of the Communist system in China. The high growth rate was easily attained owing to a fairly low volume of foreign trade. During the 1960s, the Cultural Revolution was the main explanatory factor for the recession. In the 1970s, after a fierce debate over whether

Table 13.1 Shanghai's trade volume, 1979–95 (US$ 100 million)

	1980	1985	1990	1995
Total	45.66	50.61	76.21	190.77
Exports	42.66	33.61	53.21	115.77
Imports	3	17	23	75

Source: *Statistical Yearbook of Shanghai* (1995), 122.

Table 13.2 Average annual growth rates of foreign trade, China and Shanghai, 1950s–1990s (%)

Period	**China**	**Shanghai**
1950s	14.00	25.67
1960s	2.56	4.55
1970s	24.65	17.51
1980s	13.45	7.70
1990s*	18.49	18.06
Average	**14.10**	**14.70**

Note:*
Based on data from 1991 to 1995.
Sources: *Statistical Yearbook of China* (1980–95); *Statistical Yearbook of Shanghai* (1980–95).

China should trade with capitalist countries or not, the new open door strategy was finally accepted by the government. The 1980s were the first decade of economic reform. The apparently counter-cyclical recession in Shanghai's foreign trade was mainly due to the decentralization of the foreign trade system as mentioned above.

According to the historical 10-year cycle of fluctuation, can we predict that the first decade of the twenty-first century will also be a period of depression? Since the endogenous factors (change of economic policy, for example) are the central features of the fluctuation, it is worthwhile estimating whether economic development will stabilize if China sticks to its outward strategy. Nevertheless, the continuing openness will inevitably introduce more external factors (such as world demand conditions and international capital flows) that will act as additional variables on the Chinese economy.[4]

Continued enhancement of the degree of openness

After a decade of reforms, China substantially increased its degree of openness.[5] Shanghai also displayed a phenomenal increase in the nominal degree of openness, from around 20 percent in 1981 to 33.7 percent in 1990, culminating at 39.3 percent in 1995. The World Bank (1987, p. 83) classified 41 developing countries into four groups, according to their trade orientation: strongly outward oriented, moderately outward oriented, moderately inward oriented, and strongly inward oriented. However, China was not classified. Kohli and Singh (1989) defined 'outward oriented economies' as those with an export growth rate exceeding 6 percent per annum, or with a share of exports to GNP greater than 17 percent.

With this classification in mind, Shanghai should be classified as an outward oriented economy, at least since the early 1980s. However, this is far from being the truth. From the technical point of view, the use of the market exchange rate to convert Chinese GDP may overstate its openness since it underestimates China's true GDP.[6] From a political point of view, an economy with strong government intervention should not be classified as strongly outward oriented (Helleiner, 1990). Moreover, the export-push strategies in the early decades were trial ones; these strategies involved the designation of special economic zones (SEZs) and cities and the determination of export incentives for foreign investors in targeted sectors (Panagariya, 1993). After the early 1990s, China aggressively implemented outward strategies. Tariff and nontariff trade barriers (NTBs) were being reduced. Since 1996, the import tax of more than 4000 products has been substantially reduced: the average reduction rate was 30 percent; the general import tax level decreased from 35.9 percent to 23 percent; the quantity of import quotas reduced from 53 to 36 after 1995.[7]

Slow restructuring of exports

Two turning points can be observed in the evolution of exports' restructuring up to the end of the last decade of the twentieth century, separating it into three subperiods, and allowing us to distinguish the pattern of economic growth and the changeover to industrialization (Table 13.3).

The first period extended over the years 1952–7. Agricultural commodities accounted for more than 60 percent of Shanghai's exports. By 1958, the structure of exports transformed from an agrarian base to being geared

Table 13.3 Structure of exports, Shanghai, 1952–2010 (%)

	1952–7	**1958[a]**	**1958–87**	**1987[a]**	**1988–95**	**1995–2010[a, b]**
Agricultural products and sidelines	61.33	38	30.44	18.15	10.17	9
Light industry and textile products	36.27	58	55.85	61.92	65.41	45
Heavy-industry products	2.40	4	13.71	19.93	24.42	46

Notes:
[a] Year 1958 and 1987 are two turning points for the structure of Shanghai's exports.
[b] Authors' estimates.
Sources: Data for years preceding 1980 from *The Construction and Development History of Shanghai Socialist Economies, 1949–1985* (in Chinese) Shanghai: Shanghai People's Press. Data for subsequent years from *Statistical Yearbook of Shanghai* (1995), 122.

towards economies with a strong manufacturing base. Light industry and textile products accounted for 58 percent of Shanghai's total exports.

The second period lasted 30 years, and spanned the years 1958–87. During this period, the proportion of textile and light-industry products went up slightly but continuously and was the largest export sector. The development of heavy-industries displayed a similar rhythm in this period. In 1987, the proportion of heavy-industry products overtook that of agriculture, and was ranked second place in the overall structure of exports.

It is hard to estimate the end of the third period since we hope to see another turning point indicating that heavy industry products will reach the most significant proportion in all export products. Since 1988, the relationship between light-industry products and heavy-industry products has been substitutive, since the proportion of agricultural products could not drop continuously. Light-industry and textile products are still dominant in overall exports. In 1995, the 10 largest export products accounting for over US$100 million were principally frozen poultry, baked fish, cotton shirts, long trousers, and toys. It appears that heavy-industry products will occupy the largest proportion of manufacturing exports up until the late 2010s.

Impact of foreign trade and other factors on Shanghai's economic growth

The models of export growth and GDP growth

The models of export and GDP growth can be grouped into 'neo-classical' and 'structural.'

In relation to the neo-classical models, a number of authors have attempted to bypass the criticisms voiced to rank correlation studies by formulating a conceptual framework based on neo-classical production functions. There are at least two approaches.

One approach is proffered by Feder (1983) who, by using a two-sector model, attempted to provide one of the first remedies to the problem of built-in correlation noted earlier by Michaely (1977). Feder's formulation included an export and a non-export sector. Aggregate GDP is the sum of the above two sectors. Using a sample of 31 industrializing economies, Feder (1983, p. 65) found that the results provided 'strong support to the hypothesis that marginal factor productivities in the export sector are higher than in the non-export sector.' Although these results were highly suggestive and represented an improvement over the simple correlation between exports growth and GDP growth, a number of economists remained highly sceptical with regard to the validity of these results (Edwards, 1993, p. 1381).

The second approach is represented by the work of Balassa (1985), Ram (1985), and Salvatore and Hatcher (1991). Rather than Feder's two-sector formulation, this approach resorted simply to a one-sector model. The authors introduced exports (combined sometimes with some other factors[8]) as additional inputs into the general production function to study the relationship between international trade and economic development. As we know today, this approach faces some serious shortcomings. Indeed, the results obtained by estimating simple relationships between exports and growth are very sensitive to the choice of samples as well as to the estimating techniques. The framework of cross-section studies implicitly assumes similar production functions across sectors and countries. This is grossly inappropriate. One conceptual shortcoming is its failing to address important questions on the exact mechanism through which export expansion affects GDP growth.

The above two approaches rely on cross-country regression analyses by testing the relationship between export growth and economic performance. In spite of the difference in methodologies and in the aspects emphasized, most of these studies seem to be in general agreement about the beneficial effects of export performance on economic growth.[9] However, these studies have been unable to measure the exact contribution of foreign trade to economic development.

Differing from the neo-classical approach, structural models are represented by the work of Chenery, Robinson, and Syrquin (1986), and base their interpretation on the role of foreign trade in economic growth. To the authors (1986, p. 16), the fundamental difference between these two approaches is that 'disequilibrium is more often manifested by the differences in returns to labor and capital in different uses rather than by the shortages and surpluses that indicate the complete failure of markets to clear. In contrast, neoclassical theory assumes that equilibrium is maintained over time, which limits the source of growth to factors on the supply side.' In spite of the different hypothesis, the study also starts from a version of the neo-classical growth formula, but adds some other explanatory variables. These analyses of sectoral evaluation have had to take into consideration the fact that in almost all less developed countries (LDCs) international trade affects their sectoral structure and external competition may affect the growth of productivity. The advantage of the theoretical basis and empirical work of Chenery, Robinson, and Syrquin is its combined consideration of foreign trade and industrialization, as well as structural change of economies.

Adaptation of Denison's model in the case study of Shanghai

In this chapter we finally adapt Denison's model, for several reasons. The exact contribution made by foreign trade to economic growth cannot be appropriately obtained by the linear regression approach. In contrast, the models by Denison and Chenery are more appropriate. The latter has indisputable additional theoretical and empirical advantages, but it cannot unfortunately be applied to the case of Shanghai, because of the unavailability of regional input–output[10] data.

The work of Edward Denison, as Abramovitz (1991, p. 148) wrote, 'presents a picture of post trends in output growth and in the development of the various sources to which the growth of productive capacity can be traced, a projection of the probable future flows from these sources, and a measured evaluation of the possible steps that might be taken to make the flows still larger.'

Denison's model is also a neo-classical one. The method of analysis was introduced by Schmookler (1952). Kendrick (1961) made a most complete and systematic statement. In the simplest form, the equation is $gY = gA + gI$, where, gY is real national income increase, gA is the increase in total inputs and gI is the increase in output per unit of input. The methodology

> was firmly grounded upon principles of cost minimization and marginal productivity analysis and in particular on the principle of proportionality which states that under fairly realistic conditions the earnings of employed inputs are proportional to their marginal products. Earnings were used as weights to combine total labor, capital and land into aggregate measures for these separate inputs. The best procedure available was sought to obtain a quantity series for each input (which was multiplied by the inputs weight to obtain its contributions to output) and to appraise the effect on output of changes in each determinant of output per unit of input. (Denison, 1993, p. 39)

On the basis of Denison's methodology we have made a few small modifications of those factors (Table 13.4). We argue that this is possible and feasible for the following reasons.

As Denison mentioned (1993 p. 39), 'apart from the weighting scheme, the series for the different sources of growth were estimated independently of one another. Hence, if anyone preferred a method of deriving the contribution of any output determinant that differed from mine, he could replace my estimate for that determinant without changing any others except the growth accounting residual'.

Table 13.4 Comparison of different sources of growth

Denison	**Hua Wang**
Real national income	Real national income
Increase in total inputs	*Increase in total inputs*
Labor input, adjusted for quality	Labor input, adjusted for quality
Employment	Employment
Hours	Productivity of labor
Effect of shorter hours on quality	Labor insurance and welfare
Education	Education
Increased experience and better use of women	
Changes in age–sex composition of labor force	
Capital input	Capital input
Nonfarm residential structures	Fixed assets (structures and equipment)
Other structures and equipment	Inventories
Inventories	
US-owned assets abroad	
Foreign assets in United States	
Increase in output per unit of input	*Increase in output per unit of input*
Restrictions against optimum use of resources	Foreign Trade: terms of trade, volume of trade,
Reduced waste in agriculture	Value added part of exports, degree of openness,
Change in lag in application of knowledge	Structure of exports
Industry shift from agriculture	Industry shift from agriculture:
Advance of knowledge	Nonregulated factors
Economies of scale: independent growth of local markets	influence of weather on agriculture
Economies of scale: growth of national market	Advance of knowledge
	Economies of scale: enlargement of economic scale, change of consumer structure

Note: Certain lines in Denison's table constituting subtotals are not reproduced here.
Source: Denison (1962), Table 32.

Some modifications of detailed factors such as labor and capital inputs are mostly due to the availability of statistical data. For example, the relevant statistics on the effect of shorter hours on quality and the owned assets abroad are not available. Another reason is the different hypothesis and reality concerning the Western country and China. In the United States, the difference of labor 'quality' between males and females is reflected through employment discrimination and pay discrimination. This is not the case in China, so there is no need to take this factor into account. The principle of this study is to go far as information, time, and energy permit, in order to explain the changes that occur in the determinants of growth.

Foreign trade as one of the 'increases in output per unit of input' was not included in Denison's work. However, Kim and Park (1977) added this factor in their work on the analysis of the Korean economy. As the adviser of their work, Denison (1993, p. 55) stated it 'is an excellent study for a period of fast growth, made the more useful because comparable to my studies for the United States, Western Europe and Japan, Walters' (1968) for Canada, and, to a large extent, Dholakia's for India (Dholakia, 1974).' In our study, the detailed factors of foreign trade are in accordance with those in Kim's work, and are the import index and export index, the terms of trade, the value-added part of exports and the degree of openness.

Data sets

All data are obtained from the following four yearbooks: *Statistical Yearbook of Shanghai, Statistical Yearbook of China, Statistical Yearbook of Shanghai Foreign Economics and Trades,* as well as *Statistical Yearbook of China Foreign Economics and Trades*. The time series runs from 1978 to 1995. It covers the qualitative and quantitative inputs of capital and labor and foreign trade, as well as the structural change from agriculture to industry and nonregulated factors.

Main results

Using the index of GDP, of resource input and of productivity, as presented in the appendices, the final results are obtained and are given in Table 13.5. The table provides results for different time periods and for various comparative studies. We focus on the results obtained for the period 1991–5.

These results can be summarized as follows:

- *The accumulation of capital is the engine of economic growth*
  In this period, the average growth rate of the index of fixed assets and of inventory were 21.75 percent, and 6.43 percent respectively, while the average annual growth rate for the index of labor was 4.28 percent (Appendix 1). The contribution of capital growth to GDP growth was 10.91 percentage points, or 83.67 percent of the growth rate of GDP. On the one hand, the above investments contribute significantly to economic growth; on the other, the imbalance between capital and

Table 13.5 Allocation of GDP growth, by sources of growth, 1981–95 (percentage points in growth rate)

	1981–5	1986–90	1991–5	1986–95	1981–95
Real national income	*9.12*	*5.70*	*13.04*	*9.37*	*9.29*
Increase in total inputs	*4.12*	*3.60*	*12.57*	*8.7*	*7.5*
Labor input, adjusted for quality of labor	1.45	1.04	1.66	2.53	2.31
Employment	0.15	0.09	–0.10	–0.07	0.05
Education	0.65	0.11	0.42	0.56	0.71
Productivity	0.21	0.36	1.17	1.59	1.03
Labor insurance and welfare	0.39	0.52	0.18	0.48	0.52
Employment rate	0.05	–0.04	–0.01	–0.04	0.58
Capital input	2.67	2.56	10.91	6.17	5.19
Fixed assets (structures and equipment)	2.13	1.87	8.42	4.67	3.99
Inventories	0.54	0.69	2.49	1.50	1.20
Land	0	0	0	0	0
Increase in output per unit of input	*5.00*	*2.10*	*0.47*	*0.67*	*1.79*
Industry shift from agriculture	1.68	0.84	0.03	0.36	0.69
Economies of scale: enlargement of economic scale	0.12	0.16	0.06	0.14	0.12
Economies of scale: change of consumer structure	0.27	1.28	0.20	0.74	0.56
Non regulated factors: influence of weather on agriculture	–0.28	0.25	–0.02	0.07	–0.03
Foreign trade: terms of trade, value added part of exports, degree of openness (export/GDP), structure of exports	0.18	0.82	1.25	1.83	1.23
Advance of knowledge	3.02	–1.24	–1.07	–2.74	–0.7

Source: Appendix (Tables 13A.1 and 13A.2).

labor was quite large (Appendix 1), especially between 1992 and 1995.[10] This made the index of total factor input rise sharply in this period. Therefore, the index of productivity changed to reflect a fairly low growth rate in the same period according to the mathematical calculation. This low growth rate in the index of total factor input led to the negative 'advance of knowledge' between 1986 and 1995 (Table 13.5). However, that does not imply a negative contribution of this factor in reality.

- *labor productivity is the most important factor in labor inputs*
  The contribution of the total labor input to GDP was 1.66 percentage points from 1991 to 1995. The contribution from its productivity

Table 13.6 Foreign trade growth and GDP growth, 1981–95

	1981–5	1986–90	1991–5	1986–95	1981–95
GDP	9.12 A (100) B	5.70 (100)	13.04 (100)	9.37 (100)	9.29 (100)
Foreign trade	0.18 (1.97)	0.82 (14.39)	1.25 (23.36[a] 24.67[b])	1.83 (19.53)	1.23 (13.24)

Notes: 'A', which refers to all the data on the left-hand side indicates the average annual growth in percentage points. 'B' refers to all the data on the right-hand side in the parenthesis, and indicates the percentage of 'A' in GDP growth.
[a] 13.24*3 – 1.97 – 14.39 = 23.36;
[b] 19.53*2 – 14.39 = 24.67.
Source: Table 13.5.

component reached 1.17 percentage points. This represents 70 percent of the total labor input, or 9 percent of the growth rate of GDP. Since 1986, the contribution of the rate of employment dropped continuously, by partly transferring its positive effects to productivity. This is despite the fact that, on its own, the rate of employment makes a negative contribution to the growth of GDP. Undoubtedly the rapidly soaring level of education makes a considerable contribution, too. It ranked as the second contributor for the labor inputs.

- *Great increase in the contribution of foreign trade*
  Between 1981 and 1985, the contribution of foreign trade to GDP was 0.18 percentage points, or 1.97 percent of GDP growth. During the following five years, its contribution rocketed to 0.82 percentage points, or 14.39 percent of GDP growth. Between 1991 and 1995, the rate of its contribution seems to have dropped to 9.59 percent of GDP (1.25/13.04 in Table 13.6) owing to excessive capital investment as mentioned above. But the result of an indirect calculation supports a rather surprising different interpretation, which indicates that the contribution of foreign trade to GDP growth was between 23.36 percent and 24.67 percent in this period.[11] From a long-term point of view, that is within the first 15 years of the economic reforms (1981–95), the annual average contribution of foreign trade to GDP growth was 13.24 percent.

More detailed information on the qualitative and quantitative factors of foreign trade is listed in Table 13.7. From a relatively long-term point of view, that is from 1981 to 1995, most of the contribution to foreign trade

Table 13.7 Qualitative and quantitative factors of foreign trade contributing to economic growth, 1981–95

	1981–5	**1986–90**	**1991–5**	**1986–95**	**1981–95**
Foreign trade	0.18[A] (100 [B])	0.82 (100)	1.25 (100)	1.83 (100)	1.23 (100)
Import index	0.02	0.29	0.43	0.64	0.22
Export index	0.20 (111.5)	0.25 (29.92)	0.77 (61.31)	0.92 (50.23)	0.91 (73.59)
Terms of trade	0.01	–0.06	0.00	–0.05	0.002
Value added portion of exports	(–7.83)	(3.68)	(–4.15)	(–1.39)	(–3.84)
Degree of openness	0.00 (1.38)	0.31 (38.11)	0.11 (8.53)	0.35 (18.97)	0.15 (12.27)

Notes: 'A' refers to all the data on the left-hand side and represents the average percentage point annual growth in the given period. 'B' indicates the data on the right-hand side in the parenthesis; it represents the percentage of factors in total foreign trade.
Source: Table 13.5 and Appendix 2 (Table 13A.3).

came from the quantitative expansion of imports and exports (as shown by the import and export index). On the other hand, these qualitative factors have a relatively low or negative effect on foreign trade. Compared with the early 1980s, the terms of trade have been deteriorating. This is not specific to China's foreign trade alone, but is a general problem encountered by developing countries and territories (United Nations, 1997, p. 42). A low-value added portion of exports mirrors another negative contributor. The importance of trade based on processing and assembly manufacturing activities, which handle production with buyer's samples, materials, and accessories, is one reason for this, although the most important reason still concerns the structure of exports. Import substitution is still the main strategy of the pillar industries in Shanghai.[12] In these pillar industries, the exports accounted for only 4 percent of the industry's gross output value in 1994, while in the textile industry (which lies outside the group of pillar industries as defined by the Shanghai municipality), exports covered 35.1 percent of gross output value in this category. We agree that the minimum level of development and import substitution industrialization (ISI) strategies are indispensable because the comparative advantage is based on the maturity and advantages of the industry. Meanwhile, we hope to see the ISI strategy for Shanghai's pillar industries switch to an export oriented strategy, and thus that the contribution of foreign trade to economic growth determined by the pace of industrialization will be even higher in the early part of the twenty-first century.

Summary and conclusions

This empirical study of Shanghai has demonstrated the impact of foreign trade on economic growth in an increasingly open environment. The contribution of foreign trade rose from 1.97 percent of GDP growth between 1981 and 1985 to 19.53 percent of GDP growth between 1986 and 1995. Most of its contribution came from the expansion of quantitative factors. Since 1981, the value of imports and exports played an important role in the total foreign trade factors, which covered more than 91 percent of the total contribution of foreign trade to economic development. The quantitative factors, such as the terms of trade and value added, have had relatively low or even negative effects, which were 0.14 percent and –3.84 percent, respectively.

Further results could have been obtained from this study, but this was outside the scope of the work. For example, the fast expansion of capital accumulation is the engine of economic growth in Shanghai. The contribution of capital to the growth of GDP was 83.67 percent between 1991 and 1995. The high ratio of capital inputs makes the value of 'advances of knowledge' negative, showing a difference when compared with other studies.

Appendices

Table 13A.1 Index of GDP, input of resources and productivity, 1978–95 (index 1990 = 100)

Year	Index of GDP	Index of input of resources				Index of total factor input	Index of productivity
		Labor[a]	Fixed assets	Inventory	Land		
1978	42.22	14.49	12.76	22.12	100.00	65.47	64.49
1979	45.35	25.45	15.72	6.21	100.00	66.55	68.14
1980	49.15	28.44	18.35	28.48	100.00	68.92	71.32
1981	51.89	35.20	22.19	29.34	100.00	70.58	73.52
1982	55.64	37.73	28.38	26.89	100.00	72.07	77.20
1983	59.98	42.25	20.01	–3.65	100.00	71.16	84.29
1984	66.94	50.79	36.52	14.86	100.00	74.78	89.52
1985	75.91	66.07	46.99	98.48	100.00	84.00	90.37
1986	79.26	77.26	58.15	113.81	100.00	83.76	94.63
1987	85.20	86.27	74.01	77.81	100.00	85.66	99.46
1988	93.80	97.50	95.41	134.15	100.00	102.64	91.39
1989	96.20	95.98	93.51	162.42	100.00	105.74	91.38
1990	100.00	100.00	100.00	100.00	100.00	100.00	100.00
1991	118.15	154.46	111.21	86.95	100.00	113.61	103.99
1992	151.13	157.78	153.82	143.63	100.00	118.09	112.98
1993	199.83	121.46	251.41	157.91	100.00	172.61	115.77
1994	260.68	145.63	401.32	210.92	100.00	244.90	106.44
1995	325.54	169.57	555.83	231.61	100.00	316.43	102.88-
Average annual growth rate (%)							
1981–5	9.12	15.31	14.82	6.62	0.00	3.79	4.59
1986–90	5.70	7.78	17.13	21.48	0.00	3.13	1.83
1991–5	13.04	4.28	21.75	6.43	0.00	19.90	0.74
1986–95	9.37	6.03	19.44	13.95	0.00	11.51	0.89
1981–95	9.29	9.12	18.12	11.86	0.00	8.94	2.13

Note: [a] The index of labor is derived from five factors: employment, education, productivity, labor insurance and welfare, and employment rate.
Source: *Statistical Yearbook of Shanghai* (1980–96).

Table 13A.2 Index of output per unit of input, 1978–95 (index 1990 = 100)

Year	Index of productivity (output per unit of input)	Allocation of resource: industry shift from agriculture	Economies of scale enlargement of economic scale	Economies of scale: change of consumer structure	Non regulated factors – influence of agriculture	Foreign trade	Advance of technology
1978	64.49	88.45	98.67	93.12	100.38	99.59	82.70
1979	68.14	88.06	98.73	93.23	100.37	95.64	87.57
1980	71.32	89.21	98.77	93.42	100.03	95.71	90.50
1981	73.52	90.83	98.82	93.46	100.11	95.79	91.39
1982	77.20	92.31	98.97	93.41	103.02	95.86	91.60
1983	84.29	93.81	99.06	93.36	101.95	95.99	99.28
1984	89.52	95.18	99.25	93.41	104.74	96.19	100.70
1985	90.37	96.46	99.32	94.59	98.97	96.53	104.38
1986	94.63	97.71	99.48	95.58	98.43	96.89	106.80
1987	99.46	98.65	99.70	96.86	98.39	97.49	108.84
1988	91.39	99.62	99.82	97.18	98.96	98.19	97.33
1989	91.38	99.84	99.92	100.00	99.64	99.00	92.86
1990	100.00	100.00	100.00	100.00	100.00	100.00	100.00
1991	103.99	100.53	100.23	100.48	99.86	101.20	101.64
1992	127.98	100.90	100.35	101.73	99.65	102.92	121.15
1993	115.77	100.93	100.47	102.53	99.34	105.41	106.34
1994	106.44	100.96	100.68	102.61	99.49	110.61	92.74
1995	102.88	100.43	100.85	102.74	99.82	118.60	83.51
Average annual growth rate (%)							
1981–5	4.59	1.55	0.11	0.25	–0.26	0.17	2.78
1986–90	1.83	0.72	0.14	1.10	0.21	0.70	–1.07
1991–5	0.74	0.09	0.17	0.54	–0.04	3.31	–2.83
1986–95	0.89	0.40	0.15	0.82	0.08	2.02	–2.73
1981–95	2.13	0.78	0.14	0.63	–0.03	1.40	–0.89

Sources: *Statistical Yearbook of Shanghai* (1980–96); *Statistical Yearbook of Shanghai Foreign Economies and Trades* (1989–96); *Statistical Yearbook of China Foreign Economies and Trades* (1991); Kim and Park (1977).

Table 13A.3 Foreign trade, 1978–95

Year	Export index (a)	Import index (b)	Terms of trade[a] (c)	Value added part of exports (d)	Degree of openness of exportation (e)	(a)*(b)*(c)*(d)*(e) (f)	Index of (f) (g)
1978	54.41	6.30	121.43	116.68	53.09	0.03	95.59
1979	69.12	9.62	108.98	116.24	59.34	0.05	95.64
1980	80.23	11.37	103.54	116.19	60.95	0.07	95.71
1981	71.60	16.26	103.14	114.58	59.46	0.08	95.79
1982	67.80	13.65	110.14	115.06	60.20	0.07	95.86
1983	68.61	23.32	116.04	112.46	60.95	0.13	95.99
1984	66.73	38.53	116.18	107.96	62.82	0.20	96.19
1985	63.21	77.30	115.02	95.79	62.91	0.34	96.53
1986	67.37	70.33	101.01	99.17	74.96	0.36	96.89
1987	78.24	85.36	109.14	98.27	84.44	0.60	97.49
1988	85.01	125.10	93.85	91.10	77.19	0.70	98.19
1989	96.64	133.50	85.36	92.26	80.94	0.81	99.00
1990	100.00	100.00	100.00	100.00	100.00	1.00	100.00
1991	108.00	109.20	100.00	99.77	101.67	1.20	101.20
1992	123.30	151.80	100.00	95.64	96.49	1.73	102.92
1993	138.80	253.60	100.00	84.41	83.73	2.49	105.41
1994	170.70	321.80	100.00	83.30	113.65	5.20	110.61
1995	217.70	354.50	100.00	89.22	116.06	7.99	118.60

Notes: [a] The terms of trade variable comes from *Statistical Yearbook of China Foreign Economies and Trade* (1991). After 1990, data are not available, but the tendency is that of a deterioration, as in the case of some other Asian countries (United Nations, 1997), 42. In this study, we estimate that it does not change.

Sources: *Statistical Yearbook of Shanghai Foreign Economies and Trades* (1989–96) *Statistical Yearbook of China Foreign Economies and Trades* (1991).

Notes

1. From the earlier works of Singer (1950), Myrdal (1957), and Haberler (1959) to the more recent contributions of Lewis (1980) and Krueger (1985).
2. As Denison mentioned (1993, p. 55), 'in 1987, a small group of Chinese economists and engineers led by Shi Qinqi began a study of the sources of growth in post-war China, on which I advised. A brief preliminary report on this, including tentative estimates, was completed and a meeting to discuss it was held in Hanuary 1990, but to my great regret, the group was disbanded before necessary modification were made.'
3. Before 1979, in the paradigm of centrally planned economies, more than 26 percent of the total Chinese total exports transited through Shanghai under the administration of the central government. Since 1980, the government has decentralized decision making regarding exports and imports to local governments or to regional foreign trade corporations. That is why, from a purely statistical point of view, there was a decline in Shanghai exports.
4. After several years of double-digit increase, China's export growth dropped to only 0.6 percent in 1998. This decline was mainly due to the decrease in the demand for Chinese exports by countries hit by the Asian economic crisis.
5. The degree of openness of economies can be evaluated by the ratio of exports to GDP. Another way consists in calculating the share of total trade in GDP (see, for example, World Bank, 1993, p. 37). The nominal openness is calculated on the basis of average annual market exchange rates. In this chapter, we use the first way of evaluation.
6. Lardy (1992, p. 51) showed that the trade – GNP ratio in China rose from about 9.7 percent in 1978 to 26.8 percent in 1989.
7. *Statistical Yearbook of China Foreign Economies and Trade* (1996–97), p. 50.
8. For Salvatore and Hatcher (1991), industrialization was an additional input, noted as *R*, the index of real industrial production. To them, *R* is used as an index of the measure of structural changes that accompany the process of growth and development, such as the transfer of labor and capital from agriculture and other traditional sectors where productivity is low to a presumably more efficient manufacturing sector.
9. Papers that have dealt with export growth under alternative world market conditions are Emery (1967), Kavoussi (1984), Gray and Singer (1988), Rana (1988).
10. From 1992–5, total investment in fixed assets were 35.74, 65.40, 112.32, and 160.18 billion yuan, respectively (1US$ = 8.37 yuan in 1995). The average annual growth rate of investment in fixed assets was 65.78 percent.
11. The indirect calculation means the contribution of foreign trade between 1991 and 1995, and it is calculated by the difference of the contribution of foreign trade between the periods 1986–95 and 1986–90, using a mathematical average method. The result is 24.67 percent. Another result comes from the same method of estimation, by the difference of foreign trade contribution between 1981 and 1995, 1981 and 1985, and 1986 and 1990. The result is 23.36 percent for the period 1991–95. There is no great difference between the above two estimations, thus the result is credible.
12. There are six pillar industries in Shanghai: (1) steel manufacturing, (2) motor-vehicle manufacturing, (3) electronic telecommunication equipment, (4) household electrical equipment manufacturing, (5) power generating

electricity equipment and fitting manufacturing, and (6) petrochemical and fine chemical processing. All of them are ISI-strategy oriented up until the end of the 1990s.

References

Abramovitz, M. (1991) *Thinking about Growth and Other Essays on Economic Growth and Welfare* (Cambridge: Cambridge University Press).

Balassa, B. (1985) 'Exports, Policy Choices and Economic Growth in Developing Countries after the 1973 Oil Shock,' *Journal of Development Economics*, 18, 22–5.

Chenery, H. B., Robinson, S., and Syrquin, M. (1986) *Industrialization and Growth: Comparative Study* (New York: Oxford University Press).

Denison, E. F. (1967) *Why Growth Rates Differ* (Washington, D., Brookings Institution).

Denison, E. F. (1962) 'The Sources of Economic Growth in the United States and the Alternatives Before Us', *Supplementary Paper*, 13 (New York: Committee for Economic Development).

Denison, E. F. (1971) *Accounting for United States Economic Growth 1929–1969* (Washington, DC: Brookings Institution).

Denison, E. F. (1972) 'Classification of Growth,' *Review of Income and Wealth*, 18–1, 1–25.

Denison, E. F. (1993) 'The Growth Accounting Tradition and Proximate Sources of Growth,' in A. Szirmai, B. van Ark and D. Pilat (eds), *Explaining Economic Growth* (Amsterdam: Elsevier).

Dholakia, B. (1974) *The Source of Economic Growth in India* (Baroda: Good Companions).

Edwards, S. (1993) 'Openness, Trade Liberalization, and Growth in Developing Countries,' *Journal of Economic Literature*, vol. 31, 1358–93.

Emery, R.(1967) 'The Relation of Exports and Economic Growth,' *Kyklos*, 20: 4, 470–84.

Feder, G. (1983) 'On Exports and Economic Growth,' *Journal of Development Economics*, 12, 59–73.

Gray P. and Singer, H. W. (1988) 'Trade Policy and Growth of Developing Countries: Some New Data,' *World Development*, 16: 3, 395–403.

Haberler, G. (1959) 'International Trade and Economic Development,' Fiftieth Anniversary Commemoration Lectures (Le Caire: National Bank of Egypt).

Helleiner, G. K. (1996) 'Trade Strategy in Medium-term Adjustment,' *World Development*, 18: 6, 879–97.

Kavoussi, R. M. (1984) 'Export Expansion and Economic Growth: Further Empirical Evidence,' *Journal of Development Economics*, 14, 241–50.

Kendrick, J. W. (1961) *Productivity Trends in the United States* (Princeton: Princeton University Press).

Kim, K. S. and Park, J. K. (1997) 'Source of Industrial Growth and Structural Change in Korea,' Korea Development Institute (Seoul), *Working Paper*, 77–03.

Kohli, I. and Singh, N. (1989) 'Exports and Growth: Critical Minimum Effort and Diminishing Returns,' *Journal of Development Economies*, 30: 2, 391–400.

Krueger, A. D. (1985) 'Trade Policies in Developing Countries,' in R. W. Jones and P. B. Kenen (eds), *Handbook of International Economics*, 1, Ch. 11 (Amsterdam: North-Holland).

Krugman, P. and Obstfeld, M. (1991) *International Economies: Theory and Policy*,

2nd edn. (New York: HarperCollins).
Lardy, N. (1992) *Foreign Trade and Economic Reform in China 1978–1990* (Cambridge: Cambridge University Press).
Lewis, W. A. (1980) 'The Slowing Down of the Engine of Growth,' *American Economic Review*, 70, 555–64.
Michaely, S. (1997) 'Exports and Growth, an Empirical Investigation,' *Journal of Development Economics*, 4, 49–53.
Myrdal, G. (1957) *Rich Lands and Poor: The Road to World Prosperity* (New York: Harper & Bros).
Panagariya, A. (1993) 'Unravelling the Mysteries of China's Foreign Trade Regime,' *World Economy*, 16: 1, 51–8.
Ram, R. (1985) 'Exports and Economic Growth: Some Additional Evidence,' *Economic Development Culture and Change*, 33: 2, 415–25.
Rana, P. B. (1988) 'Export, Policy Changes and Economic Growth in Developing Countries after the 1973 Oil Shock: Comments,' *Journal of Development Economies*, 28: 2, 261–4.
Salvatore, D. and Hatcher, T. (1991) 'Inward Oriented and Outward Oriented Trade Strategies', in H. D. Evans and D. Greenaway, *Developing Countries and the International Economy, Issues in Trade, Adjustment and Debt* (London: Portland).
Schmookler, J. (1995) 'The Changing Efficiency of the American Economy, 1869–1938,' *Review of Economic Statistics*, 34, 214–31.
Singer, H. W. (1950) 'The Distribution of Gains between Investing and Borrowing Countries,' *American Economic Review*, 40, 473–85.
United Nations (1997) *Handbook of International Trade and Development Statistics* (New York and Geneva: United Nations).
Walters, D. (1968) *Canadian Income Levels and Growth: An International Perspective* (Ottawa: Economic Council of Canada, Queen's Printer Ottawa).
Wei, S. W. (1995) 'The Open Door Policy and China's Rapid Growth: Evidence from City-Level Data', in T. Ito and A. O. Krueger (eds), *Growth Theories in Light of the East Asian Experience* (Chicago: University of Chicago Press).
World Bank (1987) *World Development Report* (Washington DC: World Bank).
World Bank (1993) *The East Asian Miracle: Economic Growth and Public Policy* (New York: Oxford University Press).

Index